#769

AF771854

This Book Presented

In memory of
Miller
Berry

by

The Faculty of the
Practical Nurse Program

Poplar Bluff School District R-1
Practical Nurse Program
P. O. Box 47
Poplar Bluff, MO 63901

THE CLINICAL PERFORMANCE EXAMINATION

THE CLINICAL PERFORMANCE EXAMINATION

Development and Implementation

Carrie B. Lenburg, R.N., Ed.D., F.A.A.N.
Coordinator
Regents External Degrees in Nursing
The University of The State of New York
Albany, New York

APPLETON-CENTURY-CROFTS / New York

Copyright © 1979 by APPLETON-CENTURY-CROFTS
A Publishing Division of Prentice-Hall, Inc.

All rights reserved. This book, or any parts thereof, may not be used or reproduced in any manner without written permission. For information, address Appleton-Century-Crofts, 292 Madison Avenue, New York, N.Y. 10017.

79 80 81 82 83 / 10 9 8 7 6 5 4 3 2 1

Prentice-Hall International, Inc., London
Prentice-Hall of Australia, Pty. Ltd., Sydney
Prentice-Hall of India Private Limited, New Delhi
Prentice-Hall of Japan, Inc., Tokyo
Prentice-Hall of Southeast Asia (Pte.) Ltd., Singapore
Whitehall Books Ltd., Wellington, New Zealand

Library of Congress Cataloging in Publication Data

Lenburg, Carrie B
The clinical performance examination.

Bibliography: p.
Includes index.
1. Nursing—Ability testing. 2. Competency based educational tests. I. Title. [DNLM: 1. Education, Nursing—Standards. 2. Educational measurement. 3. Evaluation studies. 4. Clinical competence. WY18.3 L563c]
RT73.L387 1979 153.9′4′61073 79-15535
ISBN 0-8385-1168-6

Cover design: Myrna Sharp Graphic Services
Text design: Greene Art Associates, Hester Greene

PRINTED IN THE UNITED STATES OF AMERICA

Dedicated to those
who cared enough to give their very best
in the development of the
New York Regents External Degree Nursing Programs,
and especially to those
who struggled to create
the Clinical Performance, the Health Assessment Performance,
and the Professional Performance Examinations

CONTENTS

FOREWORD

Evaluation of the student's program toward achieving the goals identified as appropriate at any level of education is a difficult and complex task. Evaluation is more than measurement although that too is included. Dewey, many years ago, noted confusion about evaluation because there are two quite different meanings to value. One is to esteem or hold dear and the other is to appraise. He further noted that the first meaning implies an emotional response and the second an intellectual act. In education the latter is the one to which to aspire. It could be said evaluation in nursing programs has frequently been the emotional response rather than the intellectual act.

In nursing, as in all the health fields, evaluation of performance takes on special meaning. In nursing programs faculties assure the public that the graduates of their programs are competent to practice nursing. The responsibility to prepare students who, upon graduation, are competent to practice nursing rests upon the faculties. They are indeed accountable. They have always been accountable, but at the present time accountability is of much concern, possibly because consumers have become more informed and are demanding evidence of competency in those who purport to serve them. Perhaps the public had more faith in the programs preparing nursing personnel than was warranted by the evaluation methods used by the faculties. Nursing faculties find themselves in a vulnerable position when asked to defend the product produced in their programs.

While evaluation of knowledge is important and difficult it is nowhere as difficult as is the fair and accurate assessment of clinical performance. It is with this problem, the fair and accurate assessment of clinical competence, that this volume is concerned.

Based on experiences in the development of performance examinations for the New York State Regents External Degree Nursing

Programs, it offers real help to all those faculties that are struggling with the problem of how best to evaluate clinical performance in the more traditional programs. It would be literally impossible for any faculty in any traditional program to spend the time or the money to develop performance examinations as has been done in the Regents External Degree Nursing Program. Hundreds of thousands of dollars, thousands of man hours of dozens of expert nurse evaluators have been devoted to the three performance examinations developed for the External Degree Nursing Programs, associate degree and baccalaureate degree. They have been tried, modified and field tested and modified again until they can be used with the assurance that they are objective and do assess accurately.

Those of us who have been involved with the development of the Regents External Degree Nursing Programs for almost eight years have found it a stimulating, challenging and gratifying experience. We have confidence in the examinations developed. Early in the development of the Clinical Performance Nursing Examination we became convinced that, while this examination was specifically designed for the External Degree Program, much of what we had learned and what we had designed was equally valuable in the traditional type of program and that this information should be shared.

This volume gives both a theoretical and practical background for developing assessment tools by faculties in all types of nursing programs. It is hoped the suggestions and help contained therein will be used by faculties as they look at the problem of clinical evaluation. Careful following of these suggestions should result in better clinical performance evaluation. The only result then would be assurance to the graduate that competence has been acquired and to the public that graduates of nursing programs are clinically competent.

Mildred L. Montag
Professor Emeritus
Teachers College
Columbia University
New York, New York

Garden City, New York
July 20, 1979

PREFACE

Developing performance examinations is becoming of greater concern to those in nursing education and nursing-service settings, to those in regular generic programs, and especially to those who implement non-traditional educational approaches. Regardless of the content to be tested, the *process* of developing and implementing a performance examination is extremely important. Identifying content, developing the performance examination, specifying conditions for implementation, reorienting teachers and learners, and successfully completing the necessary transition are major aspects of the process that require understanding and attention. Potential problems can be minimized if they are anticipated and appropriate action is planned in advance.

Because performance examinations are applicable to all levels and types of basic nursing education programs and to various uses in nursing service, a fundamental and comprehensive approach to the subject has been used in presenting the content of this book. The *process* of how to go about the development and implementation is emphasized in every chapter. The material is deliberately designed to assist a variety of faculty groups, including those in associate, baccalaureate, and master's degree programs, as well as individuals involved in certificate programs, in-service education, refresher courses, continuing education, and similar programs.

The primary example used throughout the text is the Clinical Performance in Nursing Examination (CPNE) developed by the New York Regents External Degree Nursing Program. It is a comprehensive, hospital-based, patient-oriented, objective clinical performance examination. Additional examples are drawn from the Health Assessment Performance Examination and the Professional Performance Examination (also of the Regents program), as well as from a few other programs. These examples provide a foundation for the discussion of a rather complex problem; they also serve as models for the development of additional examinations. Thus, those responsible for particular types of programs can apply these basic concepts, principles, and suggestions in adapting procedures to meet their special requirements. Collectively, these examples represent performance aspects of both technical and professional competencies in nursing practice.

The generalizations about objective assessment of performance are based on the experience of several years' duration with both associate and bachelor nursing programs, and on the interaction with hundreds of nursing faculty members. After the fundamental process of development and implementation are presented, one chapter is devoted to illustrating how these basic concepts, criteria, and suggestions can be applied to other situations. Multiple uses of performance examinations are discussed: e.g., to test for more complex professional dimensions of practice; to screen RN students seeking admission or advanced placement into bachelor programs in nursing (or LPNs into associate degree programs); to test nurses in the service setting for employment, promotion, or other purposes; and to test students in highly technical and/or advanced certificate programs or special-purpose programs.

To meet the diverse needs of various groups interested in objective performance assessment, deliberate efforts have been made throughout the book to address *common* problems, concerns, and approaches. Individuals are encouraged to translate the language and specifics of the examples to accommodate their particular purposes, programs, and needs.

It is clear that the use of objective performance examinations is one way to hold students, faculty, and practicing nurses accountable for their practice-related behaviors. Carefully constructed and consistently administered examinations set the standards for performance and guide the learning of those competencies expected of individuals in different categories. As illustrated throughout the book, the quality of service rendered can be influenced substantially by the appropriate use of objective clinical assessment tools. However, this goal requires a period of transition for all of those directly involved; the traditional imagery of clinical assessment, the roles of teachers and students, and the use of examinations must be reconsidered and redefined. This transition toward accountability potentially touches the behavior of the learners, the teachers, the practitioners, the administrators, and the recipients of nurses' service. Even though it is difficult, it is a transition worth the efforts it requires.

Because they have influenced the content of this manuscript, all of those associated with the New York Regents External Degree Nursing Programs merit my tribute for their untiring efforts. The members of the Overall Nursing Faculty Committee and the three performance examination subcommittees deserve special acknowledgment for their creativity and courage to pursue an uncharted course—and to do so successfully. The clinical associates and clinical evaluators also have made major contributions by demonstrating that sustained implementation of objective performance examinations is not only possible but also is quite functional. Much of the content of this book emanates from the shared experiences of these subcommittee members, associates, and evaluators; moreover, their efforts and mine have been substantially enhanced by the tireless efforts and the cheerful and intelligent support of Deborah Rapaport, my Administrative Associate, along with the assistance of many other staff members responsible for various aspects of the program. Special thanks are given to Jackie Raysor for typing the manuscript. These people not only helped me to accomplish the project but also helped me to learn and to grow in the process.

Special appreciation is given to those staff members of the New York State Education Department responsible for the College Proficiency Examination Program and the Regents External Degree Programs. They are exceptional people whose daily work is focused on the educational needs and aspirations of adult and nontraditional learners. Appreciation also is given to the Department for permission to draw from the *Monograph on Nursing* and other materials related to the development and implementation of the programs.

Mildred Schmidt, Executive Secretary to the State Board for Nursing, also deserves special mention because it was she and her staff who had the insight and courage to apply the external degree concept to nursing. Without her confidence and trust, neither the program nor the performance examinations would have been created, and this book would be an unborn idea.

Acknowledgment also is given to the W. K. Kellogg Foundation for funding the development of the external degree nursing programs. Without their commitment to new ideas and their faith in the abilities of qualified leaders to shape the future, the project would not have been completed so readily.

Finally, the friendship, vitality, and encouragement of Rita Kopf provided the sustenance required for the challenge of completing this manuscript. Her enthusiasm for the concept of performance examinations and her struggles to create versions of her own provided valuable insights. Her feedback and responses usually resulted in rich new perspectives—or at least a humorous story and suggestions for still another draft.

THE CLINICAL PERFORMANCE EXAMINATION

CHAPTER 1

Overview of a Nagging Problem and a Long-Sought Remedy

WHAT'S PAST IS HISTORY

For as long as teachers have been engaged in structured nursing education most of them have felt frustrated with the task of ultimately evaluating the ability of the student to perform as expected or desired at the conclusion of the course or program. They have looked for techniques, developed forms, used checklists, and saved and analyzed every scrap of paper with recorded anecdotal notes, and still felt uneasy about many of the clinical evaluations rendered. They have shared anxieties with colleagues, asked for advice and consensus, worried at work and at home about "problem students," and sometimes even experienced some sleepless hours regretting the verdicts reached. All too often decisions made in favor of weak students are as difficult to rationalize as those made against marginal students on the negative side. In either case, the instructor realizes, consciously or unconsciously, that in the absence of a structured and absolute standard, personal opinion and preference have weighed heavily in the clinical evaluation. This realization engenders guilt for such personal involvement as well as anger at "the system" for the lack of a more objective method of deriving such important decisions. Taboos against both of these feelings are long-standing in the nursing culture, which further compounds the Catch-22 situation of final clinical evaluation.

Probably no other topic is of more concern to clinical faculty than the problem of determining a fair and accurate assessment of students' clinical competence. The plethora of complaints about the lack of ability of new nursing graduates (from all types of programs) and the concurrent demands for more accountability in practice have increased the pressures on nurse educators to reevaluate both content and the teaching–learning process. In fact, these and other pressures are stimulating a new internal analysis of nursing itself and the kinds of educational programs required to prepare nurses to function effectively in today's society. But, at least one central problem that must be resolved is how to assure the public, and the profession, that new nursing graduates are both knowledgeable and competent to administer nursing care. Academic institutions and their faculties are being subjected to a new level of accountability for the behavior of their graduates and the quality of their practice.

The need for a standard of performance against which students can be consistently evaluated is abundantly clear. Faculty members throughout the country have expressed it as a recurrent theme in workshops, seminars, and continuing education conferences. At every meeting focusing on clinical evaluation, planners can be sure of achieving their attendance goals. It is, and has been for a long time, a frustrating and complex problem the remedy for which is as elusive as an annoying mosquito on a warm-summer-night cookout.

Part of the problem of objective performance evaluation is that it is part of the complex whole of the educative process. It is not a separate entity that can be dealt with in isolation. To begin to resolve the problem of clinical evaluation also requires that other fundamental components be analyzed and perhaps altered. Some of these fundamental aspects include the roles and responsibilities of both the teacher and learner, the differentiation between the teaching–learning process and evaluation, and the distinction between clinical evaluation and clinical examination.

Finding the perfect tool to evaluate students' clinical abilities objectively resolves one part of the problem, but it also sets in motion the need for other changes, or the would-be solution is no solution at all. The deliberate use of a clinical examination necessitates changes for the students, the faculty, the teaching–learning process, and in some cases, perhaps even the content to be learned. The objective assessment of clinical competencies requires a different approach than is typically used by most programs today. It requires full application of the concept of examination and the principles related to it. A clinical examination must be viewed with the same perspective of objectivity that applies to theory examinations. To be fair, the test must be uniform and equivalent for all students and judged by the same criteria, by all of the faculty involved. It must be administered at a designated time and place with specific and preestablished conditions that are known and accepted by both students and faculty. The expected performance behaviors are clearly and explicitly stated and known in advance by students and faculty. Students are responsible for learning the entire array of performance behaviors prior to the examination, but are tested on a sample of those that have been systematically derived according to stated criteria, and are consistent with program objectives.

In applying the concept of objective final examination to the clinical portion of the course (or program) all of the time and attention preceding the action can be focused on learning the standard of performance predetermined by the faculty as appropriate to the students' level in the program. However, as with theory, this means that there is a designated time for learning and a different time for testing; a time to practice (and perhaps make mistakes) and a time to demonstrate mastery of expected abilities; a time to ask questions and seek guidance and a time to perform with the expected degree of confidence. During the actual examination students either perform the stated behaviors and pass or they do not, and consequently fail. The guessing of what should be learned is removed for the student and the guilt so often associated with failure is removed for both the instructor and the student.

As indicated earlier, acquiring an objective tool is only one part of the problem, and in fact is the more concrete part of the complex integrated whole of making clinical assessment objective. Using an examination requires that the focused time for learning and testing be differentiated and scheduled separately; it also requires changes in the attitudes of teachers and students in reference to learning the practice of clinical nursing. Modifying the long-standing habits used in subjective evaluation requires that instructors develop a sensitivity to their own individual assessment behaviors as well as the motivation and commitment to change. Use of an objective clinical examination, therefore, makes final evaluation easier—but it demands changes in attitudes, habits, and performance roles for both students and teachers. At this juncture the real difficulty begins because of variations in individual preferences, personality characteristics, personal and professional values, and the complexity of the situations in which clinical evaluation takes place.

Thus moving in the direction of more objective clinical examinations requires a deliberately planned transition period. All of the groups involved will be able more fully to participate and cooperate only if they are sufficiently oriented to the process of objective assessment and their role in it. Clinical faculty probably can learn their new evaluator role best by being involved in the development phase; furthermore, it is doubtful that successful transition to objective assessment can be achieved without the ultimate involvement, understanding, and compliance of the total clinical faculty. This can happen only through a well-planned and scheduled transition, which requires one, two, or more years before it is fully operational and free of major difficulties.

In addition to work with the faculty, students also need an extensive orientation and a period of transition. Typically, in the beginning, students do not take the new idea of "examination" in the clinical setting seriously enough; consequently, many fail unnecessarily. Their orientation, like that of the faculty, requires repeated discussion of the substantive and process differences between the old system of subjective observation and the new system of examination in which explicit behaviors are measured against a predetermined standard of performance. Students, as well as the teachers, need some practice sessions in limited situations prior to the administration of the comprehensive final clinical examination in which all criteria, conditions, and demands are fully applied. Word of mouth (the grapevine system) will help subsequent student groups; but for the first group this will be a most difficult time. The transition period probably will be more likely to succeed if it allows time for a variety of practice sessions, small testing experiences, and discussions essential to concretize the new expectations.

One other group also requires an extensive orientation during the period of transition. If the performance examination is to take place in the clinical setting (instead of in a simulated laboratory situation), the entire array of nursing-care personnel needs to be informed about all of the details associated with the clinical examination and their role in it. Not only should the director, assistants, supervisors, and head nurse be involved, but also staff nurses, LPNs, aides, and orderlies need to know their part in the process. Members of the nursing staff, physicians, as well as those from other departments could obstruct the examination—deliberately or unwittingly—and cause major difficulties if they do not know or understand the entire process and the consequences of their behavior on the outcomes. Therefore, during the planning phase, careful consideration needs to be given to all of these groups and when possible they should be involved in the development—as a part of the total reprogramming for objective assessment.

Also during the transition, or early implementation phase, all of the conditions essential to the conduct of performance examinations can be modified and refined, based on student experiences. All of the documents, forms, directions, and criteria can be tested for functional application and the various drafts can be made final prior to actual use during the final pilot testing and implementation of the final version of the examination. Of course, most of the early drafts of these examination materials have to be developed along with the early drafts of the statements of expected performance behaviors (the examination content) because they are essential to the evolution of the examination itself. A sequence of "minipilot tests" is necessary for both content and process statements during the developmental phase and well into the transition period.

THE TOOL IS ONLY PART OF THE ANSWER

Thus far, it becomes clear that developing or acquiring the testing tool itself is only one part of the process of introducing an objective clinical performance examination. A wide range of other considerations is equally important. The succeeding chapters of this book are devoted to a full discussion of the factors essential in the planning, development, pilot testing, implementation, and evaluation phases of changing to an examination approach for clinical evaluation. This transition can provide a major step forward if it is instituted with thoughtful and comprehensive attention to details and to those persons directly and indirectly affected by the examination. Neglect of these considerations could result in a situation even more frustrating than the one that previously existed.

Regardless of the type of educational program, or the level of the student being evaluated, the process of developing and implementing a performance examination is the same. The content, or the specific behaviors to be examined, may vary considerably and can best be determined by the clinical faculty directly responsible. As indicated earlier, the emphasis in this book is focused on the process rather than on identifying specific content at particular levels for particular types of education programs. However, a major part of the process is concerned with answering three questions: (1) "What should be tested?" (2) "Who should determine what should be tested?" and (3) "How can you tell whether or not you're testing enough of the right thing?" In the long run, assisting faculties to think differently about clinical examinations and to deliberately apply the process of determining content and technique seems to be more essential than simply prescribing lists of behaviors for various levels and stages of educational preparation. Logically, deriving the specific content would seem to be the creative function of the particular faculty involved, once they are given certain general guidelines or criteria for development and implementation.

Some academic programs—whether at the associate, bachelor's, or master's level—may require more than one performance examination. Staff development, continuing education, and certificate programs probably will require only one test. However, when multiple tests are used, much of the potential duplication, omissions, and confusion can be avoided if the entire instructional group is involved in determining content for each examination to be developed. Performance examinations are costly, both to develop and to implement, and therefore are best used to evaluate only essential, previously untested performance abilities. Overall coordination of what is tested, as well as when, and how it is tested are important considerations and are directly related to such factors as the type of educational program, the content and competencies being learned, the students' level in the program, and other assessment procedures being used. Unit or department nursing faculty members are responsible for determining the particular content to be learned and tested for specific courses, but the entire nursing faculty serves an important function by coordinating efforts in planning and implementing performance examinations wherever they are necessary in the program. The complex and long-term nature of the project and its potential benefits make it essential that the entire faculty get involved in one way or another. The same principle applies to the service setting: instructors need support and input from those in authority positions and those who will participate in the implementation of the performance examination.

DISTINCTIONS IN APPROACH

As used here, performance examinations are criterion-referenced rather than norm-referenced examinations. There is a marked distinction between how these two types of tests are developed, administered, and graded. In general, norm-referenced tests use a written format and focus on a sampling of topics to be covered without requiring that any particular topics be answered correctly for the person to pass. Once developed and pilot-tested, these tests are administered to a large number of successful students comparable to those who will take the test; the results form the standard for pass/fail. Therefore, students taking the test (for its intended purpose) are in competition with the norming group.

In contrast, criterion-referenced tests focus on a standard to be achieved by all students, as established by the faculty. Once the appropriate content and level of achievement is established, students who take criterion-referenced tests are in competition with the standard, regardless of the performance of their peers. The exact standard is known by students well in advance and they study and prepare for the test with that reference point in mind. Their goal is to meet the criterion (standard) established by the faculty as minimally acceptable for that particular course or program. The discussion of clinical performance examinations in this volume is based on the above-described general understanding of criterion-referenced testing. For more theoretical discussion of both types of examinations, references on educational measurement should be consulted (see Bibliography).

The advantages of objective and consistent performance examinations seem obvious. Instructors are more able to obtain an accurate and fair assessment of the students' clinical abilities without the burden of wondering whether or not they make the right decisions, and their personal biases are reduced to a minimum. Students are more apt to be evaluated similarly by different instructors with a comparable degree of stringency applied to each testing situation. Students know in advance the array of competencies they are expected to perform and therefore do not waste time trying to second-guess what the instructor will evaluate. Their efforts can be devoted to learning and achieving the specific objectives outlined for the course or the program.

However, performance examinations are not without their problems and disadvantages. As already pointed out, they are costly in faculty time to develop and to implement, primarily because teachers typically were not taught how to conduct such examinations and consequently have had little or no experience in doing so to date. The initial introduction of performance examinations, therefore, requires time for new learning by the faculty and the opportunity to develop new attitudes and skills. Once the first attempts are worked out successfully, the process becomes less difficult, less time-consuming, and a more productive experience for all concerned.

COMBINED ASSESSMENT

Clinical performance examinations are not the panacea for all the problems of evaluation. They are what they are: one method of determining a reasonable assessment of a student's current clinical competence. They do not take the place of other evaluation techniques used throughout the course or program to help students realize their strengths and weaknesses and areas for continued learning. When administered at the end of a course, they provide feedback for learning the specific course objectives; when given at the end of an entire program of study, they are used to determine more comprehensive achievement. Regardless of when they are given, students learn from the experience of taking performance examinations and some feedback is given following completion, but learning is not the primary objective of the examination experience.

Anecdotal notes still can be used productively to assist students in the learning process, but they are not the source for determining the final clinical evaluation. Case studies, nursing-care plans, diaries, logs, and other learning devices also continue to serve their function in student learning. However, they are not the source for determining the final evaluation of clinical competence. In the typical program, instructors are convinced that every time the student goes into the clinical area for practice, an evaluation note must be written. At the end of the term these evaluations, usually in the form of anecdotal notes or checklists, are tallied and quantified for a grade.

With use of this system, students actually are graded every time they attempt to learn. Students are easily intimidated by this system, which interferes with learning and creativity; they are frustrated when they fail—even though they have not yet had sufficient opportunity to learn. The cart has been put before the horse. Learners need an opportunity to try, to practice, to fumble, and even to fail occasionally as a part of the learning process without being judged (graded) while doing so. Throughout the semester (or program) the learning process should be emphasized; at the conclusion of this phase, however, both theory and performance examinations become the objective tools for determining the students's achievement in both knowledge and competence.

Used in this fashion, clinical examinations help to make students and instructors more accountable for their individual behaviors. Instructors determine which competencies shall be expected and students are responsible for learning them to the expressed level of proficiency. When students know what is expected and have the opportunity and guidance necessary for learning it, they can be held fully accountable for achieving expected behaviors. On failure, they no longer can resort to using unfounded complaints, misunderstandings, biases, or legal threats to get the instructor to change the evaluation. With use of a properly constructed performance examination, failure can result only when the student fails to meet the expected, previously established clinical behaviors. The teacher does not fail the student; the student fails because critical elements in performance have not been met.

Beating the System

The use of objective documentation of performance against a known standard of expectations satisfies another significant purpose. In recent years, students have increasingly resorted to legal action when they failed a course, especially one involving clinical evaluation. In many cases these complaints were well founded and appropriate. However, the subjectivity that characterizes typical evaluation procedures functions favorably for some students but negatively for others. Students whose attitudes and values are inconsistent with those of the instructor frequently find it difficult to perform "satisfactorily" regardless of what they do. On the other hand, some students do not apply themselves and subsequently fail to learn, but nonetheless they look for ways to manipulate the instructors into giving a passing grade. They are content to just "get by" and look for the least demanding way of meeting the course objectives. Their attention is drawn to other than academic pursuits or their commitment is less than sufficient to learn the minimum requirements of clinical practice. Still, they look for ways to "beat the system" and to attack the faculty at one of their weakest points: clinical evaluation. Once they find an obvious inconsistency, instructor bias, or a value-laden evaluation, they have grounds for seeking legal action.

The threat of legal suit by students against instructors undoubtedly has made the job of clinical evaluation more stressful. Instructors in some situations have responded to the threat by lessening clinical demands or by giving C or D rather than F grades. The student subsequently is passed to the next course and ultimately through the program. Therefore, many students have been graduated from the basic education program and then either fail state-board licensure examinations or barely achieve the minimum score. Their incompetence is passed along to the consumer and to the employer, resulting in frustration to both and to the ill-prepared practitioner. No one has been served satisfactorily by the initial action of passing clinically incompetent students—whether they are liked or disliked by instructors, and whether they know or don't know the theoretical portion of the course.

SUMMARY OF PURPOSE

Clinical performance examinations serve a unique function: they are designed to compliment other types of student evaluation procedures rather than to duplicate them. They are not intended to test cognitive learning per se but to determine the students' ability to apply theory in the clinical context. Theory is best evaluated by objective written examinations, and even though clinical situations and vignettes can be presented in verbal form to test application and synthesis of theory, that in no way constitutes and actual performance examination. The direct, observable implementation of theory in the care of clients cannot be evaluated by written examinations. The objective determination of clinical competence requires that students actually perform a representative sample of those skills identified as essential for the practice being tested, while being observed by a neutral evaluator. The objectivity of the evaluation is greatly facilitated (though not completely guaranteed) by the use of the previously established standard of practice against which the competence of each student is consistently measured.

A MODEL: THE NEW YORK EXTERNAL DEGREE PROGRAM

The New York Regents External Degree Nursing Program (of The University of the State of New York) has established new possibilities and standards for the assessment of nursing knowledge and competencies. Because the program is designed to evaluate learning rather than to provide instruction, the full attention of the faculty and staff is devoted to identifying essential content in theory and practice appropriate to the specific degree being awarded (associate or bachelor's) and to creating objective ways to measure the achievement of that learning. Several cognitive paper-and-pencil examinations have been developed to test the comprehensive range of theoretical content consistent with that taught in conventional programs (seven for the associate and five others for baccalaureate nursing programs). But the development and use of such proficiency examinations per se are not new to higher education in general or to nursing education in particular. However, the integrated nature of the external degree examinations, their purpose, and the way they were organized and developed are usual if not unique. This is the first time a total assessment program in nursing has been undertaken and successfully completed. Some aspects related to the development of the program and the examinations will be discussed later.

The most innovative and far-reaching facet of the Regents program, however, is the development of objective, clinically oriented performance examinations. The idea of performance testing in nursing is not new, but the extent to which it has been developed and used is changing remarkably, largely because of the original and creative work done by the Regents External Degree Nursing Faculty and Staff. The Clinical Performance in Nursing Examination (CPNE), developed between 1972 and 1975, provides a comprehensive model for other performance examinations, for different levels and types of programs, and for conventional as well as for nontraditional students. This performance examination is used as the fundamental model throughout this book; it is the basic reference point from which other versions can be developed.

Many years ago state boards of nursing required the passing of a "practical test" and the five theory tests to obtain professional licensure. These practical tests, however, generally were restricted to the demonstration of one or more particular procedures in a simulated situation, assigned on a random basis. While a practical demonstration undoubtedly contributed some validity to the evaluation of candidates for licensure, the time, personnel, and mechanics involved were excessive for the limited payoffs, especially as the numbers of graduates increased. The limited data obtained by observing a candidate go through the motions of simulating the application of a dressing, giving a douche or enema, or preparing medications, for example, simply were not worth the difficulties and expense encountered for such a large-scale operation. Although the basic idea of testing for clinical competence, even though applied in a markedly circumscribed way, was and is a good one, it seems logical that the responsibility for competence testing belongs to educational programs and subsequently to nursing service rather than to licensing authorities. Numbers alone mandate the change.

Many nursing programs have developed some sort of practical test of nursing skills that is used in one or more clinical courses. Typically, students are tested at the conclusion of the introductory or fundamentals course in the first year of the nursing sequence. They are assigned, perhaps on a random basis, to demonstrate one or more skills in the learning laboratory under the observation of an instructor. Technical or behavioral checklists usually are used, more or less related to the specific objectives of the course. Students may or may not be graded, may or may not have an opportunity to repeat when they are unsuccessful, and may or may not have a comparable experience with an actual patient. Instructors may or may not be objective, may or may not apply the same degree of stringency to each student, and may or may not select comparably complex situations for the examination. The test itself may or may not be written explicitly to ensure comparable application, may or may not be worded unambiguously, and may or may not include simple, discrete, specific behaviors for consistent observation. Many students may never have another "practical" test subsequent to passing the one given in the fundamentals lab. Their remaining clinical evaluations probably will be based on anecdotal notes, nursing-care plans, process recordings, case studies, and the subjective analysis of instructors and clinical staff.

Such limited use of performance testing is typical—but it certainly is neither satisfactory nor satisfying for most clinical instructors. What is needed, and desired, by most faculty members is a comprehensive and objective test of the students' ability to apply knowledge and principles of nursing care and to make judgments in a variety of actual clinical situations. But the pressures of other priorities and time commitments, as well as a lack of funds coupled with the absence of a successful basic model, have prevented the development of adequate clinical performance examinations. Most faculties are struggling to keep up with the daily demands of classroom instruction, laboratory and clinical supervision, and the host of other faculty responsibilities. Little or no time is left over—much less the energy—to tackle the complex problem of identifying the specific behaviors to be tested and designing the tool to test those behaviors. Even if some instructors could be given time-release to work on such an examination few, admittedly, have the evaluation expertise to complete and implement it. Rarely have graduate students preparing to be nurse educators been exposed to the subject of clinical examination, much less given the experience of developing, implementing, or participating in one. Little wonder that teachers feel so uncomfortable and threatened by the prospect of developing and conducting clinical performance examinations.

The Regents External Degree Nursing Program was able to develop a clinical performance examination successfully because it had a specific and imperative goal and was able to obtain sufficient developmental funds to buy the time and expertise necessary. While it was agreed that an assessment program in nursing could be developed to serve the needs of nontraditional adult learners, it also was agreed that paper-and-pencil examinations were insufficient to test nursing competence. Therefore, the development and use of a performance examination became a necessity rather than a luxury. The clinical evaluation problem had to be confronted head-on and had to be successfully resolved if the external degree concept was to be applied to a practice profession such as nursing. The individual and collective intelligence and experience of all those associated with the program were summoned to the fundamental but complex dual assignment: specifying both cognitive and performance competencies essential to the practice of nursing, and developing objective tools to measure their achievement.

The entire eight-year project to develop both the associate degree and the bachelor's degree nursing programs, was generously funded by the W.K. Kellogg Foundation. The New York State Education Department, the agency responsible for developing the project, assumed most of the other costs of the project. Additional financial assistance was provided through capitation grants from HEW. These resources provided the time and access to highly qualified nurse educators and psychometrists, thus facilitating the job of developing both theory and performance examinations. The detailed process of development will be described later; the point here is that all of the essential ingredients were brought together and focused by a compelling purpose, at a particular time and place, and in the context of the growth of nontraditional higher education. As a result, a remarkably innovative assessment program in nursing was created, which included both written and objective clinical performance examinations to test the total content of nursing at the associate and bachelor's levels.

Many aspects of the Regents program are exemplary and useful to conventional programs, but the most outstanding contributions probably are the performance examinations. They cannot be compared with the practical or skills tests familiar to nursing instructors or to those who took licensure examinations a few decades ago. The Clinical

Performance in Nursing Examination (CPNE) is a particularly useful model that has the potential of serving the needs of many different types of education programs (associate, bachelor's, specialty, etc.) and different levels of students, including those in basic, advanced, certificate, refresher, or continuing education programs. Its development and successful implementation is a landmark contribution to nursing of all kinds, and to the consumers served by nurses. It provides a new kind of model that already is changing the direction for clinical evaluation in programs throughout the country. Because it was the first of the Regents performance examinations to be developed, it also was the model for both the Health Assessment Performance Examination (HAPE) and the Professional Performance Examination (PPE) developed for the B.S.N. external degree program. It is the CPNE (and to some extent the HAPE and the PPE) that provides the basis for much of the content of this book.

QUESTIONS AND IMPLICATIONS

In spite of the apparent advantages of using an objective examination to test competence, some critics have raised questions about possible negative implications. These complex questions deserve some consideration, although the full response to their queries forms the substance of this entire volume.

One question raises the possibility that using a criterion-referenced performance examination will entice students merely to study for the examination and disregard the pursuit of broad learning and creative discovery. That is a possibility for some students, just as some students in the current system look for ways to minimize the scope and depth of learning expected by their mentors. Already, some students spend more time evading their assignments than learning to become competent in nursing. They try to discover the pet subjects, topics, and concerns of specific teachers and focus on these points. Their concern is not with the creative application of nursing theory and skills, but with getting through the course (and "the system") with as little effort as possible. To those dedicated to the teaching and the learning of nursing, this is a sad but factual reality.

No one questions that students with this frame of mind are enrolled in and graduating from nursing programs. The question, however, is: Will the use of a clinical test proliferate such behavior? One must reply that it is a possibility. Students who are inclined in that direction will follow that path anyway, but others will continue to apply their habits of the pursuit of learning as they have in the past. Those who are enthused about nursing, those who are committed to excellence, those who are dedicated to a purpose, those who have a natural learning attitude will not be easily persuaded simply to study enough to get by. Their study habits and personal goals were long ago etched into their personality. Having an explicitly written standard against which they will be tested helps them to focus their learning and helps them distinguish between minimum and superior practice.

This consideration, however, also appropriately introduces the notion that one of the responsibilities of a "good" teacher is to excite students and to challenge them with the goal of excellence in learning. That does not change with the implementation of a performance or any other type of examination. While the responsibility for learning and gaining competence belongs to the student, the teacher serves as a significant guide, counselor, mentor, and facilitator. An important instrument is the teacher's own enthusiasm for, competence in, and persuasiveness in imparting the importance and applicability of the subject being learned. Although not necessarily an imperative (as illustrated by those who have completed the Regents External Degree Program), a teacher, especially an able one, is most beneficial for the majority of students. Most students enjoy the luxury of having someone else do the hard work of prelearning for them, and of personally guiding them in the process. The addition of an objective performance examination at the conclusion of a course or a program refocuses teaching and learning. Teachers instruct and guide, supervise and then test the learners; students are held accountable for mastering the content that has been established as mandatory.

One of the most significant changes that occurs when a performance examination is used is that students *know* what is expected of them without having to follow a trial-and-error path to discover it. In addition to the customary behavioral objectives, outline of assignments, lists of references, and the like, they also know from the beginning of the course which clinical skills are required, and under what circumstances and to what extent they are expected to apply those skills in a scheduled examination period. Thus they can begin to relate objectives, theory, and clinical competence from the beginning of the course. They do not have to be concerned whether they will correctly decipher the instructor's intentions and personal objectives. They will know almost from the outset which areas will require most of their practice time, as they already know some of their own inadequacies from previous experiences. Once they comprehend the expectations for the current course, they can focus most attention on weak areas, and still take sufficient time to satisfy areas in which they already feel more competent. By knowing the behavior to be mastered and the competencies uniformly expected by the faculty, students can deliberately concentrate their efforts on learning. Theoretically more learning should take place—more efficiently and for more students. More time, therefore, should be available for the creative student to apply that learning in other situations.

The succeeding chapters present the fundamental concepts and criteria essential in the process of developing and implementing performance examinations as well as exploring the problems that can be anticipated. Some suggestions are given for preventing or minimizing these problems during the entire transition period. While emphasis is placed on clinical-technical assessment, examples are used throughout to illustrate applicability to all types of nursing education and service programs.

CHAPTER 2

A Review of Faculty Surveys

There is no doubt about the widespread interest in clinical performance examinations among nurses in education and service settings, regardless of geographic region or particular type of nursing endeavor. At every meeting with CPE as the announced topic, individuals from educational programs, nursing service, nursing organizations, and regulatory agencies come in large numbers, seeking help with one of their most difficult problems: how to evaluate clinical competence objectively. Because of my involvement with the development and implementation of the New York Regents External Degree Nursing Programs, I have been invited by numerous groups to discuss the topic at state and national meetings and to conduct workshops on performance examinations throughout the country.

WIDESPREAD INTEREST

Between 1975 and 1977 approximately 25 such meetings were held in which the primary focus was clinical performance examination. A few of these meetings have been with individual faculties, but most have been statewide, regional, or national conferences. They have been held in all parts of the country from New York to Florida, Texas and New Mexico, California, and even Hawaii. Similar meetings have been held in Canada, from Toronto to Vancouver. Participants have come from all types of programs, agencies, and institutions, but their interest and needs are the same: how to develop and implement valid, accurate, and fair performance examinations in the clinical setting.

In New York State many sessions were held during a three-year period, primarily to prepare the pool of evaluators needed to administer the Clinical Performance in Nursing Examination (CPNE) for the external degree. Approximately 60 nurse educators have received an extensive orientation and serve in this capacity on a per diem basis as needed. Other meetings also have been held with faculties of New York associate-degree and baccalaureate programs, to help them learn from the experience gained during the developmental phase of the Regents External Degree Program.

In the South, several meetings were conducted by the Council on Nursing Education of The Southern Regional Educational Board during the period from 1976 to 1978. More than 400 nurse educators for the 14-member states attended those meetings. In addition, sessions were held in several other southern states for more than 300 faculty and service representatives. These meetings were conducted in Virginia, North Carolina, South Carolina, Florida, Texas, and Alabama.

In the Midwest, performance examination workshops were conducted in Ohio, Indiana, Illinois, Wisconsin, and Minnesota for more than 550 education and service representatives. In the West more than 300 people attended the meetings held in California, Washington, Utah, New Mexico, and Hawaii. In Canada—spreading from Toronto to Vancouver—more than 200 individuals in various aspects of nursing education and service attended workshops conducted on the topic of performance examination. Literally hundreds of basic nursing programs, special programs, in-service, refresher, and continuing education programs were represented at these meetings. Approximately 1700 educators and leaders from nursing service and nursing organizations have attended—all of them seeking clarification, information, direction, and assistance in the difficult area of developing and using objective performance examinations. Without question, this is a subject on the minds of many persons in nursing.

During several of these workshops, questionnaires were administered in an effort to obtain some insight into the kinds of problems and concerns and the areas of need experienced by those in attendance. No effort was made to obtain a random sample or to make this a serious statistical survey. However, through these questionnaires considerable insight was gained from the participants and it is possible from the responses to determine the kinds of problems being faced and to categorize them for discussion. Information gained from early workshop groups helped to crystalize the concerns and needs of those engaged in performance evaluation and served as the basis for later workshops and for the content of this volume. On the assumption that the general summary of these surveys will be helpful, this chapter is devoted to exploring the comments and perspectives of those who attended the meetings. The participants were nurse educators (from both associate and baccalaureate programs), nursing-service representatives, those from in-service and staff-development programs, and those involved in other special kinds of programs in which objective clinical assessment is critical.

A SAMPLING OF CONCERNS EXPRESSED

NURSING SERVICE

The need for objective assessment in nursing service pertains to those who have participated in complete refresher courses, in-service programs, orientation programs, as well as to those who are going through periodic service review or evaluation procedures for purposes of promotion. One of the general concerns expressed by this group relates to the amount of time required for individual performance evaluation. Another problem is the need to be everywhere at once, with too many nurses to observe and evaluate at the same time for the personnel available. This is probably a universal problem, affecting those in nursing education or any one else involved in evaluation, not just those in nursing service. Those individuals in service settings also expressed a need for specific criteria as a basis for making judgments about nursing performance. They complained that the process is too subjective, that the current forms being used (at least in their agencies) are too general and too ambiguous, and that there is a lack of standardized procedure and format. All of this, of course, prevents the desirable level of consistency and comparability in evaluation by the staff.

Perhaps the two most troublesome complaints voiced by the service participants was the degree of subjectivity and inconsistency inevitably associated with performance assessment. Almost everyone expressed a nagging feeling of anxiety about having to make judgments that sometimes were quite critical but were based on seemingly subjective information. Often the information was admittedly inadequate. Different time spans were used along with different kinds of assessment situations, procedures, and forms, which troubled those responsible for making judgments about the performance of nurses in the service setting. Another problem they identified was the need to evaluate employees without simultaneously undermining confidence in their practice. Obviously unwarranted and unfair criticism causes increasing anxiety; therefore, these participants wanted an objective instrument that could be shared in advance both with those being evaluated and with the individuals responsible for the assessment. This practice would allow the examinees to practice according to the preestablished standard and then be assessed objectively on their ability to comply with it during the designated testing time.

When there is no known explicit standard of performance it is very difficult for individuals who come from many different kinds of backgrounds and who have varying degrees of interest in their work to conform to an ambiguous standard. Therefore, those people in service settings felt that it would be tremendously helpful from the point of view of improving the quality of practice if an instrument were available that could be used consistently and with full knowledge by those involved.

Currently the evaluation reports prepared in the service setting depend upon evaluations rendered by any one of several staff members who may or may not directly observe the practice of the nurse being evaluated. Again, the lack of consistency is very troublesome. If there were a standard known and expected of everyone it could be applied during the evaluation process in a consistent and comparable fashion.

When asked specifically how nursing service personnel might make use of a clinical performance examination the following kinds of comments were reported. Some thought it could be used in the evaluation of training assistants or aides, including those who come straight out of high school into the service setting as well as those who are experienced adults finding their way into the service setting for the first time. Others suggested that it could be used as a daily evaluation of performance and a tool for counseling students as well as young, inexperienced staff members. An objective instrument for evaluation also could be used by all nursing employees to establish the level of desired competence and qualify of care expected on behalf of patients. It could include the expected behavior for all staff, with variations depending upon individual positions and responsibilities. Some participants even suggested that employees could write goals for themselves, identifying areas for continued improvement and then use the evaluation instrument as a way of upgrading their own self-monitored improvement and career development. Almost everyone agreed that the orientation of new staff members would be greatly enhanced by having an objective instrument that makes explicit the standard expected of nurses in that particular institution. In this way employees would know from the outset that the routine periodic clinical evaluations would be based on an established standard of competence. In effect, then, one would have another form of on-the-job improvement and career development for staff in a service setting. It sets the minimum behaviors expected of nurses (or designated others) in that agency.

NURSING EDUCATION

Generally speaking the participants from nursing education had similar concerns: the lack of objectivity, the time requirement, the lack of standardization, and the lack of a definition of the required standard of performance. Basically they felt that there needs to be a decrease in the guessing game and the negative approach currently so predominant in clinical assessment in nursing education. They agreed that where there is no standard form and process, inconsistency and subjectivity will naturally result. Unfortunately, faculty members frequently do not seem to know precisely which practice behaviors are universally expected of students; therefore, they are inconsistent in their expectations as well as in the kinds of written comments and evaluative judgments reached for particular students.

Some of the problems expressed by participants from nursing education relate to what happens if all students do not have the same learning experiences prior to testing. It is possible that this concern reflects the common problem of testing too much too frequently with inadequate opportunity for students to learn and become minimally competent. Consequently, an examination given at the conclusion of a program (of whatever sort) probably is best because it allows cumulative learning in the clinical setting over a period of time. There also was an expressed concern for evaluating "one-time experiences." The fundamental questions, of course, is: How essential is the testing of one-time experiences that primarily serve learning needs? These concerns are additional indicators of the confusion that exists between what should be included in clinical learning and what should be included in objective testing of clinical achievement.

Some faculty expressed the need for one tool for daily clinical laboratory use and another one for final evaluation. To what extent, however, can the same instrument be used? Is the daily form basically to be used for testing purposes or to guide student learning? These questions also suggest uncertainty about the difference between clinical experience for learning and a clinical examination given at the conclusion of the learning period.

Another problem identified relates to the differences in evaluation of knowledge and of clinical skills. Clearly the responses from the workshop participants indicate the need for differentiation between theory examinations and performance examination. The position taken in this book is that they are best tested separately because of the different nature of the tools and processes essential to test each one. The clinical performance examination needs to be as explicitly developed as written tests, with objective and observable criteria. A test of the students' ability to apply knowledge and learning mandates this kind of specificity and objectivity.

Fundamental in all of this is the basic problem of defining safe nursing practice and expectations for the particular level of preparation for the individual being examined. There is a clear need for differentiation between associate-degree and baccalaureate candidates, between generalists and specialists, between the beginner and the advanced practitioner. Furthermore, as the participants indicated, testing for "attitudes" and "appearance" (in compliance with the rules) needs to be developed as a category separate from those areas related to theory and clinical-performance competencies.

When workshop participants were asked how those in nursing education could use a clinical performance examination, the response was very clear. Clinical teachers stated they would use it to guide learning experiences as well as the daily and final evaluations in the practice setting; this would focus clinical assessment on predetermined, objectively stated behaviors applied consistently to all students in all types of situations. They felt confident that such an objective assessment would increase the chances for a better product of the educational system and also would assure better quality of patient care. Such a tool also could be used to help students to know what is acceptable as safe nursing practice expected of everyone at a given level of preparation. This practice would provide more direction for students' growth because once they master these minimal expectations, their time and effort can be focused on practice areas and skills in which they are less competent and need to improve. As faculty and students learn how to use performance examinations as a tool for increasing competence they also can become more creative and expansive in using clinical laboratory time to enrich the total learning experience.

WHAT MOST FACULTY WANT TO KNOW

At the beginning of each workshop, participants were asked what they most wanted to learn about performance assessment. Responses were amazingly similar despite the fact that the meetings were held from coast to coast and participants were from various types of basic and special educational programs or nursing-service settings. Some of their specific comments highlight the most troublesome areas and point to the categories requiring the most attention.

RESPONSES ABOUT PERFORMANCE EVALUATION

The responses of individuals at a midwestern session are typical. Unquestionably the need for objectivity was most prevalent. Almost everyone wanted a fair and objective examination tool to test students' ability to perform in the clinical setting. A second problem was the lack of consistency, regardless of the kind of student and the setting. Those responsible for assessment wanted more control of the variables; i.e., to hold certain factors constant to be sure each student received fair and equal treatment during the test. But they didn't quite know how to do it. Almost everyone wanted to learn how to develop a consistent evaluation tool and how to apply it equitably.

Furthermore, they also were concerned with accuracy as well as validity and reliability. They wanted an instrument that would increase confidence in the decisions they were required to make about student performance. Many reported that the format and process of evaluation methods currently being used were unsatisfactory. They also were concerned about how to administer objective clinical assessments in "the real world"—with all of the constraints of the academic schedule and clinical setting.

Two other concerns related to how to determine the level objectives and how to apply the objectives of clinical courses (or the program) in the process of clinical assessment. Other problems mentioned include how to determine the clinical grade and how to measure the strengths and weaknesses (or the growth factor) of students over a period of time. Many participants acknowledged the impossibility of the instructor's being with every student all the time and they talked about the need for a designated examination time. But they wondered about several questions: How does this get worked out? How much time does it take? How many "examiners" are needed? Some educators expressed concern about the rights and responsibilities of faculty members in the evaluation process and the legal aspects of clinical assessment. Others felt the need to find ways of decreasing the pressures from students for positive evaluations, and some wanted to learn how to help students improve their chances for professional and personal growth. The problems of placement, timing, and scheduling of performance examinations were repeatedly mentioned.

The same question was asked of participants at a western statewide meeting on performance evaluation: their concerns were quite similar. They wanted a more objective tool that was both fair and accurate; they also wanted to move in the direction of discrete times for teaching and testing but they didn't quite know how to work out the seemingly overwhelming problems this suggested. They wanted to know how to evaluate large numbers of students simultaneously, and still be correct and comprehensive. They wanted to know which behaviors are critical and are essential to include in the evaluation. They expressed a need for consistency among the faculty in administering the examinations and they wanted to know how to evaluate values and attitudes. Other concerns related to determining clinical grades, deciding on a reasonable sample, using staff reports, avoiding legal problems, evaluating the slow learner, and assessing those with previous nursing preparation.

Some participants also asked about the extent to which students should be involved in the development of clinical examinations. Other questions included: How frequently should such tests be given? What are the best techniques to use? How can a performance test be used with new employees? How can such an examination be used for advanced placement, especially with LPN and/or RN students? How can it be used to pinpoint the learning problems of students?

TYPICAL VERBATIM RESPONSES

A selection of verbatim comments written by workshop participants further elaborates the needs of those responsible for clinical assessment. In response to the question: "What do you want to learn about performance evaluation?" a baccalaureate educator wrote:

> What it is in the strictest sense and what it can be in reality; how to plan for it; how to write objectives that will really tell students what we expect of them; how to be the most objective evaluator and how to identify valid criteria for evaluating student's performance.

Her response states the problem quite succinctly and comprehensively. Another baccalaureate educator at the same meeting indicated that she wanted to learn "how to maintain objectivity and evaluate without getting involved.'' Still another one wrote: ''How to use criterion-reference evaluation in the clinical setting; how to determine the critical elements in performance.'' Another educator was concerned with selecting performances that are of about equal difficulty, suggesting the need for comparability of testing episodes. Other concerns expressed include: ''When should students be evaluated? . . . When does she learn before the final evaluation? . . . How many opportunities should the person have to meet the objectives?''

From one of the conferences in the East, designed especially for associate-degree educators, some of the questions and comments expressed included the following:

- The most effective way with the least amount of stress to the student.
- The methodology, and standardization.
- How to measure student performance objectively and fairly when different students have varied learning experiences.
- What is included in performance evaluation related to attitudes and behavioral components?
- The student's ability to synthesize knowledge which can be reflected in performance.
- How to select areas to be evaluated.
- The most efficient and objective ways to evaluate.
- Defining the criteria which are most important to evaluate.
- How to sort out what is necessary to be evaluated for a given course or level.
- Consistency in evaluating performance in a clinical area.
- What is the role of the instructor at the time of the evaluation?

Again, these kinds of responses were repeatedly recorded, regardless of the location of the workshop. The comments ranged from the cryptic (''anything I don't know'') to lengthy responses reflecting a great deal of frustration, as illustrated by the following:

> I would like to be able to have objective tools to use to evaluate clinical performance and not rely so much on subjective observation. I also would like to know if there are other means besides anecdotal notes to keep students' progress notes. I would like to know what emphasis is placed on nursing-care plans as a means of evaluating clinical performance, and how is clinical graded?

Participants at the workshop in Minnesota commented as follows:

- A valid means with students not under so much pressure, an evaluation of their true ability.
- Techniques for clinical evaluation that reduce or eliminate the tension factors as well as the factor of contrived evaluation.
- How to evaluate specific competencies when constant observation of ten students in three different areas is impossible.

- How to achieve consistency among testers or evaluators.
- How to evaluate using valid measures which are not unrealistically expensive and don't give away credit and competency.
- How can it be used in the area of psychiatric nursing?

One participant captured the essence of what everyone else was saying in one short statement. With a pen that obviously was gliding easily over the page, she expressed her need: "How to write performance objectives in one easy lesson."

However desirable, the one-lesson approach is no small task! Quite obviously, when all of these points are brought together and put into focus, the challenge of developing a clinical performance examination is a difficult, complex, and highly integrated process. Clearly, it cannot be accomplished in one easy lesson and yet everyone—particularly those who come to a one- or two-day workshop—seems to be looking for easy answers in dealing with the nitty-gritty problems they face every day.

EVALUATION PROCEDURES CURRENTLY BEING USED

Responses obtained from two other questions asked on the same preworkshop survey are equally enlightening. One of these questions asked about assessment procedures currently being used and the other asked for the most difficult areas confronted in performance evaluation.

The second question raised on the preworkshop survey was: *Briefly describe the procedures and/or activities you use in performance evaluation which you think are really good and you want to maintain.* Although many did not think that the procedures were good or that they should be maintained, the following list indicates the most frequently itemized methods of clinical evaluation. Once again, there was considerable continuity and similarity of responses regardless of the workshop location or background of the participants.

- Observation
- Anecdotal notes
- Student evaluation
- Skills checkoff in the lab
- Criteria with stated behaviors
- Feedback from others
- Behavioral objectives
- Process recording
- Diary

- Nursing-care plans
- Case studies
- Conferences with students
- Written examinations
- Faculty impressions
- Published learning systems performance tests

In addition to the more common procedures listed above, the following also were suggested:

- Medication cards
- Pre- and postconference discussion
- Talking with patients after care
- Checkoff of tasks from a list of expectations
- A weighted system
- Role playing
- Return demonstrations
- Student self-evaluation
- On-the-spot questioning
- Critical incidents
- Demonstrations in the lab

Responses to this question at a midwestern workshop indicate the seriousness of the deficiencies in the current practices used for clinical evaluation.

- We use no form, only subjective statements helpful with some objectives but nothing uniform for all students. Each instructor evaluates differently because of the lack of a form.
- Problems with the present tool are it's too lengthy, not specific, has satisfactory and unsatisfactory as a grade.
- We use an evaluation tool based on the nursing process; it utilizes a rating scale of 0 to 5.
- We try to use a critical criteria list for each skill; however, I don't think everything on the list is critical.
- What I now use is personal observation on the unit after a return demonstration in the classroom.
- Direct observation of the student and reports by unit personnel concerning students.
- We now use weekly evaluation of students; the problem is not enough time to adequately observe the students to evaluate them better.
- We have no preestablished criteria for performance evaluation; we use anecdotal record sheets and daily notes.

Participants at a workshop in the Far West described some procedures they currently use and their opinions of them. These comments further elaborate the current status of clinical performance evaluation. One participant simply wrote the word "none," almost in despair and frustration. Another one wrote several comments, scratched them out and then wrote "definitely needs revision." Still another said "anecdotal notes, but a better way would help." Another one wrote: "We don't have an independent examiner therefore a bias is always present.'' Further comments follow.

- I'm open to any new suggestions because I'm not pleased with what I am currently using. Procedures I like include observation in terms of criteria, nursing-care plan evaluation and a written clinical quiz. A brief discussion with the student prior to the procedure where they tell me what they plan to do and the pertinent safety, teaching, and technical points they intend to practice. A brief discussion after the procedure discussing what they did and emphasizing those things they did well and suggestions for improvement of those points that were omitted.

One final quote from this workshop group expresses still more feelings of frustration. After listing several activities used in the evaluation process, the nurse educator wrote: ''Sometimes I feel it evaluates the faculty's ability to evaluate rather than the student's ability to practice nursing.''

From these and other comments on hundreds of questionnaires that were submitted, it is clear that faculty members across the country are unhappy with the procedures currently being used. They feel frustrated and are convinced that what they are doing is unfair. They realize that simply using a checklist, anecdotal notes, subjective observations, reports from others' written papers, care plans, studies, diaries, and the like are insufficient means to document actual ability. Some of them readily admit that judgments are based on ''feelings'' about students and anecdotal notes that they further acknowledge are subjective. Thus the problem is there: it is bothersome and it is national in scope.

The methods of clinical evaluation described by the participants stand in direct contradiction to the goals they previously listed for the first question on the questionnaire: objectivity, consistency, comparability, accuracy. The conflict expressed in the responses to these two items on the survey makes it abundantly clear that a great deal of work must be done to implement objective clinical performance in education and/or service settings. The stress encountered, as well as the anxiety and the frustration described, are abundant both on behalf of students and faculty members. Based on the experience of the Regents External Degree nursing faculty and others who have been working toward a similar goal, it now seems possible to develop and implement objective performance examinations in a variety of education and service settings. The academic benefits and the psychological relief are more than remote possibilities. These prospects for improvement are incentive enough for many who want to begin the development process immediately.

DIFFICULT AREAS IN CLINICAL PERFORMANCE EVALUATION

Another question included on the surveys used at several of the workshops asked participants: What do you think are the most difficult areas to cope with in evaluating clinical performance? As a way of specifying areas of concern, eight structured responses were provided with space for checking all that applied. Data were obtained at six different workshops conducted in: central New York State, Chicago, Minneapolis, Utah, Sacramento, and San Jose. Participants came from a wide geographic area in their state or region, and represented many different education programs. Most were from associate-degree and baccalaureate programs, although some represented in-service education and continuing-education programs. A total of 178 individuals answered this particular question, responding to one or more of the eight problem areas listed. While most of the other questions on the survey used an open-ended format to obtain unrestricted comments in the individual's own words, this question provided the opportunity to determine specific and structured responses. The results from this survey question have been tabulated and are presented in Table 2.1 and Table 2.2.

In one sense Table 2.1 provides a summary of all the foregoing information. It gives an indication of the concerns about subjectivity, lack of available objective instruments, lack of comparability in the testing episodes, inconsistency in the evaluation process, and time problems associated with conducting explicit performance evaluations. It will be clear from the table that individuals have responded to 1, 2, or up to 8 different entries. Consequently, total percents are not reported. When one looks at the total columns, it is clear that subjectivity, the lack of available testing instruments, and inconsistency among the faculty are the major concerns. A total of 134 (75 percent) participants checked subjectivity, 61 percent checked faculty inconsistency, and 60 percent indicated lack of objective tools as the most difficult areas in performance evaluation. Lack of specific testing time was noted by 54 percent; 49 percent checked lack of comparability in testing episodes.

TABLE 2.1
What do you think are the most difficult areas to cope with in evaluating clinical performance?

Problem Areas	Central New York State N=24*		Chicago N=30		Minnesota N=55		Utah N=20		Sacramento N=22		San Jose N=27		Total N=178	
	No.	%	No.	%	No.	%	No.	%	No.	%	No.	%	No.	%
1. Subjective nature of clinical evaluation	17	71	26	87	39	71	9	45	20	91	23	85	134	75
2. Lack of available objective tools	14	58	21	70	30	54	10	50	12	54	20	74	107	60
3. Lack of comparable patient situations for all students	9	38	20	67	29	53	8	40	11	50	11	41	88	49
4. Inconsistency among faculty in evaluating clinical ability	18	75	15	50	30	54	12	60	16	73	18	67	109	61
5. Pressure from students for positive outcome	7	29	10	33	13	24	9	45	6	27	7	26	52	29
6. Pressure from faculty or school for positive and/or negative outcome	3	1	4	1	13	24	2	1	2	1	2	1	26	15
7. Lack of time to conduct clinical evaluation separate from instruction	11	46	17	57	37	67	3	2	11	50	17	63	96	54
8. No designated time in schedule for period of performance exam	6	25	12	40	15	27	2	1	10	45	7	26	52	29

*The N at the top of each column indicates how many participants responded to this particular question. Some checked one entry and others checked from two to all eight problem areas.

TABLE 2.2
Rank Order of Problems in Six Workshops

Problem Areas	Central New York State	Chicago	Minnesota	Utah	Sacramento	San Jose	Summary Rank Order
1. Subjective nature of clinical evaluation	2	1	1	3*	1	1	1
2. Lack of available objective tools	3	2	3*	2	3	2	2
3. Lack of comparable patient situations for all students	5	3	4	4	4*	5	5
4. Inconsistency among faculty in evaluating clinical ability	1	5	3*	1	2	3	3
5. Pressure from students for positive outcome	6	7	6*	3*	6	6*	6*
6. Pressure and faculty or school for positive and/or negative outcome	8	8	6*	6*	7	7	7
7. Lack of time to conduct clinical evaluation separate from instruction	4	4	2	5	4*	4	4
8. No designated time in schedule for period of performance exam	7	6	5	6*	5	6*	6*

*Same ranking.

Another way of summarizing this information is to place in rank order (Table 2.2) the problems as perceived by the participants in the various geographic areas. The summary rank order column makes it possible to get a clear impression of the areas of concerns (nationally), among the faculty members regarding the problems associated with clinical performance evaluation. For example, as indicated earlier, subjectivity is ranked as Number 1 by those at four of the six workshops. At two other meetings it was ranked as either second or third in order of frequency. The two workshops that did not list subjectivity in first place both listed inconsistency in the evaluation process as number one priority.

The second most frequently listed problem area (as seen in the total column) is the lack of available objective tools for evaluating students. At three of the workshops it was in second place, and at three others it ranked third place. The third most frequently mentioned area is inconsistency among faculty members in evaluating students and in the methods used. While two workshops valued it in third order of priority, two areas (central New York and Utah) listed it as the highest priority. The Sacramento-area participants ranked it as fifth in the order of frequency mentioned. The fourth most frequently mentioned problem area was the lack of time to conduct clinical evaluation separate from clinical instruction. In four of the area workshops it was ranked as fourth. Those in the Minneapolis area, however, ranked it in second place while the Utah participants ranked it as fifth. The fifth most frequently mentioned problem area was incomparability of testing episodes, i.e., of patient situations used during the evaluation process. While participants in two workshops rated it as Number 5, three other groups ranked it as fourth; those in the Chicago area listed it as the third most frequently encountered problem with which they had to cope. In this summary of rank orders, both the pressure from students and limited time in the schedule for conducting examinations corank in sixth place. The least frequently checked problem area was that related to pressure from faculty or the school for either positive or negative outcomes for the performance examination. It consistently achieved the lowest rank order of responses; clearly it is less of a problem than most of the other concerns.

To summarize, the following areas are listed in descending order of frequency mentioned as the concerns of those who attended workshops to learn more about the development of objective performance examination:

1. Subjectivity in clinical evaluation.
2. Lack of available objective tools.
3. Inconsistency among the faculty in the evaluation process.
4. Lack of time for evaluation as separate from that designated for instruction.
5. Incomparability of the testing episodes used during performance evaluation.
6. The pressure from students for positive outcomes and the lack of time designated in the schedule for clinical performance.
7. Pressure from faculties for particular final outcomes of the evaluation process.

Other open-ended questions on the survey asked when clinical examinations were given in the programs and where they were conducted. For the most part faculty members do not use clinical examinations but use clinical evaluation procedures, primarily during most nursing courses. Some simulated tests are given in the laboratory setting. Some participants indicated the use of patient-care areas but, again, this probably related to clinical evaluation (not examination) and reflects the confusion that exists between explicit examinations and the ongoing day-to-day clinical evaluation procedures. Some program participants indicated the use of simulated situations in the nursing laboratory and mentioned that repeat demonstrations of specific procedures were required after failure on the first attempt.

SUMMARY

One may conclude from the structured surveys used at a number of workshops that the problems encountered by nurse teachers seem to be essentially the same. They are faced with the stressful and difficult task of assessing the clinical competence of students during and at the conclusion of the education program, without the benefits of preestablished instruments, with inadequate preparation and guidance in objective observation, and with little or no time in the schedule for accomplishing it. Almost universally clinical instructors have had no formal (or even informal) preparation in the techniques of developing or using objective performance examinations. Typically, the clinical experience schedule is overextended, with a multitude of learning objectives that leave no time for a separate clinical examination period. Furthermore, teachers do not want to relinquish clinical practice time for testing purposes.

But even more fundamentally, there is remarkable confusion between the teaching–learning process and objective performance testing. This is both an academic and a philosophic issue but the confusion and lack of understanding about the necessity for both activities has hindered the much-needed progress in resolving the long-standing problems associated with the situation. Because of a lack of clarity about teaching and testing roles and about learning time and final demonstration time, multiple specific problems can be identified. These include: subjectivity in both teaching and testing; gross inconsistency in the evaluation process; use of ambiguous and inappropriate methods to derive a clinical grade; neglect of the development of explicitly written objective tools for clinical assessment; and insufficient time schedule for clinical testing. Furthermore, it also means that students receive inadequate guidance regarding the standard of expectations for their practice—both as learners and subsequently as practitioners.

All of these problems can be resolved. The need for and interest in doing so has been much discussed in the nursing literature over many years. Recently a renewed interest has been clearly demonstrated at nationwide meetings concerning performance testing. These meetings were sponsored by specific schools and agencies, statewide or regional groups, and by national nursing organizations. It is clear that the experience gained in developing the performance examinations for the Regents External Degree Program has generated some fundamental concepts and approaches that may assist teachers and administrators of nursing in the difficult job of improving objective performance assessment. These specific experiences have been elaborated further during the workshops and other meetings and provide the basis for many of the ideas, criteria, principles, and generalizations developed in this volume.

CHAPTER 3

Constellation of Basic Concepts and Their Influence

The effective development and use of performance examinations involves a complex integration of several essential concepts. Each concept is important in and of itself and the use of any one of them will facilitate better clinical assessment. However, the comprehensive application of all of them will maximize the process of developing and implementing an objective performance examination. Some of them may appear to be more pertinent than others, and some may be more relevant than others for specific evaluation purposes or for different groups requiring assessment; however, each one forms a significant part of an integrated whole, a constellation of key variables, a gestalt. Each deserves serious consideration by any group planning to develop a clinical examination, regardless of how limited or comprehensive it is or the situation in which it is to be administered.

The extent to which an individual instructor or a faculty group, applies or neglects each concept has a major influence on clinical evaluation per se and on final behavioral outcomes for individuals as well. The same factor also influences the effectiveness of the total program, which ultimately is reflected in the profession generally. Individual teachers, faculties, and total programs can be characterized by the manner in which these concepts are integrated into clinical evaluation. By self-admission, many faculties want to change their current image as well as their assessment procedures. Thus an understanding of these concepts, their potential structure that enables individuals and faculty groups to modify and improve current evaluation procedures. The degree of faculty commitment to implementing these concepts is a strong indicator of the success that can be expected in the transition from subjective to more valid and objective clinical assessment.

Among the many variables that deserve consideration, ten fundamental concepts will be considered in this chapter: (1) performance examination; (2) areas of care (or dimensions of practice); (3) critical elements; (4) objectivity; (5) sampling; (6) comparability; (7) level of acceptability; (8) systematized conditions; (9) flexibility in structure; and (10) consistency. While some of these areas pertain to content, some to characteristics of the text, and others to structure and process, all of them emanate from and are inherently related to the concept of performance examination. The notion of "examination" seems to be the most fundamental concept and yet the one most misunderstood in the context of clinical assessment. Even though it is used routinely to evaluate achievement of theoretical knowledge, a comparable examination in its full application (as described here) is a relatively new idea in the assessment of clinical competence.

PERFORMANCE EXAMINATION

Traditionally, instructors have applied the term "evaluation" to the clinical portion of a course and reserved the term "examination" for the theory portion. They have little or no difficulty in recognizing the need for a specific time to "test" a student's comprehension of the theoretical aspects of a given course, and in realizing that such a test should be developed and administered in as objective and consistent a fashion as possible. In this way each student is assured of an equal opportunity to document achievement of the objectives and content of the course. Teachers also acknowledge that students need a given period of time to learn, without constantly being examined. Therefore, written tests are scheduled periodically and students usually know in advance the date on which they are expected to demonstrate their mastery of the content. Sometimes a "spot quiz" is given, but by and large it does not count for a major portion of the course grade, and students usually are told—by the teacher or by previous students through the grapevine—that such quizzes should be expected without prior notification. When the course grade is largely dependent on midterm and final written examinations, students can study accordingly—briefly reviewing those areas in which they feel confident while spending most of the available time and effort on areas in which they feel insecure. They have an outline of the course objectives and the content to be covered and can study according to their needs. Faculty are expected to inform students of the content and conditions of the examination and students are expected to learn and demonstrate their achievement on the test.

Not so with the clinical portion of the course. From the first day students enter the arena of clinical "practice" they are expected to perform exactly as instructed and are observed to be sure that they do so. In fact they not only are observed as often as the instructor can get around to them, but descriptive notes are also written beginning on the first learning day, and kept in the student's file as an official dossier to be used from that day forward. Whether those early attempts at practicing as a nurse are successful or abysmal failures, they are recorded and used in the final summary of the student's performance. While the student is still learning and trying to apply theory in practice situations the instructor is keeping score through anecdotal notes or behavior checklists. At the end of the course all notes—including those from the insecure beginning of the novice—are tallied to derive the all-important clinical grade. Judgment about final achievement is based on learning time as well as the last performance. Translating this to students of drama, it would be comparable to deciding a "clinical" grade on the basis of the first script reading and early practice sessions as well as on the final performance of the play.

Furthermore, students frequently have only a vague understanding of exactly what is expected of them during the early portion of the course or program—except that they are to perform with skill, regardless of the situation that evolves in the real world of client care. How fortunate are those whose assigned patients remain stable and uncomplicated by the unexpected! Unlike the classroom (where the content to be learned is outlined and reasonably precise), the clinical experience is immersed in ambiguity and evolving complexity. And well it should be, say some instructors, to facilitate the student's learning of how to cope with the stress of the real world of nursing. That point of view, however, is open to question.

LEARNING AND TESTING

This view, of course, presents clearly the point being made: the time for learning clinical practice is not the same as the time for being tested on competence to perform in a given situation and according to a specified standard. As with theory, there is a time for unjudged learning and a time for demonstrating achievement in the clinical setting, whether actual or simulated. Observations, anecdotal notes, checklists, and the like are valuable tools in the teaching–learning process. Students need the guidance and experienced advice of their teachers if they are to grow in their understanding of nursing and in their competence to practice it at the designated level. Their awareness of how well they perform is enlarged by accurate and analytic perceptions of instructors. Constructive feedback from teachers following each clinical episode is most beneficial in helping the student to learn, to change, and ultimately to become a nurse.

Sometimes students receive too little observation and resultant feedback because instructors are assigned to supervise the clinical experiences of too many students at any one time. Their learning potential, therefore is diminished, and the anecdotal notes of necessity become vague and generalized. Nonetheless, these notes typically are tallied along with all others in arriving at a final summary of the students' clinical abilities at the end of the course. In other situations when instructors have too many students they focus on those students assumed to be "weak" or less capable, to the neglect of the others. This method automatically means that those students not observed are assumed to be practicing satisfactorily, so long as nothing to the contrary is reported and nothing devastating happens. While teachers experience some degree of anxiety about such situations, they feel there is little alternative and simply go on writing blissfully ambiguous anecdotal notes based on assumption and hearsay rather than on direct observation. So-called "good" students therefore may be fortunate in one sense: they don't have the instructor constantly hovering over them, looking for problems; however, at the same time, they unquestionably are deprived of the benefits of critical analysis of the expert (teacher) and the feedback so essential to confirm their level of competence and self-confidence. It is this interaction that helps them during the learning process, and enables them to expand both knowledge and skills in nursing practice.

Although technically most of the time in a program is spent in the learning phase, it is clear that what goes on during this period influences the final judgments made about the student, regardless of whether significant direct observations were made or appropriate feedback for the student was exchanged. While "good" students are left to learn on their own, the "weak" student typically receives the undivided attention of the instructor, lest something unfortunate happen to the patient. However, this of necessity means that the instructor knows much more about this student—positive and negative—and writes more specific notes to be included in the tally for the final score. It is not uncommon for these students to feel that the instructors are focusing excessively on them, which only makes them more and more nervous and vulnerable. It is quite understandable that they develop feelings of mild paranoia that compounds their stress and consequently their ability to perform to the level of their potential. More errors are made, which perpetuates undesirable behaviors of both students and teachers. This spiral effect can become overwhelming, especially when the students realize that incorrect actions or inactions made while trying to learn are being recorded for future reference. They constantly feel the stress of being in a testing situation, even though they are still learning and have not yet mastered the expectations held for them. The situation is further compounded because in many instances they are not even sure of the explicit behaviors they are expected to perform. Students subjected to this kind of "tyranny of the tally" find it difficult to escape if they get a poor start. The longer the negative tallies are accumulated the more stifling the tyranny becomes.

PERPETUATING PROBLEMS

By very definition, students need a time to learn as well as a time to be tested on theory and clinical performance. During the learning phase they need repeated guidance, assistance and feedback—without the fear of negative anecdotal buildup that can be used against them, and that doggedly will follow them all the days of their life in the program. While anecdotal notes can be useful in the learning phase (to help students realize how someone else perceives their actions), they are typically too subjective to be used as the basis for final decisions about the students' actual abilities. Too many variables are uncontrolled, or even acknowledged. As previously pointed out, those already judged to be "good" students generally received positive (albeit frequently ambiguous) notes derived from scanty observation while those already labeled "poor" students receive excessive supervision that results in more specific and more numerous notes. Regardless of the students' current abilities or potential for mastery, such prejudgments and resulting teacher behaviors greatly influence both learning and evaluation in the clinical setting. So often students are subjectively stereotyped very early in the course of events and thereafter are observed accordingly by busy instructors who are relieved to find some "good" students who do not have to be supervised constantly. The student is unaware of the ultimate importance of performance during these early clinical experiences.

When clinical learning and clinical testing are differentiated and respected as separate but essential parts of a whole, both learning and the valid demonstration of competence have a better chance of success. However, when faculty are asked when they conduct clinical examinations, they typically confuse examination with evaluation and respond that they are in the clinical setting.

Traditionally, the use of continuous evaluation procedures (anecdotal buildup) has been a substitute for an explicit examination of clinical performance—and with good reason. Until recently, few if any faculties had developed objective, comprehensive performance examinations. For one reason or another, the idea of an examination of actual performance has remained latent or at best ignored for many years. Some faculty members probably believe a clinical examination is not appropriate while others believe it is too difficult to accomplish and therefore do not even try. For many, the definitions and functions of examination and evaluation have been confused and unconsciously merged, to the detriment of the concept of clinical examination and student assessment. For all intents and purposes, cumulative, subjective evaluations have been assumed to constitute a clinical examination.

This unwitting confusion has been promulgated in graduate-school courses preparing clinical teachers and administrators and is further compounded by actual current practice in all types of nursing education programs. Student teachers are not taught how nor do they learn how to develop and use performance examinations from role models in the academic setting. Thus they merely perpetuate the system—even though most of them experience some degree of discomfort and anxiety with it.

As stated earlier, in recent years an increasing interest has been expressed in the development and use of objective performance examinations. There seems to be a yearning for a better way. Among other things, the movement of competency-based education, the need for increased accountability in practice, the growth of the adult education and the nontraditional movement, and the marked increase in the need for flexibility in educational programs, have all brought the idea of competency testing to the attention of nursing educators and leaders throughout the country. The development of the New York Regents Degree Nursing Programs and its unique clinical performance examination was like an insistent wedge that opened the way for conventional programs to adopt such examinations suitable for their own students. The need for more objective assessment of clinical competence has repeatedly been acknowledged. How to accomplish it (the central concern of this book) is the problem and the concern of most nursing faculties, as well as those in in-service and continuing education.

DISTINGUISHING DIFFERENCES

The first and most fundamental step, however, is the clear understanding of the difference between—and the functions of—evaluation and examination in the clinical domain. Only when the faculty (individually and collectively) resolve this issue can the other essential concepts be applied, resulting in more valid and equitable clinical assessment. But it must be clearly understood that the use of such examinations is best accompanied by a designated learning time, free of penalty or the perpetuation of faculty comments made while the student struggles to learn. The tyranny of the tally system must be broken, with anecdotal notes being used only to help students see their behavior through the eyes of a caring and responsible expert.

Also essential to the idea of clinical performance examination is the clarification that written tests about the clinical experience do not constitute a performance examination—nor do written case studies, nursing-care plans, process recordings, diaries, or similar papers. In most cases these devices are beneficial during the learning experience; they help students to integrate and expand their knowledge, apply principles, engage in analysis and synthesis, comprehend the complexities of nursing, and become more secure in the role they are learning. But they serve a learning function and are cognitive in nature; they do not provide the opportunity for students to demonstrate, or for instructors to observe, actual clinical performance. They can, and should be used as appropriate learning techniques and as evaluations of cognitive achievement, but they must be differentiated from an examination of the student's competence in the practice of nursing. This separation is fundamental.

Just as the construction and administration of written theory examinations are governed by certain rules, so are performance examinations. For example, written tests are given on prespecified dates, and cover prespecified content, both of which are known to the students in advance. Prior to giving the test, the teacher determines exactly what questions will be asked based on a sample of the content from the several topics covered. Furthermore, the exact answers that will be accepted as correct are specified, and so is the tolerance for error to be allowed for a passing score. Also the process for grading and the mechanics of administration are known in advance by teachers and students.

Similarly, in an appropriately designed objective clinical examination, students should be informed in advance of the possible array of competencies on which they will be tested. They should know in advance the critical behaviors (critical elements) that will be examined and the extent to which they must be satisfied to achieve a passing grade. They also should know all conditions under which the test will be given, and should expect evaluator bias to be controlled by the specific "test items" and by the predetermined rules of administration. Consequently, passing such an examination is based on the student's ability to demonstrate expected behaviors in predesignated categories, known well in advance of the test. This ensures objective assessment instead of anecdotal buildup. If students fail it is with their full awareness of the standard, leaving little grounds for criticism or complaining. It is a criterion-referenced test, not a guessing game, and its purpose is to document the student's achievement of an expected standard of performance.

Regarded with this perspective, performance examinations, whether actual or simulated situations are used, require the same kinds of objective considerations as written tests. When regarded as an explicit objective examination, the faculty can concentrate their efforts to ensure clarity in what is to be examined, the extent of student involvement, the level of acceptability, the degree of tolerable error, the array of possible inclusions, the conditions under which the examination will be given, and the appropriate structure and process for administration. Just as with written examinations, the emphasis here is on predetermining content as well as procedures and criteria for success, in order to provide an objective, equitable, and appropriate opportunity for the learner to demonstrate achievement of the stated goals. Consistency in developing the test, in administering it, and in judging students' behavior is imperative for performance as well as for written examinations.

AREAS OF CARE

The process of how to determine exactly what will be tested will be discussed later, but one way of organizing that content is to identify the array of discrete areas of nursing care or dimensions of practice* that are appropriate for selection during the examination. Instead of listing all of the possible specific tasks, procedures, or behaviors that fall within the domain of nursing (appropriate to the course or type of program in which the examination occurs), the concept of areas of care or dimensions of practice clusters similar activities under one of several simple headings. Generally the clusters are formed around activities that incorporate similar principles or competencies. By clustering several nursing activities under one heading, the number of categories to be developed is reduced to a manageable list and the focus is on nursing behaviors rather than procedures per se. Each dimension is specifically defined in terms of the scope and purpose of the examination and all of the nurse-related behaviors essential to its implementation (called "critical elements") are itemized. This approach allows any of the specific activities included in that particular area of care category to be used to test the competencies required in that area.

Applying the concept of areas of care to performance testing is helpful both during the development and implementation phases. As already indicated, it reduces the number of areas in the array and therefore decreases the amount of time required to develop the test (once the idea is understood and accepted). Obviously, the fewer the categories to be defined the fewer the critical elements to be specified, which technically is the single most difficult problem confronting the committee responsible for developing the test. It is this identification of areas of practice to be included—and, consequently, those that may be excluded—that sets in motion a list of other developmental activities.

---

*In some types of programs the term "dimensions of practice" may be preferable because of the scope of the behaviors being tested: other programs may prefer the term "areas of care." In this book, the two terms frequently are used interchangeably because the concept is the same.

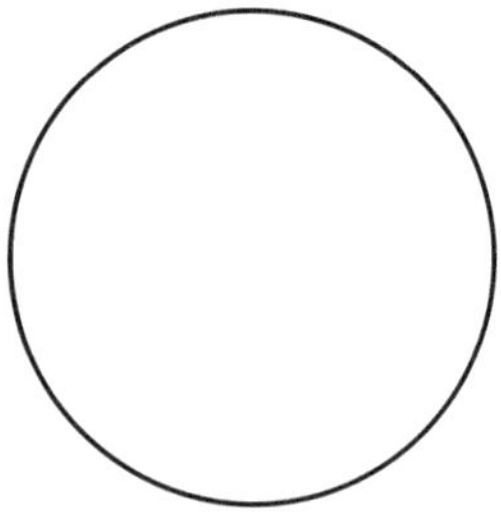

Fig. 3.1. The image of what is being investigated is complete of itself—as represented by a perfect circle. Whether simple or complex, it is viewed as a discrete totality.

To understand how dimensions of practice (areas of care) and their associated critical elements are related to the examination itself, some helpful concepts will be borrowed from sociology and adapted to fit the purpose.

In his graduate courses, Paul F. Lazarsfeld, a noted sociologist long associated with Columbia University, taught an approach to survey research that is beautiful in its straightforward simplicity and directness.* While the fit is not exact, the idea is nonetheless appropriate to the current discussion, and will be described briefly for the perspective it provides. When one is trying to find the answers to a researchable problem, it is essential at the outset of planning the research to conceive the complete image of the notion (problem, concept, theory) being explored—e.g., to isolate it as a single discrete entity that can be envisioned by itself, regardless of how complex or simple. Whatever the problem, it must be conceived as a whole, consisting of whatever parts it naturally possesses. It can be represented by a closed circle (Figure 3-1).

The second step in clarifying the research image is to identify all of the dimensions of that image—i.e., all of the integral parts that are included within it, essential to it, and that collectively comprise it. Identifying the dimensions and carefully defining them helps the researcher to be sure that all facets are covered and that the image is indeed complete (Figure 3.2a). Consciously or unconsciously omitting dimensions skews the perception of the image and distorts the development as well as the resulting findings and interpretations. Every

*The ideas discussed here are extracted from class presentations in sociology and survey research courses with Dr. Lazarsfeld between 1968 and 1971 at Columbia University, New York City.

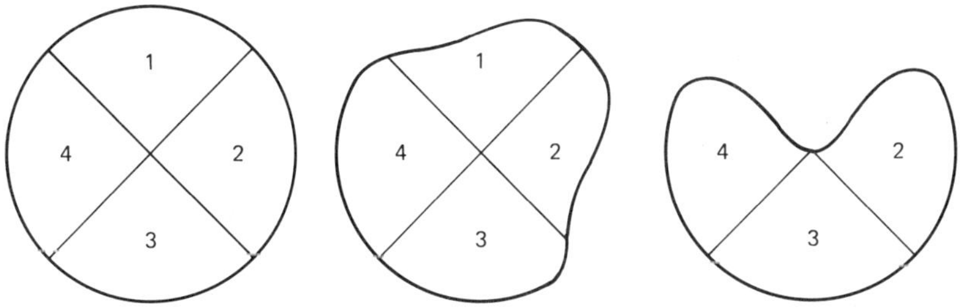

Fig. 3.2. The dimensions of the image. A. When all dimensions are accounted for, the result is a perfect circle. B. When some dimensions are omitted or overemphasized, the image is distorted; consequently, so are the content and results.

effort should be made during the planning phase to discover and to include all dimensions integral to the image (concept, problem/test) being explored or developed. Omitting or overemphasizing dimensions distorts the integrity of the whole, as illustrated in Figure 3.2B.

The third step is to decide on the most appropriate indicators of each dimension. In survey research these are the specific questions to be asked during the interview or to be included in the questionnaire. Collectively they provide the data essential to understanding the dimensions and consequently the image itself. The precise number of indicators needed varies from one dimension to another, but they must be sufficient to represent the particular area. Care must be taken to ensure that none of the dimension is misrepresented by too many, too few, or by inappropriate indicators (Figure 3-3).

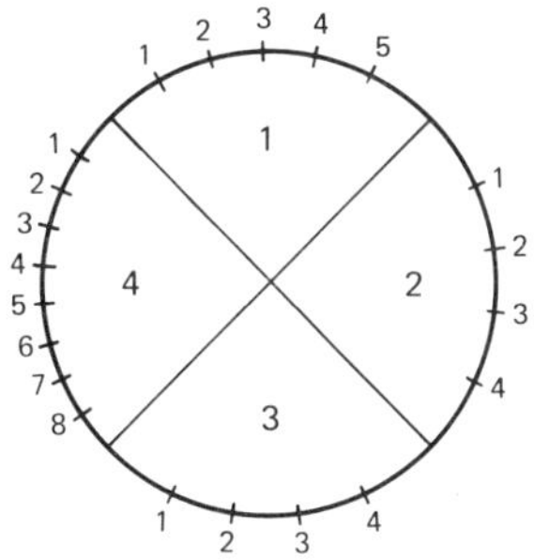

Fig. 3.3. Indicators of the dimensions of the image. Sufficient and explicit indicators for each dimension are specified to ensure that the image is comprehensively explored and understood.

This organizational approach is also applicable to the development of an objective performance examination. The examination itself corresponds to the image being investigated (or, in this case, being developed). As a matter of fact, the teacher is exploring the students' competence to perform that which has been designated as essential. The examination is the method for obtaining the data required for making a judgment as to whether or not acquired competencies match the desired expectations. The examination is seen as one complex image, a complete whole, regardless of whether it pertains to the competencies expected at the end of a course or at the end of an entire program. The dimensions of the examinations are the major areas of care to be included and which collectively represent the total content to be evaluated. The indicators of each dimension are the appropriate critical elements; i.e., those discrete behaviors of the student to be observed during the examination, and which clearly indicate competence.

MERITS OF SUCH ANALYSIS

This simple approach has considerable merit as a way of organizing the development of the examination content. It is functional regardless of whether the test uses actual or simulated situations, is circumscribed or comprehensive, or is designed for general students, special students, or learners in the service sector. It is a concise way of pursuing the problems and obtaining relevant data for analysis.

Just as developmental time is reduced by clustering activities, so is implementation time. Furthermore, the examination is made more functional if evaluators are free to select situations that test the competence required by the category (areas of care), rather than being required to find a series of particular procedures to be tested. This is particularly true when the examination is administered in an actual clinical setting and when it involves comprehensive performance, such as at the conclusion of a major portion of the total nursing program (regardless of the type of program).

The selection of particular dimensions to be included in the array depends on why, when, and where the examination is to be administered. If it is used at the end of the entire program the array of areas will differ considerably from an examination given at the end of an introductory nursing course. If it is administered in a hospital setting it will differ from one given in the nursing laboratory or a community setting. If it is given to test the students' ability to administer technical aspects of care to hospitalized patients, it will differ from one given to test competence in health assessment or leadership. The purpose and placement of the clinical examination are important aspects to consider during the planning and development phases, as they have a major influence on the dimensions to be tested and the specific behaviors to be measured. Some dimensions of practice in a comprehensive clinical performance examination might include: administration of medications (regardless of what, why, and how); use of fluids (regardless of what, why and how); measurements of mobility or vital signs; the use of irrigations; or the need for oxygenation. Some dimensions of comprehensive professional practice might include: health assessment; teaching; leadership; collaboration; or decision making.

The selection of dimensions to be included is the first level of sampling. At this point it is sufficient to note that the concept of dimensions of practice facilitates the development of the performance examination in that it samples from among the entire universe of possibilities of practice as well as clustering the specific tasks into manageable units for assessment.

For utilitarian purposes, areas of care to be included in the examination may be divided into three categories: required areas, selected areas, and overriding areas of concern. Required areas include those dimensions that all students are expected to perform; they are usually readily available and give a degree of uniformity to the examination. Selected areas are other dimensions that may be chosen, depending on the situation and availability; several selected areas are identified from a preestablished array and are reasonably comparable but allow the flexibility and variety necessary to conduct the examination in a clinical setting. Overriding areas describe behaviors that are continuously monitored throughout the examination, including asepsis, physical jeopardy, and emotional jeopardy. Subsequent sections will describe the process of developing and using these categories of behaviors.

CRITICAL ELEMENTS

Essential nursing behaviors or "critical elements," are the most finite units by which clinical performance is measured during the examination. They are the single, discrete, observable, and mandatory behaviors that collectively comprise the standard against which an individual's competence is measured. They are the essential elements of nursing practice for a given area of nursing care. When one of them is violated or omitted, patients are actually or potentially endangered and care being rendered is less than satisfactory.

The concept of critical elements is quite different from the more traditional approach of steps to be followed in the procedures of nursing care. Nursing-procedure manuals are filled with the sequential steps necessary to carry out the nursing care required by patients. They outline, sometimes in quaint minutia, the multiple and precise movements judged by the particular committee who developed them to be necessary in implementing a procedure or task. They are meant to help the novice practitioner realize the need to organize and efficiently move through the behaviors to accomplish the procedure in the best interest of the patient. For instance, 36 steps to make a bed have little in common with critical elements. A total of three critical elements may be sufficient because they do not describe how to make a bed but rather identify the essential points that must be assured.

Critical elements are *not* steps in implementing procedures. They require a different mind-set, come from a different perspective, and have a different purpose. If one could wipe the mental chalk board clean and start afresh, the basic question would be: What actions are essential to apply the relevant principles and implement the particular nursing care required? Stated otherwise: What is the essence of the desired nursing care for this type of situation stated in specific behavioral terms? What behaviors cut through the periphery and get to the heart of nursing practice required by the client? What is it the nurse really needs to accomplish? What does the patient need most?

For example, in the area of medications, rather than outlining all of the steps essential in preparing and administering drugs, the critical-elements approach states the behaviors that must be enacted to ensure safe practice, without details about the "how to." One of the benefits of this approach is its straightforward simplicity. The following critical elements developed by the Regents External Degree nursing subcommittee are applicable to evaluating the administration of any type of drugs, by any route, to any patient, under any circumstance:

1. Secures the correct medication.
2. Measures the correct dosage.
3. Administers the correct drug to the correct patient.
4. Uses the correct route and/or site for administering the medication.

5. Administers the medication within one-half hour of the scheduled time.
6. If IV medication:
   a. Clears air from tubing before initiating flow;
   b. Verifies patency of needle or tube before initiating flow;
   c. Administers or regulates flow to deliver correct amount in correct period of time.
7. Records medications.

MERITS OF THE APPROACH

By focusing the points of the examination on the critical elements, considerable subjectivity and variation in evaluator judgment is removed. Value judgments and differences of opinion frequently center on the multitude of less vital aspects of nursing care when any one of several techniques or approaches potentially might be acceptable. While faculty members themselves often disagree about "the best way," clear statements of expectations remove ambiguity and confusion and make the test more objective. Only the essential or critical elements are identified and precisely itemized; and thus they govern the only behaviors tested during the examination. They establish the measure of acceptable performance and the tolerance for error during the examination. All other aspects of care representing the ideal or epitome of practice are taught and practiced during the learning period, but during the examination, it is the essential behaviors that establish the basic standard. By very definition, however, a violation of a single critical element means that the patient has been jeopardized or received unsatisfactory care and that the student's level of competence is unacceptable in that episode. Failure to meet all critical elements constitutes a failure to meet the standard. Therefore, it is imperative that all behaviors designated as critical elements must, indeed, be essential for the client's well-being.

The areas of care and their respective critical elements identify the content of the implementation phase of the performance exam. Depending on the type of examination, specific guidelines (instead of critical elements) may be identified for the competencies to be examined during the planning and evaluation phases because these two phases are less concrete, and require more latitude to be evaluated. Guidelines are no less important, they simply require a different type of statement.

Such overriding areas as asepsis, and physical or emotional

jeopardy apply here as well as to all other areas of care. Violation of a single critical element listed for medications (or one of the overriding areas) automatically results in failure of that situation because an essential aspect of care has been omitted or incorrectly performed. The patient's well-being has been compromised, which constitutes unacceptable practice.

In contrasting this approach with the procedures approach it becomes clear that gathering the equipment and using sterile technique for example are omitted as "steps" not because they are unimportant but because they are subsumed under the stated critical elements. It is impossible to administer the correct drug without having the drug and the equipment necessary to dispense it—whatever is required. It also is impossible to give the correct drug and dosage without calculating and preparing it. These procedural steps are subsumed in the specific critical elements. However, though they are more general in one sense: they are worded as concretely and objectively as possible.

Asepsis provides another example. In nursing practice asepsis applies everywhere, all the time; it is second nature to a competent nurse. Consequently, critical elements for asepsis are written in a separate overriding category but apply in all situations. When they are violated, regardless of whatever else is being done, it is considered grounds for failure because the patient has been jeopardized. Their simplicity is remarkable when compared with the multiple repetition and sequential steps found in any procedure manual. Repetition and sequence may be essential for learning, but the use of critical elements during an examination is a different matter.

The critical elements for asepsis developed by the External Degree faculty include:

1. Protects self from contamination.
2. Protects patient from contamination.
3. Disposes of contaminated material in designated containers.
4. Confines contaminated material to contaminated areas.
5. If a sterile field is required: establishes and/or maintains a sterile field including instruments, equipment, and working area.

These statements do not tell the student or practitioner *how* to accomplish the task, but rather they focus on the behaviors that are mandatory for the patient's protection. In a performance examination, which by definition is a nonteaching situation, what is actually done takes precedence over the steps used to accomplish it as long as critical elements are not violated. Presumably the student already has learned "how"; the examination concentrates on whether the performance is acceptable as specified in the critical elements. As typically there is more than one way to conduct any procedure, any one will be accepted during the examination so long as the critical elements are performed and the patient is not otherwise jeopardized. For example, a dressing can be changed without contaminating the patient's wound whether the student uses gloves, forceps, another dry sterile dressing, or clean hands on the corners of the dressing. The objective is to change the dressing without contamination of the wound or otherwise spreading microorganisms to the patient, the nurse, or others in the environment. *How* this is accomplished may vary. The critical elements are general enough to allow the use of different techniques, but is absolutely specific in their mandate to prevent contamination or the spread of pathogenic organisms.

There is no standard number of critical elements for the dimensions of practice; the number varies with the area being examined and is subject to the discretion of the faculty developing the examination. Generally, it is desirable to keep the number of critical elements to a minimum and to focus on essentials.*

It is imperative that those responsible for developing and implementing a performance examination constantly remember that critical elements are the mandatory behaviors expected in acceptable practice. Frequently the committee developing the examination regresses into thinking of sequential steps or points to be covered in teaching the particular area. Although such material may be written in a logical and sequential flow, the intent is to identify what should be performed—not the detailed steps of how those actions care to be accomplished. The frame of mind (or direction of thought) for writing critical elements is quite different from past experience; faculties typically revert back to a more familiar mode unless their attention is periodically refocused.

While the discussion here is focused on using the concept of critical elements to identify behaviors to be tested, the same approach also could be applied to the teaching–learning phase. Because these lists are crystalized behavioral imperatives, they help both faculty and students to concentrate on the behaviors essential to desirable outcomes. To be sure, the specific techniques are helpful and should be presented in one form or another, but some instructors may find these

---

*A subsequent chapter will focus on the process of developing, writing, sorting and screening critical elements.

comments useful for teaching students the clinical aspects of nursing in the classroom and/or in the nursing laboratory.

ORGANIZING BASIC CONCEPTS

Thus far the concepts of examination, areas of care, and critical elements have been presented. Application of the concept of performance examination has the potential of revolutionizing (and improving) both clinical evaluation and clinical instruction. Using the concepts of dimensions of practice and critical elements helps to determine and organize the content to be included in the performance examination. The content to be included is also influenced by the type and level of the students being evaluated, the purpose and placement of the examination, and the test's relationship to other assessment tools being used. However, once these overall parameters are identified, the content is organized around dimensions of practice that are explicitly defined and for which all essential nursing behaviors (critical elements) are meticulously specified.

While the above-discussed concepts relate to content, the four concepts to follow characterize the examination and are applicable during both the development and implementation phases. They apply to the examination itself and to the manner in which it is administered. Omission or violation of these and the other concepts will almost certainly guarantee the failure of the faculty's efforts to achieve an objective and equitable performance examination. All of them are essential and cannot be emphasized too much. Every effort should be made during both the development and implementation phase to apply them deliberately and continuously. The four concepts that characterize the examination include: objectivity, sampling, comparability, and level of acceptability. The three remaining concepts relate to structure and process: consistency, systematized conditions and flexibility of structure (Figure 3.4).

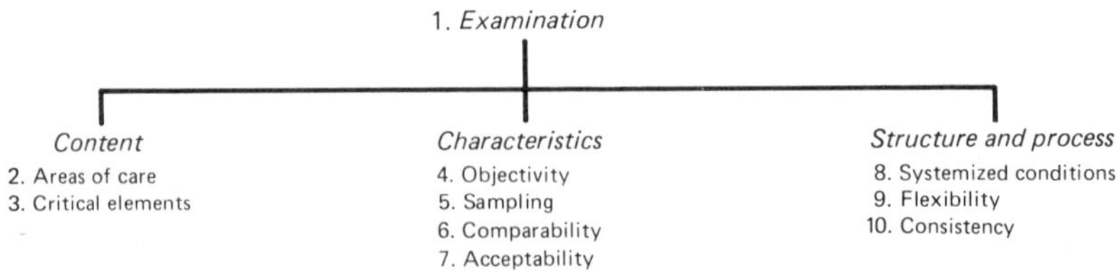

Fig. 3.4. Organization of ten basic concepts.

OBJECTIVITY

One of the most frequent complaints lodged against current clinical evaluation procedures is that they are too subjective and influenced by the biases of instructors. As revealed by the responses of nurse educators all over the country (discussed in Chapter 2), it is the number-one concern about clinical evaluation.

As previously pointed out, evaluation frequently is dependent upon how many times and under what conditions the student is observed. It is also subject to word-of-mouth and written commentaries passed along from previous instructors ("talk tyranny"), and may not necessarily take into account subsequent growth and changes in the student's behavior and actual learning. Once a student's behavior is characterized, the label frequently remains attached and compounds the difficulty of "becoming" and of maturing in knowledge and competence. Ensuring objectivity in clinical assessment is equally as important as in written examinations of theory. The development and use of an explicit performance examination, which outlines both content and process, is the most direct way to move toward objective clinical evaluation. When specific behaviors to be demonstrated are identified and stated without ambiguity for both students and faculty, the degree of subjectivity will necessarily be markedly diminished. When the conditions also are objectively stated and applied, subjectivity can be minimized further.

Use of an objective clinical examination does not negate the use or importance of faculty judgment, as some might infer from this discussion. It does, however, exert some control over the variations and discrepancies in faculty assessment of nursing performance in similar situations. One aspect of control is that the instrument itself dictates the behaviors to be evaluated as well as the degree and extent of performance that will be considered acceptable. This leaves little room for last-minute changes in what is expected and how it will be evaluated. It minimizes personal opinion about the student's performance, except as it explicitly relates to the stated behaviors being examined. It also provides a control on what students think "should be" or "shouldn't be" included in the examination. By explicitly identifying all essential behaviors, personal preferences and biases of individual teachers are minimized and the examination is made more objective.

Just as the concept of examination is pivotal in clinical evaluation so is the concept of objectivity. It is an attitude, a posture, a fundamental belief, a specific frame of reference that influences the faculty and that characterizes their approach and the resulting performance examination. Without this basic attitude—the objectivity frame of reference—the concept of examination as previously described cannot be implemented successfully. Without measures to ensure objectivity, the examination loses its power and is reduced to ambiguous evaluation.

Objectivity is achieved primarily through the development of a standard set of critical behaviors to be performed during the examination; these are written explicitly and used in preparation for the test. The critical elements are comparable to items on a written examination. They are stated in such a way that the expected behaviors, as worded, have a precise and uniform meaning for the faculty and the students. The "correct" answers also are clear both to students and to the faculty, and can be documented in the nursing literature; furthermore, they are appropriate to the students' learning and level in the program. To minimize subjectivity, "value words" and ambiguity are eliminated insofar as is possible. Once the critical elements ("items") are identified and accepted by the faculty, they are *not* changed by individual teachers during the examination because of the student, the situation, or any other variable. They apply to *all* students, *all* the time. To a large extent, then, objectivity during the performance examination depends on the specific identification of critical elements to be tested, which elements are worded as unambiguously as possible and applied without qualification to all students. Other concepts related to developing content and process also influence objectivity. Each of these concepts is part of an integrated whole and in the real setting should not be considered in isolation. The complex interrelatedness of concepts and their influences on objective assessment will be discussed after all ten basic concepts have been defined and discussed separately.

SAMPLING

While the concept of sampling has always applied to written examinations it usually has not been a major consideration in clinical evaluation. In developing theory examinations, test items are written on a variety of topics included in the course-content outline, with no intention of reflecting every bit of knowledge the student was expected to learn. Technically, written tests are constructed by first developing a blueprint and specifications to ensure that the questions asked represents the entire array of content to be covered. The blueprint outlines major topics to be tested and the specifications indicate the number of items to be written to be certain that each topic is tested proportionate to its overall importance. The questions, therefore, test a sample of the total body of knowledge. Students have the outline of content covered (course outline and objectives) and have studied the entire array of topics, but they do not know which specific items will be included until they take the examination. They must study all of the content but they are tested only on a sample taken from the whole. The sample, if properly developed, represents the whole array of learning and precludes the necessity of testing every discrete bit of knowledge.

When the notion of examination is applied to clinical evaluation, the concept of sampling also can be fully incorporated. During the development of the performance examination, major content areas appropriate to the purpose and placement of the test are outlined. Only those aspects that require performance (observable application of theory) and only those topics most reflective of the content are included. In the first level of sampling the most frequently used and most appropriate performance areas are selected from the entire universe of possibilities for potential inclusion on the test. Students are informed that this array constitutes those areas of care (or dimensions of practice) on which they potentially will be tested. The second level of sampling takes place at the time the test is administered. Ultimately, the particular configuration of areas on which students are tested depends on the available patients who meet the criteria for selection. The flexibility required for the second level of sampling accommodated by the number and types of areas required by the faculty.

Students preparing for the examination are expected to learn and to perform all areas of care listed in the array, accurately applying all critical elements (first-level sampling). However, during the actual examination they will be required to implement only a specified number of areas of care, but they will not know until the start of the test which ones they actually will have to perform (second-level sampling). The assumption is that if students can perform areas *A*, *B*, and *C* correctly they probably can perform *D*, *E*, and *F*—so long as the assignment of patient situations is done on a random basis.

The concept of sampling, properly applied, saves considerable time in developing clinical examinations and in their subsequent administrations. Definitions and critical elements have to be written only for those areas of care potentially to be tested, rather than for the entire universe of possibilities.

All other areas of care covered during the course or program are no less important during the learning phase, but may not be representative or found frequently enough in the clinical setting to be included in the performance examination. By using sampling technique the number of areas to be tested is reduced to a manageable number. It permits the examination to be given in a reasonable time period and greatly facilitates comparability of testing episodes (another concept to be discussed later). Each student, therefore, is tested on a configuration of areas of care that are selected from a sample array but modified by the available patient situations. However, in order to control this second level of specific sampling, specific criteria govern the selection of patients and the number of areas to be tested in each situation.

COMPARABILITY

Objectivity is essential, but a performance examination also must ensure that each testing episode is comparable in the demands placed on the students. The degree of complexity of nursing care required probably will not ever be exactly the same when the examination is administered in the clinical setting. The problems presented by clients are as variable as their number. Each patient has a unique array of nursing-care needs and the clinical examination realistically has to take this into account if it is to function within the real world. One of the problems, therefore, in developing a comprehensive test of clinical competence is that of devising a mechanism that takes into account variability in client care needs, while expecting comparable behaviors in the students' performance. To be fair, the test evaluates the students' competence to administer nursing care that is of equivalent complexity, with no one situation remarkably different from another. The degree of stringency must be controlled to the extent possible to prevent some students from having excessively difficult patient situations while others have excessively easy ones.

The concept of comparability applies both to the development of examination content and procedures, and is relevant during the planning phase as well as during its administration to students. In addition to requiring similar nursing competencies, efforts also have to be made to assure comparability in such conditions as the time allotted for care, specifications for written plans and evaluations, reporting and interactions with the staff, and other procedural matters. Such assurances can be implemented only if they become part of the instrument itself and the documents describing how it is to be used by students and faculty. These procedural aspects will be discussed in detail in subsequent chapters; here it is sufficient to note that another one of the major considerations in developing a clinical performance examination is the comparability of required expectations, regardless of the diversity of client situations being used during the test, or other variables.

Ensuring comparability is more difficult when the examination is administered in an actual patient-care environment; however, the same concept applies to simulated situations conducted in the nursing laboratory in which the scope of abilities being tested is limited. Whether the performance test covers one or two basic skills or the entire comprehensive care of a patient, comparability of testing episodes is a key consideration. Specific methods must be used to be certain that every student has an equal chance of passing, and that no students will be singled out for more difficult or for easier patient situations.

LEVEL OF ACCEPTABILITY

The concept of acceptability also is important in developing a performance examination because it gives direction for determining the degree of excellence expected of the students during the test period. It also guides the faculty in selecting the areas to be included and in writing the critical elements. One of the primary considerations in developing a performance examination is to insure that the level of performance demanded of students is reasonable and is neither too excessive nor too minimal. Establishing the level of acceptability controls the degree of toleration for error during the test, or the amount of deviation from perfection that will be judged as possible.

Determining what constitutes acceptable or reasonable performance depends on the purpose and placement of the examination, the level of student in the program and the areas to be included. It also is a function of the philosophy of the faculty/committee preparing the examination. They determine the degree of accuracy or perfection expected of the average student and reflect this decision in the precise wording of critical elements. Therefore the critical elements, once finalized, explicitly state the essential nursing behaviors that constitute acceptable practice—therefore they must be performed with 100 percent accuracy. How reasonable, how accurate, how stringent the performance must be in order to be labeled "acceptable" is a major responsibility of the faculty as they write critical elements. The difference between ideal behavior that is taught and the acceptable behavior required during the examination must be discussed and agreed upon during the developmental phase.

The standard of acceptable performance, therefore, is specified by the precise wording of the critical elements. Furthermore, as critical elements also control evaluator bias, they regulate the level of expectation by clarifying what is acceptable and what is unacceptable behavior. The interrelatedness between the concepts of examination, objectivity, critical elements, and acceptability now becomes more evident.

Cognitive ability is evaluated through written tests, and correct answers are specified prior to their administration to students. A passing score may require as little as 70 percent accuracy. This means that a student may answer only 7 of 10 items correctly and still receive a passing grade, even though the test covers only a sample of all the knowledge covered in the course. Whatever the established passing score, it designates the teacher's decision of what constitutes acceptable performance. It defines what is considered reasonable on the examination and sets the limits for tolerance of error. Perfect, or ideal, performances are not required, even though that would make both students and teachers very happy. Less than ideal is acceptable, within the stated limits, even though perfection is preferable.

The same concept is applicable to clinical performance examinations. The faculty decides the tolerable limits of errors or the degree of "perfectness" that will be required or judged acceptable for the given examination. The student whose performance is less than that identified as essential in the critical elements does not pass the test. The student whose performance matches or exceeds the established expectations passes the test. The degree of tolerance for deviation from the ideal is determined before the examination is given. It is a conscious decision and stated without ambiguity or confusion for the prior information of both students and faculty.

The critical elements and other guidelines specify what is considered acceptable behavior and once they are written to the satisfaction of the faculty they must be performed by the students with 100 percent accuracy, without exception. None of the specified behaviors may be omitted or performed incorrectly, for together they define the acceptable standard of competence expected of all students. Failing to meet critical elements therefore is comparable to missing items on a written test in excess of the preestablished cut-off point; it is going below the "70 percent" point.

Acceptability, therefore, is another essential concept for the development and implementation of clinical examinations. It helps faculty to draw the line as to what will be considered competent and incompetent performance, while at the same time preventing the excess of idealism to render the examination unrealistic. It establishes a reasonable and acceptable standard of performance appropriate to the purpose of the examination and helps to control value judgments of individual instructors. As with written tests, the clinical examination tests reasonable performance, based on the ideal that was taught during the teaching–learning phase.

During the teaching–learning phase the epitome of ideal nursing practice is taught and pursued; it is the goal for students and teachers alike, both as learners and practitioners. It is the prized "A+" behavior so difficult for novices to achieve. During the examination period itself, total perfection is unrealistic to expect of all students, hence written criteria designating the acceptable standard of nursing care are central to ensure that clinical performance is reasonable, though not necessarily perfect. No one is allowed to behave less competently than specified by this standard for it establishes the baseline of acceptability.

Objectively, sampling, acceptability, and comparability are concepts that characterize the examination itself, especially the development of content. The remaining three concepts, systematized conditions, flexibility in structure, and consistency, apply primarily to the structure and process of administering the examination.

SYSTEMATIZED CONDITIONS

The examination content could be explicitly itemized and worded, but if the conditions under which it is administered are left to emerge spontaneously as the test unfolds, the entire endeavor will fail. What to examine is critical, but how it is measured is equally important. The faculty committee responsible for developing the content also has a responsibility to develop the conditions that will guide the administration of the performance examination. These conditions are systematically identified, defined, and worded in clear, unambiguous language and become another crucial part of the study guide used by students and evaluators.

Some of the conditions to be described concern the following: the time allotted to each portion and to the entire examination; scheduling of time and place; criteria for the selection of patients; criteria for pass/fail; and codes of dress and behavior.

To the extent possible, problematic situations that potentially could develop should be anticipated and preliminary responses for them worked out in advance. For example: What should the evaluator do if the patient becomes noticeably worse just prior to or during the examination? Or if the student or evaluator become ill? Or if some unforeseen circumstances interrupts nursing care and the student cannot complete care within the designated time? Situations that frequently occur during the regular administration of nursing care are just as likely to happen during the clinical examination if it is given in a real setting; therefore, every effort should be made to systematize the response to them to ensure that the validity of the test and its objectivity and consistency are not compromised.

Systematized conditions, stated in the study guide, help to avoid spontaneous responses that differ from one evaluator to another. Diverse solutions to the same kind of situation potentially nullify the previous efforts to maintain the objectivity, consistency, and comparability of the examination, even though evaluators try to be "fair." The only solution is to think through as many problems as possible that might occur and to specify the expected responses for evaluators and students. Additional problems that have not been anticipated could occur but comments about the most common ones will give guidance regarding how to handle others.

Stating the time allowed for each subpart and for the total test precludes the possibility that some students could take a longer period than that allowed. Explicitly stating criteria governing the kinds of patients that will (and won't) be selected prevents evaluators from selecting a patient who would be "good" for teaching purposes but whose condition (the care required) is too complex and time consuming for examination purposes. Identifying at the outset the interrelationships between evaluators and service staff, between student and staff, and between evaluator and student also prevents potential misunderstandings that could skew the examination. Clear statements of what constitutes passing and failing will inform the student in advance and help to minimize conflict and emotional situations at the conclusion of the test period.

Systematizing the conditions, like specifying content (competencies) to be tested, also greatly reduces the possibility of legal actions being taken against faculty by those involved; to the extent that evaluators comply with the specifications, students who fail have little or no grounds for legal action. This is another major advantage of requiring an objective performance examination—especially in a society in which people are quick to seek legal redress for assumed as well as actual grievances. Of course, the most important reason for specifying content and conditions is to ensure the valid and objective assessment of the student's clinical competence.

FLEXIBILITY IN STRUCTURE

Another concept to be considered in the development and administration of the examination is that it must be flexible in order to fit into the real clinical environment. Its structure and process must be functional, given the setting in which it takes place. This concept is less critical in simulated situations but nonetheless is worth consideration even in those highly controlled situations. Without thought to the degree of flexibility necessary to administer the examination, problems will be encountered once it is pilot-tested and/or implemented. For example if the requirements for patient selection, the number and type of dimensions to be included, and the types of nursing care units to be used are too rigidly specified, the examination will be nonfunctional and/or impractical to administer. Excessive and unwarranted restrictions do not make the test more valid; they only make it unnecessarily difficult to implement.

For example, it is not possible (and is not necessary) to have all students evaluated on exactly the same areas of nursing care while testing their clinical competence. It is more functional to require some common areas that are readily available in the clinical setting to be used along with a prescribed number of other areas selected from a given array and which match the patients' nursing-care needs for the particular time and day. The combination of a set number of "required" and a set number of "selected" areas makes the examination both comparable in demands and also flexible enough to fit into the clinical setting without excessive difficulty. Furthermore, having a built-in half-hour time cushion between each discrete part of the examination (i.e., between each patient-care situation) allows flexibility to accommodate for the interruptions that typically occur during the implementation phase. The criteria for selection of patients also are developed so as to ensure sufficient flexibility in that aspect of implementation.

The degree of flexibility and the way it is incorporated depends on several factors, just as with all of the other concepts—i.e., the purpose and placement of the examination, the level and type of student being tested, etc. Regardless of exactly how it is actually implemented, the concept of flexibility deserves considerable attention in order to avoid serious difficulties in administering the examination.

CONSISTENCY

One of the most frequently identified problems of clinical evaluation is the lack of consistency among faculty in conducting clinical evaluations. The concept of consistency primarily applies to the role of the evaluator during the process of administering the examination. It is concerned with making sure that each and every evaluator complies with the preestablished rules of conduct. Regardless of the personal opinion or preference of the individual instructor, once the content and conditions are specified and accepted by the faculty, every effort must be made to ensure consistency in administration of the examination. If one or more faculty members decide they have the authority to change the rules or critical elements on the spur of the moment, the effectiveness and objectivity of the entire examination will be compromised. The purpose of explicitly identifying content and process and using clear, unambiguous language is to secure objectivity, comparability, and consistency. When evaluators apply the tool each in his own preferred fashion, the test is no longer fair, valid, or objective.

Because there is a tendency to confuse the concepts of consistency and comparability, a distinction should be made. Comparability refers to the relative equivalence of the content to be tested while consistency refers to the uniformity among evaluators in administering the clinical examination. The first primarily relates to content and the second to conditions and procedures of testing.

Those who function as evaluators almost always are clinical instructors at times other than the examination periods. It is therefore not uncommon for them to revert to teacher behaviors during the performance examination, knowingly or unknowingly. There is the tendency to "regress to the mean," to automatically return to behavior that is most often practiced and that is habitual. Some will have more difficulty than others in divesting themselves of the teacher role while they occupy the role of objective evaluator. Some may never be able satisfactorily to perform both functions with equal ability and ease. (This problem area will be discussed in subsequent chapters.)

Thus during the development of the clinical performance examination ways to ensure consistency in administration must be considered. The particular solutions to the problem will vary—depending, again, on why and when and to whom the examination is given. But more than likely statements will have to be written addressing the problem, along with specific criteria for evaluating the evaluators. It also probably will be necessary to assign someone generally to supervise the conduct of evaluators to note their compliance with the rules of conduct (at least until everyone is thoroughly familiar with the new process and is able to perform the new role). Having a coordinator to supervise the entire examination process will greatly augment the probability that all content and process criteria will be consistently applied by all evaluators.

SUMMARY OF BASIC CONCEPTS

The value of the performance examination is influenced by a number of interrelated concepts and how the faculty uses or abuses them. These factors include the notion that final clinical competence is best assessed by an examination that is objective in that content and process are explicitly stated in a document available to both students and evaluators prior to its administration. Other concepts focus on ensuring an adequate sampling of areas of care and their related critical elements, and that each testing episode is comparable in the complexity it demands. Other concepts deal with establishing the level of acceptability of performance, while being certain that the examination is governed by systematized conditions, is flexible enough to be functional in the clinical environment, and that all evaluators consistently administer it as approved by the faculty. These concepts apply throughout the development and the implementation phases. Singly and collectively they exert a major influence on process and outcomes of student evaluation. They are so fundamentally important and their value is of such magnitude that they will be referred to time and time again in this book. Experience has shown that neglect of any one of them endangers the goal, and that collectively, if appropriately applied, they ensure an accurate and fair assessment of the clinical competence of students.

FACULTY SELF-ANALYSIS

Early in the process of constructing an objective examination of performance abilities, it would be helpful for the faculty to engage in a period of analysis of their current knowledge and use of the ten basic concepts discussed above. This is a two-pronged analysis: the first requires that each teacher identifies the extent to which she/he individually applies each concept, while the second phase requires analysis of the extent to which the entire faculty (in the aggregate) incorporates them in the assessment of students' abilities throughout the program. Both individual and group analyses are dependent upon the willingness and ability of each faculty member honestly to confront her/his behavior and that of colleagues as it relates to the role of clinical evaluation. It may be less threatening if the individual analysis is done privately before one participates in a probing group analysis; however, this indoubtedly depends upon the security of the individual and the cohesiveness, group effort, respect, and support system within the group. These activities can be unsettling because—if conducted seriously—they both have the potential of revealing and labeling behavior that previously was suppressed as a vague feeling of dissatisfaction. It is the identification and crystalization of behavior associated with each concept that is immediately helpful and simultaneously threatening. However, if the faculty (individually and collectively) is determined to deliberately move toward more objective and explicit assessment of student achievement of clinical competence, such an analysis is essential rather than optional. As with other behavior-modification efforts, deciding the direction to be taken is often determined only after a serious review of the current situation.

As illustrated in the following pages, it may be helpful to think of each concept as a continuum, stretching from one extreme to another. By drawing a straight line and labeling each end-point, the spectrum between opposite behaviors is clarified. The idea of the continuum is necessary because the behaviors are dynamic and changing (rather than static). The line represents a continuum of degrees—an imaginary scale of, say, one to ten. The process requires the faculty (individual or aggregate) to analyze the extent to which each particular concept is actually incorporated in current clinical assessment and then to designate that approximate location on the line by marking it with an *X*. This is done separately for each concept, one at a time. Honesty and openness to learn from this experience are required, both with one's self and in sharing the revelations with colleagues. The analysis will be only partially successful unless all clinical faculty members participate. This can be the turning point and the beginning of the transition toward more objective clinical performance examinations.

To begin, take for example the concept of examination. At the extreme right hand end of the line is testing as a behavior; moving to the left the behavior increasingly is characterized by teaching behaviors. At the extreme points neither incorporates aspects of the other.

Teaching ←——————————→ Testing

SPECIFIC QUESTIONS AND GOALS

Each faculty member asks and responds to the following kinds of questions: When I am actually evaluating the students' clinical ability at the end of the course (or at any other designated time), to what extent do I still engage in teaching? When I say I am conducting the final evaluation, how much do I show and tell, coach, assist, and give verbal and nonverbal clues? To what extent do I regard that assessment as an objective examination, in which teaching behaviors are totally inappropriate? Is this assessment period envisioned as just another day in the clinical setting where students are expected to do their best but also where teachers have their last opportunity to pass on any last-minute advice and assistance? Succinctly stated, the question asks: Am I teaching or testing during the period devoted to final clinical evaluation? (This discussion does not pertain to the teaching–learning phase in which assisting, showing, and advising are desirable and beneficial; rather, it is the final examination time.)

In thinking critically about their actual behavior during the evaluation phase, many instructors come to realize that they give repeated verbal and nonverbal clues or automatically assist students. They may or may not comment negatively on the student's inadequate performance, "depending on the situation." Where teaching and assisting occur, the following analysis would result:

Teaching ←X———————→ **Testing**

The focus is more on teaching than on explicit testing, even though this may have been unconscious behavior on the part of the teacher. The influence of the teacher's behavior on the objective assessment of the students' ability is clear. When instructors get involved with teaching during the presumed "testing period," objective observation is negated and, perhaps more importantly, students learn to anticipate faculty assistance even when they are expected to perform independently.

In contrast, when faculty engage in a final evaluation that is strictly devoted to providing an objective opportunity for students to demonstrate their clinical competence in a precisely defined and unassisted episode, the analysis looks like this:

Teaching ←———————X→ **Testing**

The same kind of analysis pertains to all of the dimensions of practice to be included in the examination: To what extent is the test focused on specific and prescribed tasks or procedures or to broader areas of care?

Procedures ←———————→ **Areas of Care**

If a clinical performance examination is given early in the program—for example, in the first semester—focusing on specific procedures is desirable. However, if the examination is placed at or near the end of the educational program it is more desirable to focus on clusters of tasks or functions that require the application of comparable principles or activities. Assuming the student is being examined at the conclusion of the program and the focus is on specific procedures, the analysis is illustrated as follows:

Procedure ←X———————→ **Areas of Care**

When broader areas of care are identified and critical elements are developed, allowing any one of several particular procedures to be used to document competence, the *X* is placed near the right hand end of the continuum:

Procedures ←——————————X→ **Areas of Care**

When procedures are the central core for evaluating performance, students will be measured on their ability to follow the steps required for successful implementation. In contrast, the concept of areas of care facilitates the use of critical elements that are equally applicable to many specific procedures.

Steps in
Procedure ←X——————————→ **Critical Elements**

If teachers focus on the discrete observable behaviors that are essential for the patient's well-being and that demonstrate competence to apply knowledge and judgment, the continuum is illustrated as follows:

Steps in
Procedure ←——————————X→ **Critical Elements**

This kind of analysis continues for each of the other concepts. Each instructor is encouraged honestly to identify her/his place on a continuum representing the remaining concepts that characterize the performance examination and its administration. By asking specific questions about each concept some revealing insights are apt to occur. The emphasis always is focused on the teachers' behaviors that actually take place during the final assessment of clinical competence, rather than the fantasized imagery of the ideal. The discussion here is brief but is meant to suggest the kind of open exploration that is necessary to understand what really goes on during so-called clinical evaluation, and the kind of changes that are necessary (individually and collectively). For best results the reader is encouraged to plunge into this exercise fully rather than to tip-toe in slowly. The experience is apt to be chilling but also refreshing.

To continue with the analysis, consider the concept of objectivity. If the instructor is inclined to be influenced by recollection of past experiences with the student (positive or negative), by personal biases related to differences of opinion, or by any factors other than those specified in the examination itself, the self-analysis requires that an *X* be placed at the subjective end of the continuum:

Subjectivity ←X——————→ Objectivity

As confessed by hundreds of faculty members (and reported in the surveys in Chapter 2), this is the most common and frustrating problem related to clinical evaluation. Lack of objective tools makes the situation essentially universal. In contrast, the consistent use of an examination with explicit statements for content to be measured, for process, and with built-in controls for evaluator bias, characteristically results in objective assessment. Predetermined observable critical elements become the basis for judgment, rather than opinion, personal preference, or comments passed along from someone else. Objectivity has been enhanced remarkably.

Subjectivity ←——————X→ Objectivity

How much to test is another problem. To the extent that teachers try to test all skills and knowledge previously taught in the clinical setting instead of randomly sampling from among that potential universe, the *X* is placed on the left end of the line. As sampling is used increasingly, the *X* moves proportionally in the forward direction. Total content is the appropriate goal for teaching but sampling is essential for most performance testing.

Total Content ←X——————→ Sampling

When the performance of students during the examination is expected to reach the ideal instead of a more realistic preestablished level of acceptability, the analysis of that concept is as follows:

Ideal Performance ←X——————→ Acceptable Performance

If the faculty devises ways to ensure comparability of testing episodes so that each student has to perform in situations that are reasonably equal in complexity, the concept is illustrated as:

Incomparable ←——————X→ Comparable

When all conditions under which the test will be administered are systematized and implemented accordingly by the faculty, the concept is illustrated as:

Spontaneous Arrangements ←——————X→ Systematized Conditions

The examination that is developed with consideration to needs for appropriate flexibility in structure and process (instead of imposing restrictions that make it nonfunctional in the real setting) is analyzed as:

Rigid Structure ←————————X→ **Flexibility (Functionability)**

When faculty members bypass the preestablished rules governing content and process and impose their individual preferences, consistency is compromised. To the extent that some instructors comply with the examination protocol and others do not, evaluation of students is inconsistent and consequently objectivity is lost.

Inconsistency ←X————————→ **Consistency**

By thinking through actual behaviors in relation to each concept and placing the *X* mark on a line, individual faculty numbers find it easier to pinpoint areas that need special attention and improvement both for themselves and for the whole faculty group. Subsequent to this individual analysis it is recommended that the clinical faculty share their individual findings and identify strong and weak points that characterize the clinical evaluation process as a whole. This activity will alert the group early in the process to difficulties that probably will require extra efforts to overcome or rectify.

INTERSECTION OF CONCEPT VARIABLES

There is more to consider than each concept as a single entity. The concept variables also interact with each other, which further illustrates their influence on clinical assessment. While some insight results from the analysis of separate concepts, a greater awareness of the complexity of providing objective performance examination is gained by intersecting one or more of these variables. This is a second level of analysis, which illustrates the resulting behaviors that can be expected and indicates the potential influences on student outcomes. For instance, intersect examination and objectivity.

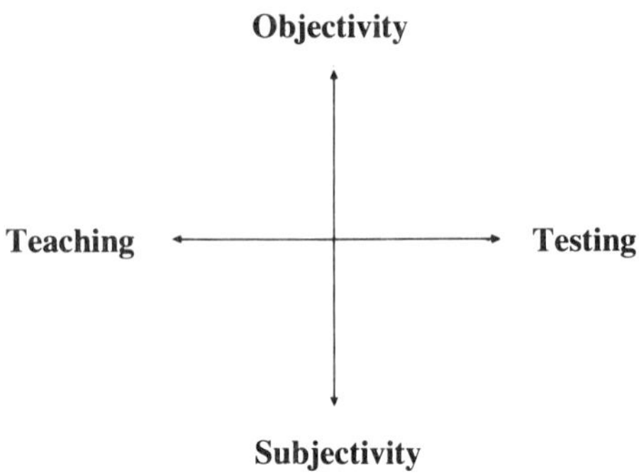

As before, analysis will be most productive when the teacher draws the lines and places an *X* at the location on each line that corresponds to assessment behavior usually practiced. Actively engaging in the process is helpful. When the instructor indulges in teaching behavior during the final evaluation period and also responds by using biases and personal opinion, the episode results in a subjective teaching experience rather than an objective examination of the student's competence. Drawing dotted lines from each axis until they intersect shows that teaching and subjectivity characterize the faculty behavior and emphasis is in the lower left-hand box. This diagram clearly illustrates that the presumed evaluation is characterized by a high degree of personal preference, bias, assisting, and coaching.

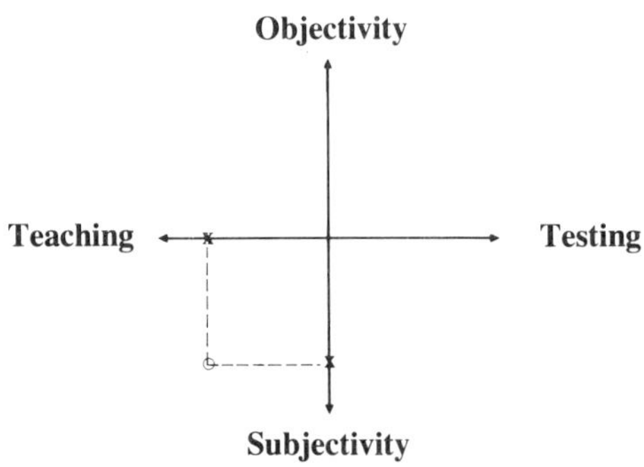

However, another image results when the teacher applies more appropriate testing behavior but continues to evaluate the student based on subjective criteria. The intersection of these variables places the instructor's behavior in the lower right-hand box. Some improvement may have been gained, but the assessment still rests on the opinion of the teacher—for better or for worse.

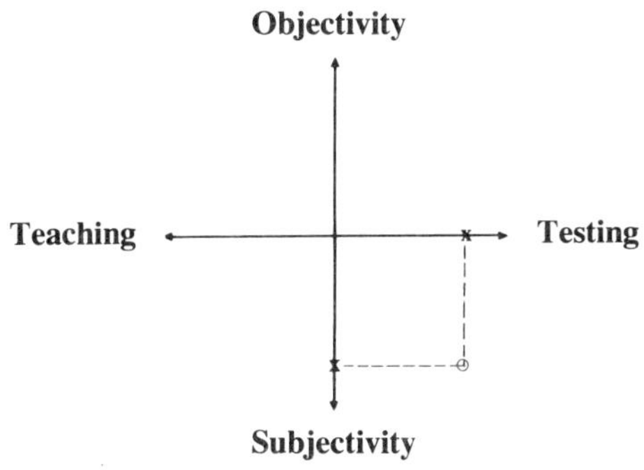

The desired behavior during the examination period is illustrated by the intersection of *X*s placed at the testing and objectivity ends of the continua, which results in emphasis in the upper right-hand box. Based on the self-analysis of many clinical faculty members, they need and want to move from the teaching/subjective box (lower left-hand box) to the objective testing box (the upper right-hand box). To have faculty and clinical evaluation characterized as objective would be a great improvement. The problem is how to do it.

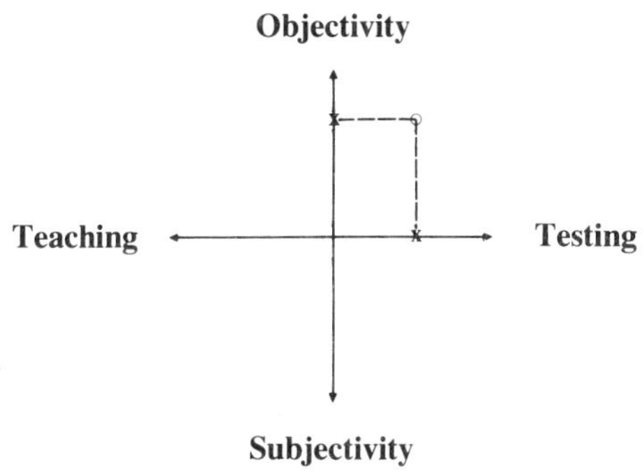

An in-depth analysis of the behaviors of clinical instructors during the final evaluation period clearly indicates the potential influence of the faculty on the reported competence of students. The evaluation may or may not actually be true but the written conclusions emanate from invalid processes and procedures when the essential concepts are violated or ignored. Again, during the teaching–learning phase it is quite appropriate for the teacher to share subjective opinion and experiences related to clinical performance. Students learn from such experiences and aspire to the best performance, but during an objective examination they should be judged on preestablished and mutually understood grounds rules and specific content. How much content is tested must be a matter of prior agreement.

Consider the intersection of the testing and sampling concepts, both from a theoretically and personal perspective.

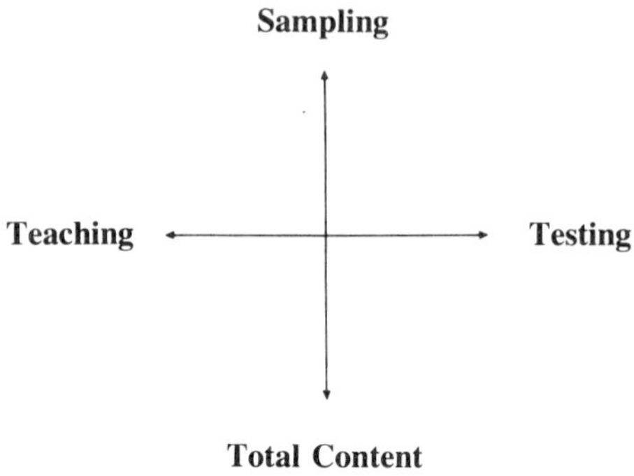

During the teaching–learning phase instruction should be concerned with the total array of content. Students are expected to become aware of the entire outline of content and competencies, and to learn and to integrate a variety of approaches, theories, skills, and techniques. Just as the entire universe of cognitive areas is not tested on written tests, not every skill taught in the clinical area needs to be explicitly examined for every student. Sampling, therefore, is used to make testing more realistic and functional. During the scheduled examination period certain designated areas of care are identified—a sampling from among the total array—on which the student is expected to demonstrate competence. When fully applied the intersection of these variables looks like this:

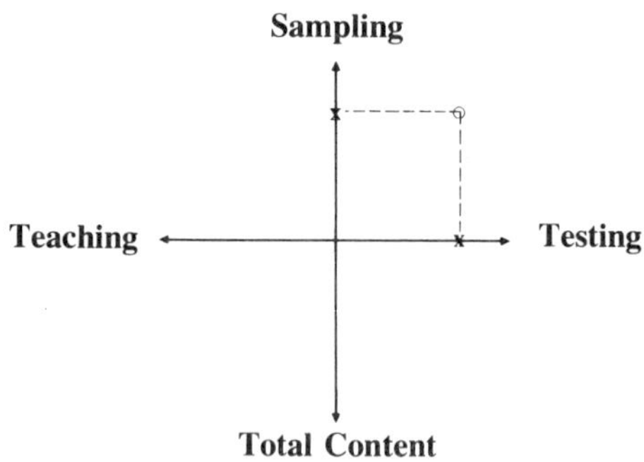

However, in most cases, based on the ‘‘evaluation’’ approach currently being used by most faculties as illustrated by faculty surveys, the behavior of clinical instructors usually falls in the lower left-hand box, as illustrated on the top of p. 73:

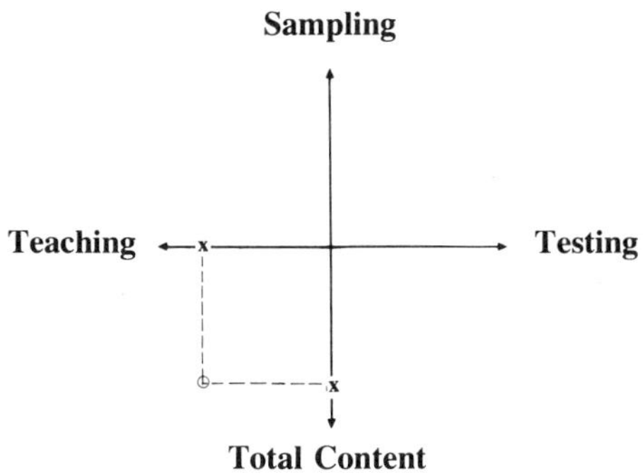

Even though this may be the final evaluation of clinical competence, the faculty is still teaching and trying to cover as many clinical areas as possible. Even if some testing is being done, the emphasis is on documenting every skill that has been taught. Typically, the clinical instructor is not comfortable omitting some areas from final scrutiny and would rather check each one off three times.

In such cases, to improve sampling in clinical assessment the faculty must move from the lower left to the upper right-hand box. Developing an explicit performance examination definitely will help. The array of areas to be tested are determined and fully developed before the test, and a representative, random sample of them are actually used during the examination.

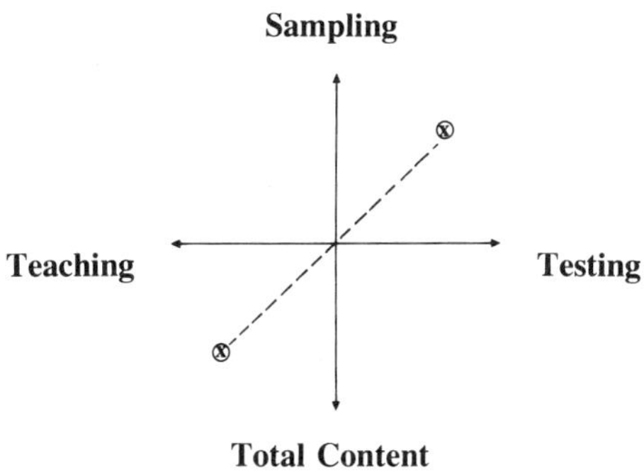

FURTHER ANALYSIS

One should consider the variables of examination and acceptability in the same analytical way and try to determine their influence on each other and then on the assessment of students.

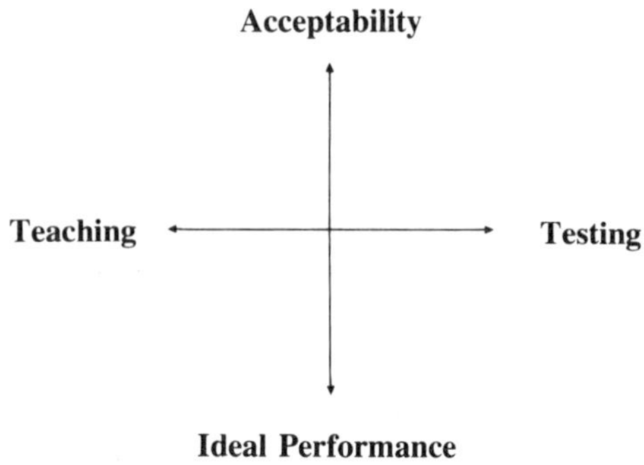

During the teaching–learning phase it is desirable for instruction to focus on the ideal behavior of the nurse. Teachers naturally are eager to stimulate students to aspire to the highest goals of achieving knowledge and clinical competence. Every faculty member would enjoy the delight of having all superior students all capable of a degree of perfection and all able to demonstrate excellence all the time. Every student would love to perform nursing care in such a way as to apply all theory and principles and to interact in the most humane and caring way as professional nurses, feeling competent, secure, and able. However, such behaviors usually result from years of practice and concentration rather than from a basic, beginning program of studies. However, students must document that they have learned sufficiently for the protection of consumers. Therefore, during the clinical examination students are held accountable for that level of competence that has been predetermined as reasonable and acceptable by the faculty, as stated by the critical elements. While teaching and learning focus on the ideal situation, the examination focuses on ensuring a reasonable and acceptable demonstration of nursing ability, given the content, process, and placement of the test.

With the inclination of some faculty members to continue teaching and to expect ideal performance, their final clinical evaluation would violate both of these two concepts. Once the standard of what is acceptable and expected is established (the critical elements) then all students must perform with 100 percent accuracy. That is the definition of acceptable, what it means in that given situation. Nothing less will be tolerated. The desired movement for individuals and the faculty as a whole is from lower-left to upper-right quadrants. Teaching should focus on the ideal, but testing is based on a preestablished level of acceptability that is less than ideal but still tolerable.

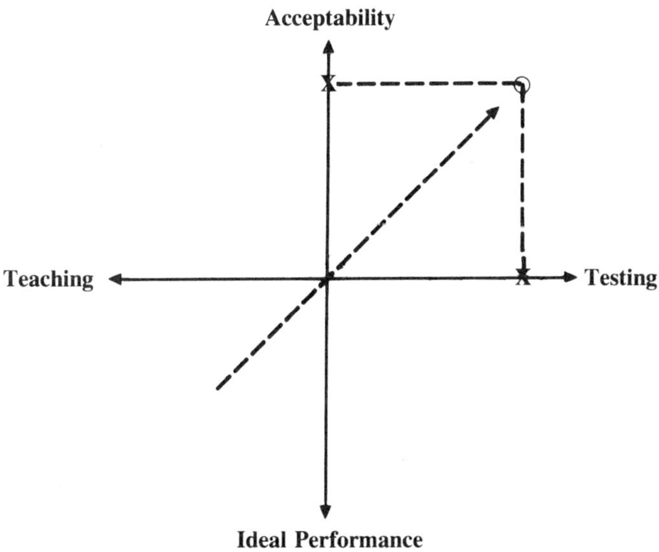

The following example intersects the concepts of objectivity and comparability.

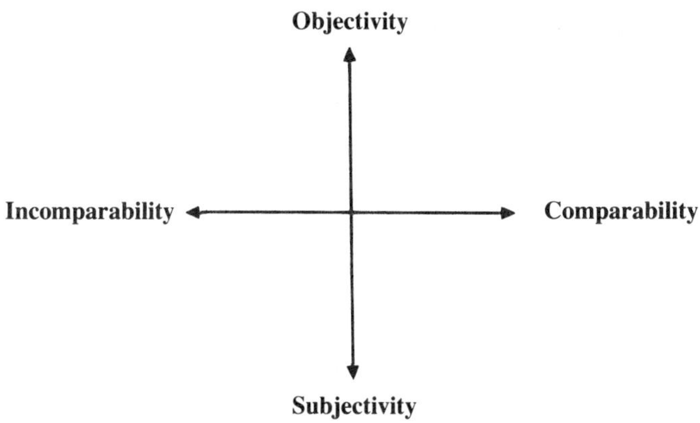

Consider the influence on student assessment when instructors evaluate students on the basis of subjective criteria and use testing episodes of variable complexity on which to document the students' achievement. Consider the influence of the faculty's behavior on the reported outcomes, which in fact may reflect little of the students' actual ability but rather the opinion of the faculty (given the subjective procedures being used).

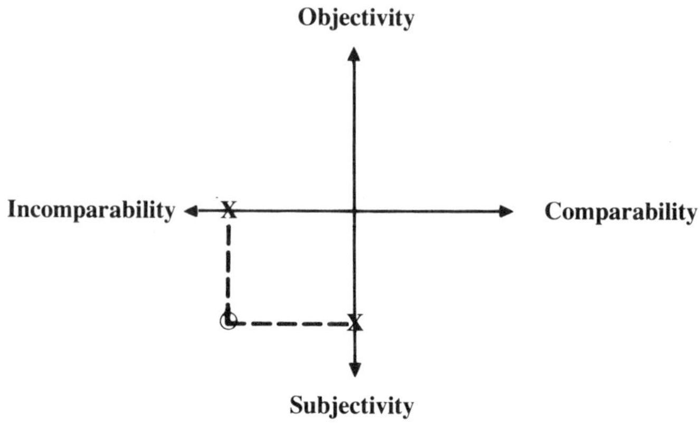

Consider the remarkable differences that would result if the faculty objectively applied an explicit instrument and used only comparable testing episodes for all students involved. The desired shift is from the lower-left to the upper-right-hand behavior box.

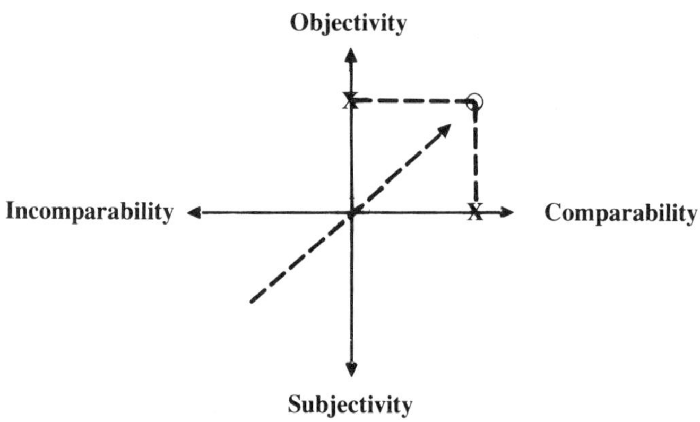

When each basic concept is intersected with another one and analyzed in depth (as suggested by the above example) the faculty can learn much about what they actually are doing, what they think they are doing, and what they wish they were doing. The parts of the puzzle must be sorted out before they can begin to be fitted together. A conscientious analysis will lay the foundation for improving clinical evaluation. But it all begins by having the faculty individually and collectively—and honestly—explore their behavior in terms of each concept variable.

THE TOTAL CONSTELLATION OF CONCEPTS

The challenge becomes even more complex when all 10 variables are intersected simultaneously. The particular configuration that results from this integrated faculty analysis characterizes the approach to clinical assessment for individuals as well as the collective behavior of the group in terms of the 10 basic concepts. This one picture, the diagram analysis, summarizes all that must be said but tends to defy verbal description. It graphically represents the extent to which the faculty needs to work on improving clinical assessment.

Figure 3.5 represents the total configuration of concepts. Each of ten lines represents a concept continuum, with both extremes of the behavior spectrum identified; the sketch has been left "blank" and may be used as a basic form for plotting individual and group characteristics; multiple copies should be made and used liberally. Figures 3.6 through 3.9 show examples of both typical and extreme configurations in order to illustrate the kind of influence faculty behavior superimposes on final outcomes of clinical assessment. In most cases,

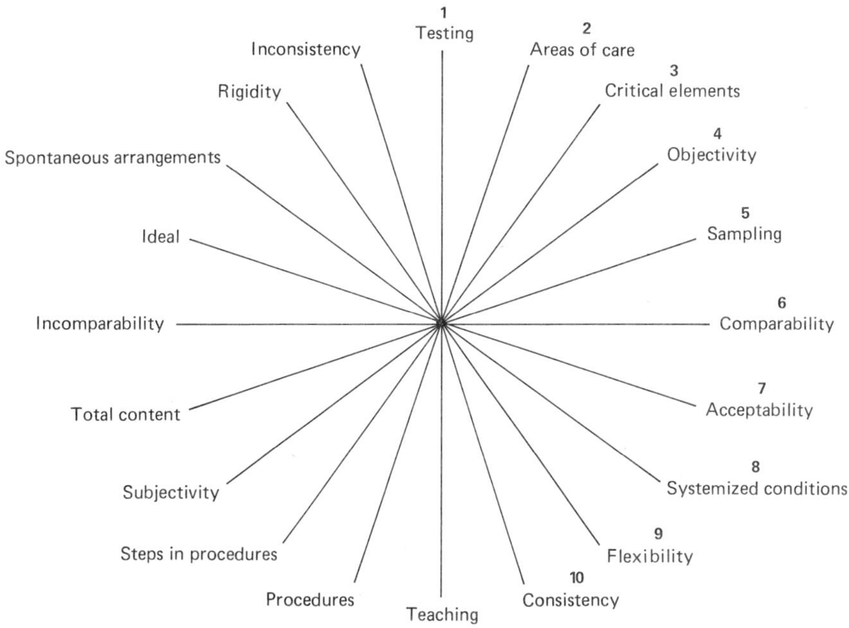

Fig. 3.5. Constellation of basic concept continua—interrelating concepts essential to performance examinations.

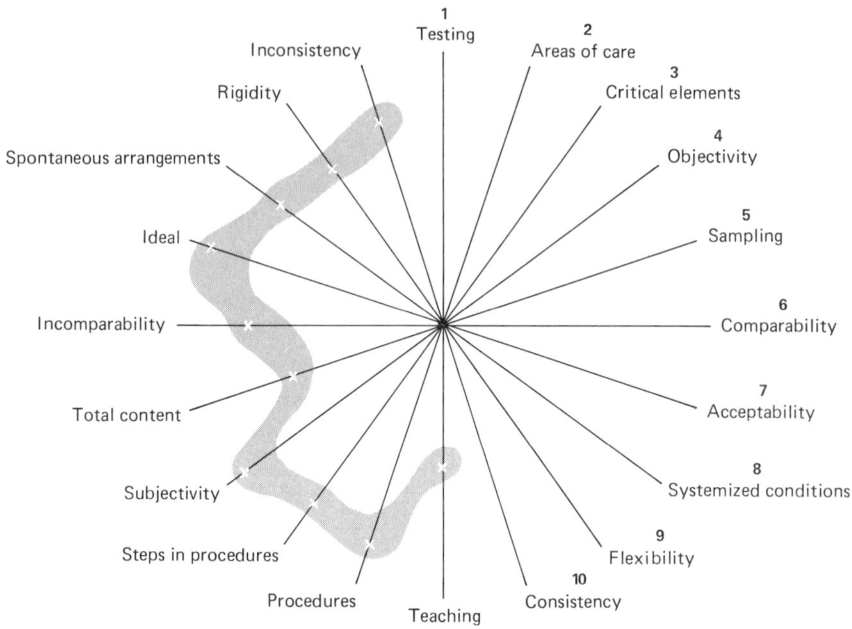

Fig. 3.6. Negative configuration showing marked violation of concepts.

faculty members probably are totally unaware of the significance of their behavior. The self-analysis suggested in this chapter—for individuals and the clinical faculty as an aggregate—is potentially one of the most helpful exercises the faculty can undertake because it forces them to confront their behavior and its influence on students.

As suggested for the previous exercises, to obtain the maximum benefit from this last phase of the analysis each faculty member is encouraged thoughtfully to mark on each line the degree to which the behavior identified is usually experienced, once for self and again on another form for the faculty as an aggregate. After placing an *X* at the most appropriate location on all ten concept continua, one draws a line that encircles all of the marks, around the outside, down and around the inside until the elongated configuration is complete. This can be a tricky process especially if the marks weave across the center area from side to side. One should be sure to draw the encircling line by each concept in a consistent pattern. The resulting image probably is tortuous and curls back and forth across the center and left semicircle of the diagram. Regardless of its design, the picture clearly reflects the current status of performance testing for the particular individual or group,

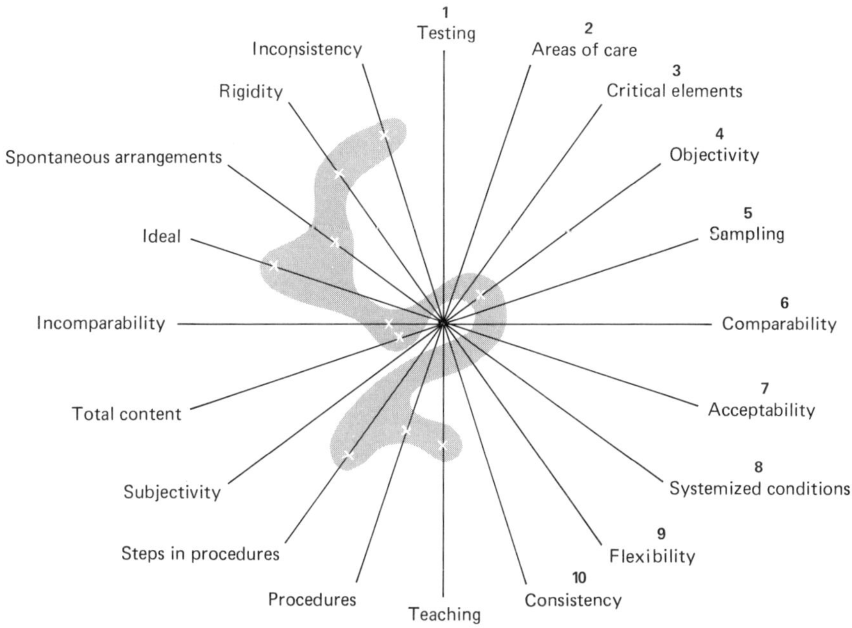

Fig. 3.7. Configuration showing improved objectivity, comparability, and sampling.

and the influence of the suggested behaviors on the outcomes for students being evaluated.

Based on the self-analysis of many faculty groups these illustrations place faculty behavior at the left extreme on each of the concept continuum. This is not atypical and it certainly provides a graphic summary of the violations of the basic concepts. Although the faculty of any particular school has a somewhat different configuration, Figure 3.6 illustrates the extreme of subjective, inconsistent, noncomparable, idealistic clinical evaluation. It clearly documents the need for thoughtful and deliberate attention to improve clinical assessment while it simultaneously points to the critical role the faculty behavior plays in the overall outcomes of student evaluation. Engaging in such an exercise, if undertaken honestly and seriously, leaves no doubt about the faculty's current position or about the direction in which they should move to improve clinical assessment. The outcome could be more optimistic—or more pessimistic—than originally thought, but having specific data helps to make a more reliable diagnosis and plan for corrections.

Figure 3.7 illustrates some attempts to move in the direction of

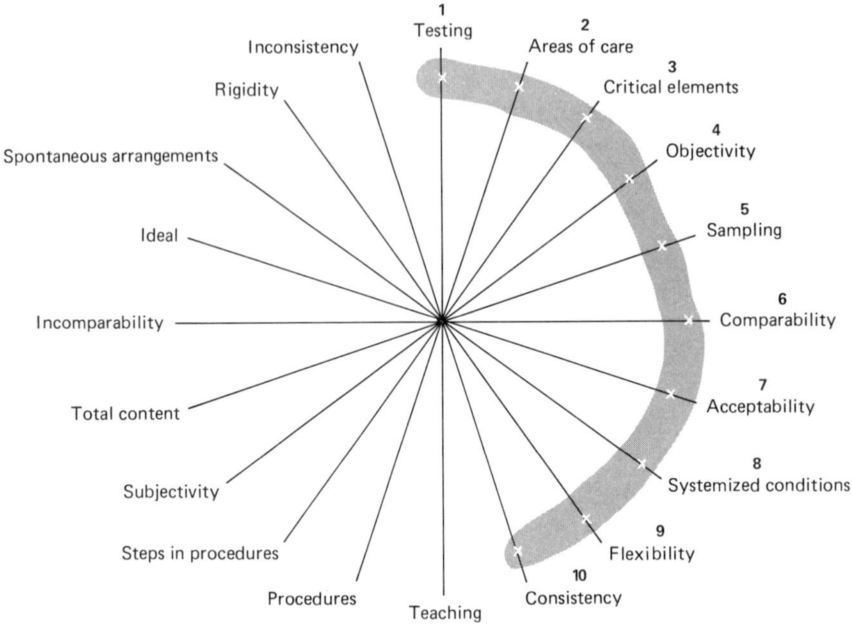

Fig. 3.8. Configuration showing desired positive positions on concept continua.

improved objectivity, sampling, and comparability while instructors still engage in teaching behaviors, are inconsistent in administering the test, and in general have considerable work to do toward achieving a truly objective examination. The *X*'s have moved toward the right semicircle but some are bunched in the center.

Figure 3.8 illustrates the desired positive position on each concept continuum. Each concept is fully applied, facilitating the possibility for a comprehensive, objective, and fair clinical examination. To the extent that faculty and students are aware of the standard of expectation and it is evaluated by using the concepts presented above, a valid and reliable clinical assessment is possible. Progress in this direction is greatly dependent upon the willingness of each faculty member to be honest in both the self-analysis and in the group analysis and to participate in evolving a system to improve concepts on which an undesirable evaluation was recorded. This systematic appraisal is essential if any serious efforts are to be made in improving clinical assessment—whether for introductory courses or for end-of-program evaluation, whether for associate or baccalaureate program, or for specialty pro-

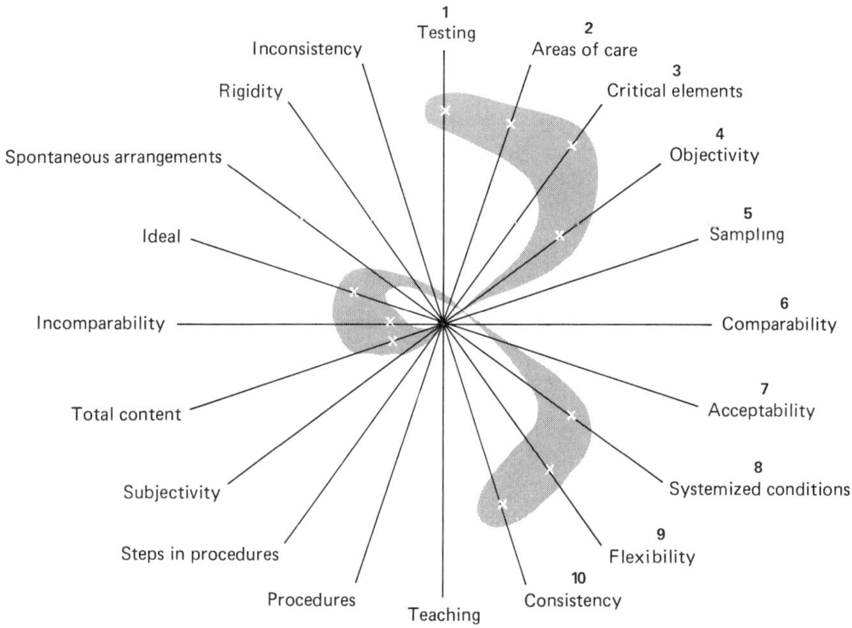

Fig. 3.9. A performance examination still in transition.

grams. The same process of self-analysis applies, just as the same concepts do. This analysis is the springboard from which all other efforts arise, and change is encouraged.

The process of analysis and then understanding the resulting implications take time. The evolution from a traditional system to another takes time. Just to begin takes courage and a commitment to a new and improved approach. During the course of the transition period it probably would be helpful if someone kept a progress diary of changes in the configurations and other aspects of the evolution. The collected incidents would make a great contribution at the celebration party once the project is concluded, while also preserving a small piece of history.

Figure 3.9 illustrates the analysis of an examination in transition. Its erratic nature shows the areas that need more work—some far more than others. During development, pilot-testing, and early implementation, monitoring of concept implementation is especially important because it highlights areas that need additional attention in the process of evolving a reasonable, functional, and objective performance examination. Faculty awareness of these weak spots alerts them to pay more attention where necessary, and to constantly nudge the *X* marks toward the right semicircle area on the diagram. Only then can the examination concepts be fully implemented.

SUMMARY

Ten concepts are discussed to illustrate their significance for the development and implementation of a clinical performance examination. Each one is important in itself but the interaction of each with the other is perhaps more relevant in the long run. The faculty's individual and collective analysis of the extent to which these concepts are applied can be a productive endeavor, leading to insights that can improve clinical assessment regardless of the type of program or the students' level within the program. Such a total analysis requires honesty, the ability to confront inefficient and unproductive behaviors, and the willingness to make a commitment to undergo a period of transition toward more objective clinical examination. It is the beginning effort, but often a most difficult one.

Individual efforts alone will not suffice. Because all of the faculty is involved in one way or another, they all must engage in the transition, even though some may be more enthusiastic than others. Effective and persistent leadership is required if the project is to succeed, for there will be frequent occasions of disappointment and frustrations, and even some hostility. The role of the leader is to keep the purpose and goal before the group and to stimulate the participants to apply their collective intelligence and aspirations to the achievement of the goal. After the work is finished the rewards are tangible and persistent, and well worth the efforts.

CHAPTER 4

Determining Examination Content: Getting Ready

Some of the most frequently asked questions about performance testing are: What should be included? How do I know it's a fair test? How much is enough really to know that competence is being measured? How many areas should be included? How complex should it be? What exactly do you measure? How do we go about developing the test? When should simulation be used?

The questions about performance testing can be grouped into six basic questions: what, when, where, who, why, and how? This chapter primarily explores the what question, with some spillover into the other queries. As the topic concerns a complex integrated whole, it is helpful to consider all of the parameters to some degree while developing one at a time in detail. For example, it is not possible to decide what to include in the performance test before determining: (1) when and where it should be given; (2) how many such tests will be given; (3) what other evaluation procedures will be used; (4) who the students are; (5) who is responsible for administering it; and (6) why it is necessary to have a performance examination in the first place.

What to include is inextricably related to each of these six considerations. The process of developing the clinical performance examination is concerned with what to test, within the context of the other variables. Ultimately, all of the pieces have to be explored and have to fit together. Finding answers to the "what" question is imperative—but the answers must be consistent with the context, and that requires a preliminary but meticulous exploration of all aspects of the process of developing a performance examination.

COMPOSITION OF THE COMMITTEE

A fundamental maxim that can be applied to the current topic is to identify the organizing questions before trying to give any answers. Because developing a performance examination is a costly and time-consuming project, and because its application has major consequences for student learning and evaluation, it would be wise for the faculty to devote a period of careful discussion to answering such questions early in the developmental process. Before attacking the project of developing the performance examination, the nursing administrator and faculty have to consider other kinds of questions, i.e., preliminary ones concerning questions related to content.

One of these organizing questions is: Who is responsible for determining the content of the performance examination? And even more fundamentally: Who is responsible for deciding who shall determine the content?

SCOPE OF EXPERTISE

Once the nursing faculty has agreed that a performance examination is desirable, a committee probably will be selected to actually begin the work. At first glance it might seem perfectly obvious who should be on the committee—namely, the clinical instructors responsible for the course at the time the test is to be given. This might be quite appropriate if the test is to be given following only one nursing course (or semester). Indeed, when the content is focused on a limited subject, the faculty with that particular perspective might be completely appropriate and adequate. However, if the performance examination is to be given at or near the end of the entire program, a different committee composition might better serve the purpose. It is commonly accepted that those who devote a majority of time and effort to a limited scope of practice not only become experts but they also tend to lose a broader perspective and frequently need help in keeping the comprehensive whole in balance. If, for example, the examination is developed only by those who teach fundamental nursing skills, it will bear the stamp of that area of concern. Fundamentals instructors tend to be more conscious of the multiple specifics of nursing techniques and tend to emphasize certain skills. Because of their focus they provide an essential expertise in developing the examination; however, their perspective needs the balance provided by other instructors whose interest and expertise are of a different nature. If clinical faculty representatives are selected from the entire nursing spectrum, the test will tend to be more comprehensive in scope and more balanced in emphasis. Once again, this contextual variable determines not only the content but also who decides that content.

Therefore, when the examination is intended to test the students' competence to administer "total nursing care," the scope of that term must be defined even before a proper committee can be convened. If its focus is on physical and technical aspects of care, experts in those areas should be appointed. If it includes psychiatric/mental-health concepts, those experts also should be appointed. And if it includes aspects of community health, health assessment, or specialty and research areas, experts with those perspectives should be represented on the committee as well. The kind of faculty experts needed to develop the test is dependent on the kind and scope of content to be evaluated. Put another way, the purpose and competencies to be examined determine who should develop the test. However, it is just as true and just as important to recognize from the outset that the appointed committee defines and develops the test according to its own collective focus of concern. Its specific composition, therefore, is an essential consideration. In addition—although this may be obvious—it should be mentioned that factors other than clinical specialization have an influence, such as personality characteristics, years of experience, the numbers of qualified faculty members available for the task, workload, cooperation from administration and service facilities, and the like.

It is conceivable that either choice or circumstances could dictate that a committee of one or two members be responsible for the entire project. The committee members may be volunteers or they may be appointed by the chairperson. They may be voted into committee by the entire faculty or by a specific clinical department. However, it should be realized that the process and the resulting instrument will reflect to some extent the individuals' particular concerns, either knowingly or unknowingly. This may be highly desirable; it also could present problems. Regardless of the size of the committee or the method of selection, the characteristics of its members exert an important influence on decisions about content and process. If this point is taken into consideration from the outset, appropriate efforts can be made to ensure that the examination is not skewed in an undesirable direction or that essential aspects are not overlooked. The composition of the committee is intimately related to the desired outcome as well as to the final product. Not every faculty group has the luxury of this kind of choice, but every group should recognize the significance of this contextual variable.

In addition to the clinical-content experts on the committee, it is extremely helpful to have a regular consultant who is competent in the field of educational evaluation and measurement. If available, such an expert usually provides a more objective perspective as typically she/he has no vested interest in a particular content area that is at stake and a more neutral stance is possible. Furthermore, such an expert brings knowledge and experience in the construction of objective examinations and other evaluation procedures, which compliments the expertise of the nursing faculty. For example, as the clinically oriented members struggle with specifying content and process, a psychometrist can serve as a sounding board, an "outside" observer and consultant, as well as a resource in evaluation methodology. And sometimes when the discussions become heated and intense—as they surely will—the consultant may even become a referee.

While a psychometrist has little or no knowledge of nursing she/he potentially could become one of the most important working members of the committee, from the beginning planning phase all the way through the final pilot testing and validation of the performance examination. Some nurse educators have an academic background in testing and measurement that is extremely helpful; having a nonnurse testing expert on the committee, however, serves several important functions and in general is beneficial. Naturally the extent of helpfulness depends on the background and personality of the particular individual available and interested in working with the committee. Individuals who are competent in testing and measurement typically are found on the faculty of colleges and universities, particularly in the departments of education and psychology. If no one is readily available on the local campus, it may even be worthwhile to employ a consultant from elsewhere to work with the committee periodically, particularly at critical points in the developmental schedule. Much can be accomplished in a few hours if sufficient preparation is made to maximize the efficiency of the time available.

ORGANIZING THE TASK

In addition to careful selection of the committee that will develop the performance examination, a number of other preliminary organizational factors deserve consideration. They influence thc effectiveness of the committee and its ability to achieve the desired objectives. Insufficient attention to these planning and organizational details will have a decidedly negative impact—especially in the early stages, regardless of the good intentions of the faculty and the need for the examination.

TIME AND SCHEDULES

One of these factors is the realization that an extensive period of time is needed to develop a performance examination "from scratch"; naturally, less time is required when an already existing instrument (such as those from the Regents External Degree Programs or other sources) is adapted to the particular situation. Both faculty and administration need to be aware of the potential time requirement and to plan accordingly. Sustained administrative support is essential to ensure that the faculty committee is given sufficient time to work on the assignment without feeling guilty on the one hand for paying less attention to other tasks or for feeling excessively overburdened on the other hand. Because of the long-term nature of the project, it is important for other faculty members who are not involved to be cooperative in releasing committee members from some of their regular duties; otherwise resentments could emerge that might hamper progress or interfere with the success of the project.

Developing a comprehensive performance examination is an evolutionary process that requires deliberate planning and scheduling to ensure that sufficient time and resources are made available for whatever period is required to complete the project. If possible, release time for committee members would help expedite completion. But even if this is not a realistic expectation, an objective tool still can be developed; it just takes longer and requires more individual commitment. Probably a minimum of one to two semesters is required, when an existing model is used but modified. Even then, persistent efforts are necessary for everyone involved to complete the entire project in one year, taking into account the planning through pilot-testing stages and the transition into implementation. The complete development and implementation of the Clinical Performance in Nursing Examination of the Regents External Degree Program took four years; the Health Assessment performance examination took two years.

Scheduling meetings of the committee on a regular basis—whether once a week or once a month—will facilitate steady progress and is highly desirable. If meetings are left to spontaneous and haphazard arrangements, whenever members can free themselves from an already overextended calendar, it is obvious that the project will suffer as a result. Scheduling meetings well in advance also is important and once the dates are determined every effort should be made by the regular members to keep them. Almost everything will conspire against this (or so it seems), and only a firm commitment to the goal will ensure its achievement. In the past there always have been other responsibilities that emerged to usurp the priority of developing a performance examination; there is no reason to suspect that this will change. Nursing faculties have a notoriously busy schedule, a situation not too likely to be altered. Therefore, administrative and faculty support—both psychological and practical—are necessary from beginning to end if success is to be achieved.

The organization of such a project can be divided into ten basic categories:

1. Selecting the committee and setting activities in motion.
2. Developing a first draft of the dimensions of care and the respective critical elements to be included.
3. Developing a first draft of process and conditions under which the examination will be administered.
4. Developing subsequent drafts of both content and process based on an evolving understanding of examination as a whole.
5. Employing minipilot-tests of each aspect of the test as it is developed, each resulting in refinements of the draft documents.
6. Developing a study guide that explicitly states all aspects of content and process.
7. Drafting the forms to be used and the manual for evaluators, as well as selecting and programming evaluators.
8. Pilot testing and validating the "final" version of the test and study guide; making final revisions in all documents.
9. Orienting students, faculty, service personnel, and others throughout the period of transition and particularly just before actual implementation.
10. Implementing the tested and approved examination at the appropriate time in the academic schedule.

Essentially all of these stages apply whether the examination covers a limited scope and is to be given after one or two courses or is a comprehensive test at the conclusion of the program. They also apply whether the examination is administered in the actual clinical setting or simulated in a nursing laboratory. Many more complex problems have to be addressed for a comprehensive examination in the actual setting, but the developmental process is just about the same. Therefore, the committee needs to contemplate the entire spectrum of activities early in the planning phase and then to organize the project accordingly by scheduling meetings and activities over a period of time. This is done on a tentative basis in the planning phase and is modified as the committee steadily moves forward in meeting specific objectives. Better to comprehend the scope and demands at the outset than to spend time and effort only to realize later that circumstances prevent completion. The Biblical story of the importance of taking stock before beginning to build a house serves as a good example. Better to take time for adequate planning than to give up half way through the project. When one is first reviewing all that has to be done to develop a clinical performance examination, it is natural to become discouraged and to feel inadequate. It is easy to think: we don't have enough time; we don't have enough qualified faculty; we don't have a testing expert; the faculty is already overextended, etc. These are reasonable and logical anxieties. However, in most circumstances the task can be accomplished so long as the faculty and administration are firmly motivated to do so and are willing to spread the developmental process over a period of time while continuing with other activities. An organized, patient, and committed chairman of the committee (or total faculty) is also imperative to accomplish the goal.

PATIENCE AND COMMITMENT

Actually getting the job done is dependent upon selecting the most qualified committee members, outlining the sequential activities required for development and implementation, scheduling regular work sessions, and finally, systematically exploring and resolving each part, one step at a time. That is a key phrase: one step at a time. Progress is made gradually by methodically developing one aspect at a time and by maintaining the attitude that the process is evolutionary. As each part evolves the committee will grow in understanding, competence in the process, and confidence in their own ability. Progress becomes more efficient as experience is gained. As each draft is developed, typed neatly on the page and reviewed, the examination begins to look better and better. It takes on a concrete form and begins to come alive with possibilities. The committee should be prepared to write several sequential drafts because, like it or not, this is an evolutionary process. Only after several major sections are completed can particular parts be realistically revised. And only after all sections are developed in the initial draft can the subparts be adjusted so that they all fit smoothly into an integrated whole. Seeing it take shape helps the committee to more fully understand how the rest of it should be developed.

THE WHAT, WHEN, WHY, HOW QUESTIONS

As previously suggested the question of what content to include in the performance examination is dependent upon such factors as when it is to be administered (i.e., at what point in the curriculum), why it is being used, and how it will be implemented. It is related to the type of nursing program in which the examination will be used (LPN, associate, bachelor's, master's, certification, refresher course, etc.). Additional factors include consideration of other evaluation procedures and how many other performance examinations are used throughout the program. To some extent it also is related to the characteristics and adequacy of the faculty, their philosophy about teaching-learning, organization of the curriculum, clinical resources, support services, and cost. All of these factors are interrelated and the final content of the examination emerges from the particular configuration of characteristics and decisions made about the when, why, and how questions.

Because this book is addressed to faculties in various types of programs, it presents a generalist perspective and relies upon the particular faculty group to specify particulars within their own context. To avoid unnecessary confusion, the discussion of what to include in the examination will be based on the conventional academic program, even though the principles are just as applicable to other educational endeavors.*

TIMING

In the early planning stage the faculty is presented with the problem of deciding when a performance examination should be given. It might be appropriate after a module or a course, at the end of one semester, at the end of a particular curriculum sequence, or at the conclusion of the entire program. Clearly, when the examination is to be given is a most important variable in determining the competencies to be included. If the student has completed only the first clinical nursing course, the test should include a sample of those skills expected to be mastered during that course. If two or more courses have been completed the array of competencies is enlarged to the clinical aspects covered up to that point. And if the examination is to be administered immediately before completion of the entire program, it

*A separate chapter will be devoted to application in in-service programs, refresher courses, continuing education, and other special situations. The basic process is the same.

will include a comprehensive sample of skills and behaviors expected of graduates of the particular type of program.

To the extent that students are expected to continue to apply prior learning in each successive course, the later the examination is given the more comprehensive in nature it can become. All previously learned skills and principles applicable to the clinical area, regardless of when they were learned, may be included in the universe of possibilities from which the sample of competencies will be drawn. However, it is possible that only the "upper-level" abilities will be tested. When these higher-order skills subsume more fundamental ones it is not necessary to test both levels explicitly. These are decisions the faculty must make in determining what to include—as well as what to exclude—from the performance examination.

The faculty may want to determine the students' competence after completion of a particular technical course or specialty rotation. In addition to testing theoretical understanding, they may want objectively to evaluate the students' actual performance of the clinical skills involved. Unless resources and time are abundant, it probably would be more efficient and more realistic to test such students in a simulated laboratory setting rather than in the complex clinical environment. In the laboratory all variables can be controlled—including some while excluding others. Each student can be tested objectively and consistently with each episode demanding comparable ability without the everpresent concern for the welfare of patients who require care. In acute specialty-care units in a hospital, for instance, the variability among patients, the lack of availability of comparable situations, and the potential dangers to patients make it almost impossible to administer an objective performance examination in that setting. The knowledge required for practice in such situations is best evaluated by properly constructed written tests and most of the skills uniquely related to that specialty area can be objectively tested in the nursing laboratory by using all of the principles related to performance examinations. While some of the reality is lost, much is gained at the same time and such a simulated test becomes one in a series of performance examinations.

AN EXAMPLE

For example, following a course focusing on maternal–infant care, a simulated performance examination could be administered in which students are tested on a random sample of required skills. (This is a performance not a theory test.) The selected competencies to be measured are predetermined and thus noted on individual cards; according to the predetermined conditions the students draw a card and perform the specified skills in a controlled setting. These might include such things as: examination of the fundus; assessment of a newborn; specified care of an infant in an incubator; insertion of a nasogastric tube for an infant; teaching the mother about postpartum and infant care; or whatever nursing competencies are expected for the level and scope of the particular course. By testing these skills in the laboratory less time is required and all students have a fair and objective opportunity to demonstrate their skills. The amount of time devoted to the topic during the entire program and the abilities expected of beginning graduates help to determine the degree of emphasis to be placed on it during performance assessment.

Competencies related to highly specialized areas such as intensive-care or coronary-care unit also may be tested most objectively, efficiently, and safely in the laboratory setting. For example, assessing the cardiac patient's status by reading an EKG strip, giving cardiac-pulmonary resuscitation, assessing the patient's need for emergency treatment, using specialized life-support machinery, or teaching the patient and his family about myocardial infarction may all be tested in the nursing laboratory by using films, models, and role playing or other techniques. Such specialty performance examinations have a self-limiting scope, and because of their complex technical nature they are ideally suited for simulation. It should be remembered that theory about a particular topic, its integration with previously learned theory, and its application can best be tested in an objective written test. The performance examination tests the students' competence actually to demonstrate the required abilities.

OTHER MEASUREMENTS

Another critical factor in determining the competencies to be measured, and closely related to the question of when the examination is to be given, is consideration of the number, scope, and type of other evaluation procedures being used in the program. It is possible that several performance examinations could be used, each one testing a narrow scope of ability and each one independent of the others. A simulated performance test could be given at the end of each semester. It also is possible to have only one comprehensive examination at or near the end of the entire program, which encompasses a random sample of a range of expected behaviors and which is constructed in such a way as to assess the students' overall nursing competence.

In specialty programs, associate degree, and practical nurse programs administering one comprehensive clinical examination is probably quite adequate because the primary focus is on giving technical nursing care to institutionalized patients, even though the level of expectation varies from one type of program to another. The nature of the expected competencies is essentially the same: the examination focuses on bedside care of hospitalized adults and/or children who have a variety of common illnesses requiring nursing care that is technical in nature. A baccalaureate program may require two or three performance examinations. As with written tests, the scope of the curriculum and course objectives will determine how comprehensive the performance examination should be and how many are needed. The type of program will dictate the complexity of the testing situation as well as the particular areas of care to be included in the test. While written tests reflect the achievement of knowledge appropriate to the type of educational program, the performance examination likewise reflects the scope and degree of competence expected of students at a given point in the program.

If selected areas of competence already have been measured in simulated tests, for example, they need not be explicitly evaluated in subsequent examinations. As stated earlier, a test of higher-order, more complex abilities is presumed to incorporate less complex skills, which therefore do not necessarily have to be explicitly tested again. Furthermore, it is important to remember that the performance test is not a conglomeration of every aspect of learning and accomplishment. Rather it is a test specifically designed to evaluate a representative sample of actual competencies of students to implement theory satisfactorily in a given clinical situation. Thought processes, memory, and various cognitive abilities are measured on objective written tests (or in other ways). For example, knowledge required to conduct an in-depth investigation, analyze data, and generate a plan can be evaluated through case studies, reports, and nursing-care plans. While these evaluative procedures are essential, they are not an explicit part of the performance examination. Rather, objective assessment of performance is another separate part contributing its own reflection of the student's achievement of the stated objectives; it should be developed and used to capitalize on its unique contribution. Interjecting an overt test of cognitive skills during the performance examination has a high probability of contaminating and confusing both the test of theory and the test of competence. Each area is essential and deserves its own unique test. Collectively, all of these evaluation tools measure the students' total achievement and ability.

A PARTICULAR MODEL

The New York Regents External Associate Degree in Nursing requires the completion of a comprehensive Clinical Performance in Nursing Examination (CPNE) after all nursing theory examination requirements have been met. It is a tightly organized, objective two-and-a-half-day examination of the students' competence to administer a wide range of technical care to actual hospitalized adults and children requiring general nursing care. By design it tests the students' ability to integrate knowledge, apply the nursing process, make clinical judgments, and implement and evaluate the plan of care. Some of these skills are evaluated implicitly while other more concrete competencies are being tested explicitly. That which is directly observed is a reflection of the internal cognitive ability as it is applied to each phase of nursing care.

This examination—as developed by the external-degree nursing faculty subcommittee—incorporates the 10 basic concepts presented in the last chapter although they were not identified as such at the time. How helpful it would have been to have had them explicitly stated and illustrated early in the development phase of that project!*

Developing performance examinations for baccalaureate (and master's) degree nursing programs presents a somewhat different situation from the focus in associate degree programs. Because the scope of theory and clinical competencies and the settings where professional nursing care is rendered are so diverse, more than one comprehensive performance examination may be required. It is possible to use only one comprehensive performance examination with other assessment procedures being used for special clinical situations. However, two or three distinctly different examinations may be needed adequately to cover the entire array of professional competencies to be assessed prior

---

*This book distills the essence of experience from those years of challenge and discovery. More details will be given about the content and the development of the CPNE throughout this book. It is a unique clinical assessment tool and served as the model for the additional performance examination developed for the external BSN program (Health Assessment and Professional Performance Examinations). The CPNE also serves as the basic model presented throughout this volume.

to completion of the program. They may be spaced throughout the program subsequent to a particular content sequence or administered as a clinical battery at the end of the program.

In the New York Regents External BSN degree program three completely different performance examinations are required to assess clinical competence. One, the Clinical Performance in Nursing Examination (CPNE), is the two-and-a-half-day test mentioned above. Because of its design and purpose, this comprehensive examination is used objectively to measure competence in the technical portion of the practice of nursing for both the associate and bachelor's external degree nursing candidates. It is an essential companion to the other two clinical examinations in the BSN external program. Each is designed to complement the others, and all three complement the required series of written examinations and the general education components required to obtain the degree.

Health-Assessment Performance Examination

The second clinical test, the Health Assessment Performance Examination (HAPE), is designed to evaluate the students' competence to conduct a comprehensive health assessment as a basis for planning to meet the health needs of clients. The student is required to obtain subjective data through a detailed health history and objective data through a physical examination of the client, both focusing on a nursing perspective. These data serve as a basis for writing an analysis of the client's health needs and recommendations for his health care. Rather than actual patients, this examination uses paid subjects who are programmed to assume the role of client with designated health-care problems; this allows more control over the variables being tested.

Professional Performance Examination

The third performance test, the Professional Performance Examination (PPE), culminates the entire nursing theory and performance examination sequence for the BSN program. It is a totally simulated examination that tests the student's competence in such areas as: leadership, collaboration, research process, teaching, management of clients, clinical decision-making, and relating with others. It primarily uses a series of video-recorded vignettes to ensure control over multiple complex variables and the multiplicity of situations, major health problems, and client settings involved. In this way the student can be tested on a range of nursing situations involving a sampling of major health problems; care of individuals, families, and groups; institutional and community practice settings; various age, ethnic, or geographic considerations; and a variety of health-care personnel.

The focus, format, and competencies of each of these examination is different. Collectively—along with the five required written cognitive examinations—the entire array of expected competencies is objectively evaluated regardless of how and when the student learned them. Based on successful completion of these examinations and the stipulated general education requirements, students are eligible for the Bachelor of Science degree in nursing.

A BRIEF REVIEW

To review, the scope and objectives of the types of program determine to a large extent the content and number of performance examinations needed. For both the Regents associate and bachelor's nursing programs the examinations are designed for the termination phase of the program. Their placement (subsequent to the entire basic teaching–learning phase) dictates that the total array of nursing competencies be included. They are not meant to test knowledge or skills comparable to end-of-course tests but rather to serve as comprehensive objective examinations consistent with end-of-program competencies. Their content was determined largely by this fact.

Closely related to this discussion of determining content is the need to clarify exactly why the performance examination is being given, and why it is being given at a particular time in the program. Specifying the purpose of the clinical test helps the faculty figuratively to draw lines of limitation around the content to be included and to comprehend the perimeters before outlining the multiple details to be tested. The competencies to be included and all other procedural aspects of the test have a direct relationship to the reason it is being used. If its purpose is to test the student's ability to perform technical skills specifically related to a particular type or area of nursing care, its content must be restricted accordingly. But if its purpose is to ensure beginning competence in a wide ranging variety of situations it must be comprehensive in nature, longer, and more complex.

To reiterate, determining what to include on the performance examination is directly related to the type of program, the purpose of the test, when it is given in the program, how many such examinations are necessary, and other evaluation procedures used. Furthermore, content for the performance examination also is dependent on the number of qualifications of available faculty, clinical and laboratory facilities, and the budget.

COST AND OTHER FACTORS

Developing and implementing a comprehensive performance examination is costly because of the faculty time involved. As previously pointed out, it probably will take a faculty committee (desirably consisting of four to seven members) at least one to two semesters—working on a regular basis—to complete all essential aspects of the project. Committee members needed and the time required are dependent upon the type of program, the complexity of the test, and the use of previously established models. However, another aspect of cost relates to the use of the examination once it is developed. If an end-of-program comprehensive examination is used, it probably will require a minimum of 3 to 9 hours of faculty time per student, depending on how the test actually is administered. This is costly in time and therefore in money. (In a subsequent chapter suggestions will be given for minimizing costs and for dealing with scheduling problems.) Consideration of cost is important to the current discussion because that factor impinges on the content to be included, which in turn is dependent upon the number of examinations deemed essential, why and when they are to be administered, and whether simulated or actual situations are necessary.

A simple end-of-course simulated examination is time consuming and less costly than a comprehensive clinical one given at the end of the program. If the skills can be examined in the nursing laboratory, less time probably will be required and this enables the available faculty to evaluate more students in the allotted time. However, using several end-of-course simulated performance tests may be more costly in the long run than a single comprehensive examination both in terms of development and administration to students. Use of one comprehensive performance examination at the conclusion of the program of learning is costly, but it is required only once a year. It is possible to divide the test into two parts, giving one during midterm of the last semester and the other at the end of the semester (and program). This saves faculty time and permits designated examination periods for the performance as well as for written examinations. More about cost will be discussed later; for the moment it is sufficient to realize that faculty time and costs are important considerations in the preliminary discussions of the overall development and content to be included in the performance examination.

ADDITIONAL CONSIDERATIONS

A few other factors also deserve brief mention because they influence decisions about the nature and content of performance examinations. One of the most important is the availability of a sufficient number of patients or clients who meet the criteria for selection (to be presented later). It would be foolish to develop a comprehensive and sophisticated clinical examination requiring the administration of specific nursing care when there are insufficient patients with those needs in the available clinical setting. The examination given in the actual setting of necessity must reflect the needs of patients. When the number and type of patients are limited, the clinical performance examination may be augmented by simulated procedures in the nursing laboratory or be restricted in the scope of its demands. One other factor that will be mentioned briefly is the availability of a well-supplied nursing laboratory. If no laboratory exists, one may have to be developed or arrangements made with an appropriate local facility to use theirs. If the college does not have a sufficiently equipped lab, perhaps a hospital staff development (in-service) unit could be considered, or at least certain essential equipment could be used there during the examination period. For examinations such as health assessment, a local clinic or the campus health-sevice facilities could be used, probably on weekends. For video-taped simulated examinations the learning-media center probably will have to be used, unless the nursing program has its own equipment and facilities. The availability of appropriate space and equipment are important considerations in determining what should be included in the performance examination.

SUMMARY AND COMMENTS

In summary, decisions about what to include—and what to exclude—on a performance examination and its overall organization are dependent upon and directly influenced by a number of factors. Each of these considerations impinges on the others; they are interrelated and mutually affect each other, as shown in Figure 4.1. They must be explored early in the planning discussions—not only as separate points but also

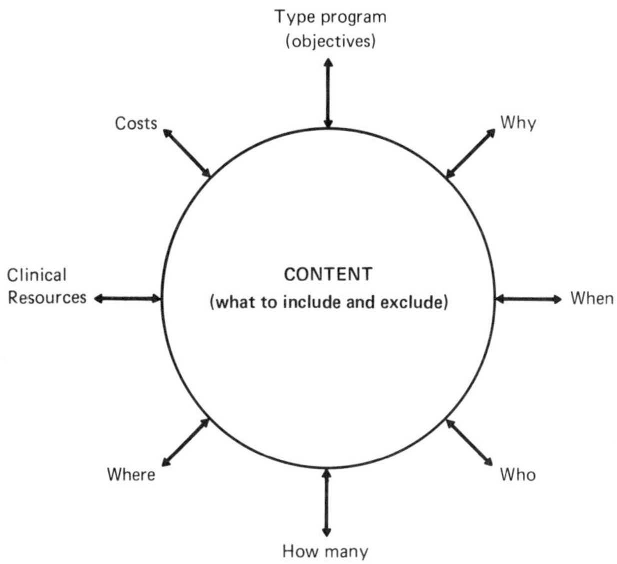

Fig. 4.1. Interrelated factors influencing the development of performance examinations.

in relation to each other if unnecessary difficulties are to be avoided during the planning/development and implementation phases.

Furthermore, determining the competencies to be examined also interfaces with the following questions.

1. What are the curriculum objectives of the program and how are they related to clinical performance? What is the type of education program and what are the expected competencies of its new graduates?
2. Why is the performance examination necessary? What purposes does it specifically serve? How does it relate to other evaluation procedures?
3. When is the test to be administered in the curriculum sequence? At what level will the student take the examination and why at that point? Will an end-of-course or end-of-program examination best serve the purpose?
4. Who will be responsible for developing the content and procedures for the performance examination? Are all essential clinical areas represented on the committee to ensure an adequate balance if the examination is comprehensive in scope? And after the examination is developed, who will administer it?

5. How many performance examinations will be given during the course of the entire program? Does each one serve a distinctly unique and complementary function? To what extent do they overlap?
6. Where will the performance examination be administered? Is the actual clinical facility or a simulated laboratory best suited for the particular examination?
7. Are clinical resources sufficient to examine the desirable competencies? If not, can simulation be used? Is a properly equipped nursing laboratory available if necessary? Are other local resources available?
8. Are there sufficient numbers of prepared faculty to develop and implement the examination? Can time be scheduled for both functions? Are sufficient funds budgeted to ensure ample time to develop and administer the examination and/or to purchase necessary equipment?

All of these factors require open discussion in the preliminary stage of developing a performance examination—especially if it is to be comprehensive in scope. Final decisions about content depend on answers to these questions, and to a large extent the answers to these questions depend upon the faculty's preferences for the examination itself. Recognition of this interdependence is important to the success of developing and implementing an extensive performance examination program.

CHAPTER 5

Specifying the Content

Some of the most frequently expressed concerns about developing performance examinations relate to specifying the content and being sure that enough is included to document competence while keeping the required time to a minimum. Questions raised to determine what content to include also invariably leads to a discussion of what to exclude. This chapter focuses on how to determine content, how to organize it into dimensions of practice (or areas of care), and how to write the explicit statements that pinpoint the behaviors to be measured. Content and the process of administration are the two major interdependent components of the examination. Strictly for discussion purposes, developing content will be isolated and emphasized here; the organizing conditions and procedures will be addressed in the next chapter.

Once areas of care are identified and defined and the critical elements are explicitly written, a major step will have been taken toward making clinical assessment not only objective but also fair and comparable. Furthermore, it is halfway home to ensuring consistency; the other half is found in systematizing the conditions and process of administration of the examination. Most of the 10 basic concepts presented earlier will be applied and illustrated in this chapter, although some are more relevant to establishing conditions and hence will be integrated later.

One of the fundamental problems that confronts the faculty committee responsible for developing a performance examination is the conflict between idealism and realism. Throughout this chapter the need to reach a reasonable balance between these two aspects will become evident over and over again. Because of the very nature of nursing, many nurse educators are caught up in an "infatuation with perfection"—even when they are working with novices during the learning period. Clearly, no one advocates care for patients that is harmful or that jeopardizes their physical or emotional well-being. However, it is a common experience among those engaged in developing performance examinations that expectations initially are set too high. Pilot-tests show that those who are qualified (as judged by other means) are unable to pass. Revising the scope and extent of expectations is not "watering down" the test but making it more reasonable and more realistic. To some, such modifications are difficult to accept because they move away from perfect practice. Repeated pilot-testing is necessary to establish a balance between perfect and reasonable (acceptable) practice. The level of acceptability for passing the examination establishes the baseline (the degree of tolerance for deviation from the ideal practice that has been taught). Students are then held accountable for that minimum acceptable level, with 100 percent accuracy of performance. The struggle to determine a realistic level of expectation is an integral part of the challenge of specifying the content of the examination.

However, before the reader misunderstands the intent of this discussion it should be recalled that the focus of attention here is the development of a performance examination, not a teaching plan, course outline, or outline of the multitude of objectives for an entire program. All of the principles about constructing an objective examination presented earlier are applicable here. Sampling from among the universe of possibilities, specifying essential behaviors as discrete observable critical elements, and ensuring comparable difficulty are important considerations in the struggle to retain a legitimate compromise between the epitome of ideal practice and the reasonable expectations for acceptable performance. If expectations for performance during the examination are too idealistic even the more able students will not pass; if the behavioral expectations are set too low, even the incompetent students will pass. It is the struggle between these two extremes that will confront the faculty throughout the project; its resolution probably will not be achieved until the final pilot-testing and subsequent revisions are completed. Because clinical instructors are unaccustomed to objective testing in the clinical setting, they may be uncomfortable with concepts such as sampling, using only critical behaviors, and expecting 100 percent compliance with the minimum expectations as acceptable performance. Therefore, throughout the transition period the entire faculty—and the students—will be called on to modify some of their previous opinions and preferences.

Once decisions are made about the purpose of the clinical examination, when and where it is to be given, and all of the other factors discussed in the previous chapter, work can begin on identifying the areas of care and the critical elements that will constitute the examination per se.

PRELIMINARIES

Before beginning the task of actually identifying content, the faculty committee responsible for developing the examination should establish and clarify certain preliminary variables. These may already have been decided by the entire nursing faculty or other appropriate person or groups. They include such factors as the purpose, level, and placement of the examination in the program; the scope of competencies to be tested; types of clients and setting desired; the theme around which the content will be organized; and the time schedule available for developing the examination. The content and format of the examination are directly and intimately related to these variables associated with context, theme, and time.

The committee also should keep in mind that this development process is evolutionary. From the outset, it is helpful for those involved to adopt the attitude that they are working on a draft version in a series of drafts. Rather than aim for perfection of one piece before moving on to another, it probably is more fruitful to develop a first draft of the whole (as it is envisioned at the time) and then return to it piece by piece to refine and improve it. This then becomes draft two; after it is typed in an organized format, the committee and others can study it, refine and modify it, try it out, and subsequently develop draft three. Throughout this evolutionary process the committee grows in understanding of what to include and how to go about testing it.

This process can be called a "developmental do-loop," because it is similar to the do-loop function in computer language. The same maneuver is applied to a series of variables one at a time, and then another maneuver is applied to the same variable; on and on the cycle goes until all variables have been fully explored, tested, or analyzed. In terms of developing an objective performance examination, the committee drafts one version, tests it out, refines it, and goes back to write another draft based on the previous analysis. Each aspect is repeatedly refined until it meets the expectations of the faculty.

There is one danger of the "developmental do-loop" applied to test development; some committees may never get out of the cycle. Faculty members who are infatuated with perfection will never be fully satisfied with *all* of it and will tend to perpetuate the process. The chairman and other members of the committee will have to monitor this tendency continually if the goal is to be achieved. While everyone prefers a perfect examination eventually, that probably is an unrealistic goal for the first round. Undoubtedly an examination that is 50 percent objective and comparable is better than one that reaches only 30 percent on the objectivity continuum.

As the faculty committee works together to crystalize the examination, developing better and better drafts, their perception of both content and procedure is enhanced. Subsequently, they have more insight about the modifications needed to meet the program objectives and the reality of the context.

PERSONAL ATTITUDES

Another problem that can be anticipated and that each committee member probably will confront is the pain of separation from a previously held "beloved idea." Each person brings the totality of his past learning and experiences, some of which are firmly held. Because these experiences differ, not everyone will cherish the same procedures, methods, words, values, or ideas. Therefore, at almost every step someone is going to have to relinquish something she or he ordinarily would not choose to give up. This is difficult to do, but perhaps the best consolation is that it happens to everyone, if the committee is balanced in the strength and capability of its members.

It actually helps to set up an informal reward system to acknowledge that someone has given up something of importance for the good of the whole. The performance subcommittee of the Regents External Degree Nursing Faculty gives imaginary gold stars to those who have the fortitude to revise an opinion when they are persuaded that it would move the project forward more positively. This is not to suggest that everyone should simply "give up" everything, but rather that each member contributes from a personal pool of experience some of which is more useful than something else. Each person should think through the point being made and try to persuade the others according to their convictions and knowledge. However, in the final analysis if the examination is to be the result of group effort, each member gives and gives up in a perpetual cycle of negotiations to extract the best contributions from each in order to achieve the common goal.

The development of an objective performance examination can be likened to an impressive problem-solving venture. It requires the collective intelligence of the group, applied systematically and logically all along the way to solve the problem. Brainstorming is very helpful, and all members are expected to share their knowledge and experience, and more importantly, creatively to invent new applications and ideas. Each aspect of the project is a part of the puzzle to be solved. If it isn't achieved before, the problem-solving attitude should become automatic during and after the development of such an examination. Each member learns to negotiate with the circumstances, to adapt, to modify, to synthesize, and to require persuasive evidence before relinquishing a point considered important.

One other point: one must remember that moving toward more objective clinical assessment requires an anticipated period of transition. Given the faculty, resources, and time available, it may be more helpful to begin with the objective of a limited test and to use that experience for faculty growth before initiating the development of a comprehensive clinical examination. For example, a simulated performance examination could be developed and administered in the nursing laboratory at the conclusion of the first one or two semesters of nursing. The steps in the process of development are the same but the complexities and problems would be much more manageable for the limited simulated test.

Beginning with a more circumscribed performance test also would be helpful for students during the transition period. They could learn how to reorganize their approach to learning and assessment, and more importantly, learn to demonstrate nursing competencies based on an explicit and objective set of predetermined criteria. They also would learn that only by satisfying the expected standard could they qualify for progress in the program, and that is a powerful stimulus to most students. The initial learning of both the faculty and students would be based on a test with limited complexities and consequences.

Once a limited, end-of-course, simulated performance test is developed and implemented the faculty could proceed with developing a more complex end-of-program examination. This approach would allow time for students and other faculty members to make the psychological and procedural transition toward objective assessment on a larger scale. Use of a limited and/or simulated test might be considered as an interim step for development purposes; subsequently, both simulated and actual performance tests could be used on an ongoing basis. Also, the initial, limited test could be used to orient students (and faculty) to objective performance testing so that they would know how to prepare for and approach the comprehensive clinical performance test at a later time.

SECRETARIAL HELP

It is important to have adequate typing and secretarial assistance. It is imperative that someone skilled in notetaking attend the meetings for this purpose, as consistently as the committee members. This person could be a regular faculty member who is assigned the responsibility of taking detailed and accurate notes; however, this role unquestionably will limit the active vocal contributions of that person during the meetings. When possible, it may be more desirable to have a secretary or an assistant, or someone knowledgeable about nursing (but not a committee member) take notes (minutes) and edit the series of drafts of documents. It is also helpful to have the same person responsible for this assignment throughout the developmental process, and to be sure that all minutes and documents are properly recorded, available at meetings, and copies appropriately filed.

In between meetings, the draft documents developed at the previous meetings should be carefully edited and typed. Starting the meeting with a fresh copy helps the members review the material more quickly and begin the critical analysis necessary for continuing and/or revising that part. It is always easier to criticize something printed on the page than to rely on memory, or poorly recorded handwritten notes. With each meeting the examination draft becomes more complete and more specific; it also seems more and more like a real possibility. Furthermore, the typed versions are more helpful if they are cumulative—that is, if each retyping includes everything developed to date. This also minimizes the time required to sort through piles of pages in search of a missing part. It is also helpful to keep separate minutes of the meetings (in chronological order) for a record of suggestions, problems, decisions, questions, ideas, etc., raised during each particular session. It becomes readily apparent that a capable recording secretary is a valuable asset to the committee in keeping the minutes separate from the examination draft and the multitude of other related documents being developed, and in seeing to it that all materials are ready for each meeting. Again, this role is best played by a knowledgeable and reliable person, but who may not necessarily be a key participant in the group.

SCHEDULING

Another preliminary procedural matter is the time frame and scheduling of meetings. The administration, the total faculty, and/or the committee has to decide how much time is available and the deadline by which the examination should be ready. Through these overall considerations the committee determines how frequently it should meet and how long each meeting should last. Because of the nature of the task, short and infrequent meetings are less desirable than longer, more frequent ones. Meetings lasting several hours, one day, or even two days allow the members to concentrate on the project and move forward more systematically. When only two to three hours are available members barely have time to review minutes and redirect their thinking from other pressing matters before the meetings are over. However, a three-hour session held regularly each week may facilitate recall and provide continuity. In some situations it may be most desirable to have an all-day session every two to three weeks. This would allow time to have the minutes and other documents typed and to try out newly developed aspects of the examination, e.g., wording of critical elements, definitions, procedural matters, clarification with colleagues, and the like.

Two of the most important points to keep in mind are the necessity of holding regular, frequently scheduled meetings that allow as much time as possible for discussion and development, and the necessity of committee members' attending consistently. Once the committee is appointed, with representatives from the desirable clinical areas, it is crucial that they accept the responsibility for attending regularly and for actively participating in the process. Nothing is more disruptive than having different committee members and substitutes at each meeting, and/or having infrequent, poorly attended meetings. These are sure signs of potential failure because they reflect a lack of real commitment by the members and/or administration actually to achieve the goal.

CONCLUSIONS

The importance of these preliminary considerations cannot be overemphasized. Each one has the potential for markedly helping or hindering the developmental process; hence they are discussed before outlining the guidelines for specifying the examination content and procedures.

Specifying the content to be included in the performance examination is divided into three major categories: (1) identifying specific areas of care or dimensions of practice; (2) explicitly defining each area selected; and (3) writing precise critical elements for each defined area. Each of these categories will be discussed in detail below. Specific criteria for each selection will be identified, with examples, and implications discussed when useful and appropriate.

CRITERIA FOR IDENTIFYING TEST AREAS

The first step for the committee in identifying content is to brainstorm extensively and to arrive at a list of potential areas of nursing care appropriate to the objectives to be satisfied by the performance examination. As previously indicated, the potential list also is contingent upon the type of setting (e.g., laboratory, specialty unit, or general hospital), type of client to receive care (adult or child), type of performance examination (simulated or actual), and other contextual variables.

CRITERION 1

Areas of care selected for inclusion emanate from stated objectives. The areas of care to be performed during the examination are derived from the established objectives, and therefore from the theoretical content and clinical learning covered to date. The objectives could be those of a single course, a block of courses, or the total program. From these total broad statements, specific objectives are written for the performance test, especially if it is to be a comprehensive one. Identifying the overall objectives to be addressed and the concomitant objectives specific to the examination would assist the committee from the outset. These statements—and the process of identifying them—crystalize the scope and complexity of the areas of care to be included in the initial array of possibilities. After a sufficient time for brainstorming, the committee should have an extensive—though not necessarily complete—list of areas of care related to designated objectives.

CRITERION 2

Areas of care are appropriate to the student (or graduate) of the particular type of program. As mentioned earlier, the use of performance examination is applicable to all types of basic, generic nursing programs as well as to refresher courses, long-term continuing education courses, or other specialty clinical courses or programs. Regardless of which one is involved, the examination committee is obliged to ensure that the areas of care the student is expected to demonstrate are essentially relevant to the practice of a person completing that type of program. Faculty have a common tendency to include in a test everything related to clinical practice within the scope of their own knowledge and competence. This seems to be quite unconsious and probably is related to the fear of omitting some valuable bit of assistance that otherwise might come back to haunt them if students are unsuccessful. Therefore, a concerted effort has to be exerted to limit even the initial list of areas of care to those expected for students in the particular type of program. This is likely to be a problem especially when the performance examination is comprehensive and given at the conclusion of the program. Pilot-testing and validation of the examination on students who already have been evaluated by other methods will help to assure appropriateness of the sample of areas being included. After the faculty committee has refined the list of areas to be included and thinks it is a reasonable and appropriate sampling, sharing it with other faculties for critical feedback is also very useful. Similarly, critiques from head nurses, supervisors, and others in nursing service provide data helpful to the committee in further refining the array of potential areas of care to be used in the performance examination.

CRITERION 3

Areas of care are consistent with the student's level in the program. In addition to assuring appropriateness of content for the type of program, the committee also has to keep in mind the level of the student being tested. Whether at the end of the first course, the end of the program, or somewhere in between, areas of care and their associated critical elements should be consistent with the level of theory and clinical learning to date. Frequently, faculty committees, sitting around tables in conference rooms conjuring up ideal situations and verbalizing their fondest hopes for their students, have a tendency to make performance expectations unnecessarily complex and unrealistic.

This criterion is intended to help the committee to be realistic in compiling the array of areas of care to be included. Clearly, however, expecting too much has to be tempered with concerns about expecting too little. Achieving a balance between these two potential extremes is one of the most difficult and persistent tasks of the committee. It does not come easy or soon, but rather emerges from repeated review and analysis of the evolving test materials. Essential feedback and solicited critiques from colleagues in other nursing programs and nursing-service areas, and from students also help to balance the demands of the test.

The areas of care to be used in an actual clinical examination are reflected in nursing practice consistent with the general content of the test—e.g., general adult care; care of children; specialty nursing care, etc. If the student is near the completion of the program, and the objective of the examination is to evaluate competence in administering total nursing care to hospitalized patients, then the list of areas of care may be extensive and inclusive. Any areas of practice taught in the program could be included, so long as they are sufficiently represented in the clinical setting and meet the other criteria for content and structure. Complexity also is added to the comprehensive examination at the terminal level by the number of areas to be performed in each patient-care situation, and by imposing time restrictions on parts and/or the whole test. Expectations are set very differently for students who have completed less than half of the nursing program. At this level the performance examination is restricted to less complex technical care; more time is allowed and fewer areas are expected in each testing episode. Simulated care in the nursing laboratory also is more appropriate and possible at this level in the program. Whether the performance examination is designed for the clinical setting or the nursing laboratory, the degree of complexity and number of areas of care depend on the level of the students as well as the type of program in which they are enrolled.

The decision about exactly which areas will be included in the array of possibilities rests with the faculty as a whole. Variations will occur from one program to another, depending on the unique characteristics of each faculty, school, student body, setting, and resources. There is no magic or foreordained list hiding in some ambiguous "somewhere" that can be painlessly ordered from a catalog. Many nursing faculties have been working on developing content areas for performance examinations and these provide invaluable assistance as examples or models. The faculty of the Regents External Degree Nursing Program decided to make the clinical performance examination available to others but to protect its integrity and ownership through copyright. Aspects of it may be used with permission and the examination in its entirety will be made available within the near future.*

It should be clear that the areas of care identified for the test will vary with the type of program and the student. The faculty is responsible for determining which practice areas are appropriate for their particular situation.

CRITERION 4

Areas of care are typical and commonly expected in the practice of beginning graduates. The examination is designed to test those aspects of nursing care that are routinely practiced by the beginning graduate. Even in highly specialized performance examinations, the content to be included is that which is expected in the practice of a beginner in that type of unit, agency, or situation. For master's programs, practitioner programs, or staff-development programs the same criterion can be applied. The examinations to assess competence should cover a representative sample of the commonly expected areas of care (or dimensions of practice) for the beginning graduate of that particular program. It does not include the aberrant, unusual, rate, or "academically interesting" areas—unless this is the purpose and focus of the test. These considerations are relevant for the teaching–learning phase, but are inappropriate for a performance examination.

Assigning patients who have just returned from open heart surgery and who have innumerable tubes and machines attached and have half-a-dozen physicians-in-training scurrying about, is not the kind of situation in which one objectively tests the students' competence with fluid maintenance, drainage, or personal hygiene. Using less critically ill patients would provide more appropriate opportunities with potentially fewer unanticipated consequences that would negatively influence the patient and/or the student assessment.

Areas of care, such as obtaining the client's family health history, analyzing a symptom, and conducting a nursing-oriented physical examination are appropriate for the new graduate of baccalaurate or practitioner program; they are not typical areas of practice expected of a graduate with an associate degree. Administration of medications,

*A monograph describing the entire CPNE study guide, listing areas of care and critical elements and all other aspects of the examination, is available for $6.00. Checks should be made payable to The University of the State of New York and sent to: Nursing Monograph, Regents External Degrees, The Cultural Center, Albany, New York 12230.

appropriate use of asepsis throughout nursing care, and provision of personal hygiene are relevant and appropriate for graduates of all academic and specialty programs, to one extent or another. Therefore, they may be included if the faculty chooses to do so—as major considerations or as aspects subsumed in other focused areas of care. Unless the faculty is alerted to potential problems in this category, some individuals may continue the practice of looking for the unusual patient situation. They fear that such learning opportunities may not turn up again in the near future and therefore may feel obliged to select them during the examination. However, this is teaching–learning behavior and is inappropriate for assessment.

A more useful approach is to consider the performance examination as a vehicle for determining the students' competence in areas of care that typically will be required in the majority of practice settings for graduates of the program. Designating commonly expected areas of care is a very functional method of controlling the kinds of situations that will be selected during the examination; it keeps the focus on testing rather than letting it drift to possible "good" teaching situations that occur during the examination period. It also keeps the focus on a rational array of potential areas, rather than allowing the list to be swollen by rare or unusual circumstances, for which the student probably has had little preparation.

CRITERION 5

Total array of areas provides a reasonable sampling from the universe of nursing activities. Because it is impossible, unnecessary, and expensive to test the students' performance in every aspect of nursing practice that has been taught in a program, a system of sampling from among that universe of possibilities is highly desirable. Unrestricted and repeated brainstorming results in the exaggerated list of potentially appropriate areas of care; this becomes the initial draft list of possibilities. During the developmental and pilot-testing period, many areas from this list will be deleted, others will be added and others may be combined or modified. Statements of conceptual framework, course and program objectives, clinical objectives, procedure manuals, and other related documents also are sources for determining the initial list of areas to be included. Determining the validity of the areas to be included is both a continuous and periodic process. It begins with the deliberate decisions made by the panel of experts developing the test and is concluded with the final pilot-testing of the examination.

Compiling the list of areas is a prerequisite step and such a list should be drafted as quickly as possible; everything else awaits its completion. With a broad array of possibilities on hand, the committee that begins to refine and modify it based on discussion and analysis of the relevance, appropriateness, availability, and measurability of each entry. Careful discussion within the committee and solicited feedback from others facilitates the process of sifting out the first-draft/sampling of areas. These are areas that meet all of the criteria discussed here. They represent the best examples of the most commonly expected areas of performance. They are neither too difficult nor too easy for the students' level and can be demonstrated within the context in which the examination will be given. The final array presents a reasonable sample of areas of practice that can be objectively examined.

However, there is another consideration related to sampling and while it will be discussed in detail in the succeeding chapter it also is relevant here. The total array of possibilities determines the basic categories of content for which students will be held accountable. With a criterion-referenced test students, faculty, and others directly involved must be fully informed of these areas in advance of the examination. Students learn and practice and are expected to be competent in all areas identified; however, in actuality they will be tested only on a prescribed number and combination of them to be determined at the time the test is given. In other words, students are tested on a sample of the areas of care listed in the array of possibilities. This is quite comparable to the use of written tests in which students know the potential content to be included but do not know the precise areas that actually will be tested. The faculty committee determines the broad sample of areas to be included in the performance test which students are expected to pass. At the time of the test the particular configuration of areas to be performed is decided by the evaluator, according to preestablished criteria for patient selection.

If the examination is comprehensive and given in the clinical setting, the patients available and actually selected (based on specific criteria) determine the particular combination of areas for which the student will be held accountable. Each patient has somewhat different needs for nursing care and this provides a natural sampling of areas to be tested. The student does not know exactly what will be demanded until the patient assignment is given at the beginning of that testing episode. Even the evaluators cannot prearrange or influence the selection except within the stated criteria. Patients are chosen as close as possible to the time of the actual starting of that testing episode (Patient

Care Situation or PCS), with sufficient lead time given to the staff to arrange for continuity of staff assignments and patient care. More on these procedural matters later.

This sampling criterion addresses the notion that the areas of care included in the potential array are a sample from among the universe of possibilities; that the entire array will not actually be tested, but a randomized sample of them will be tested without specific preknowledge of those to be included by the faculty or the student until immediately before the test begins. Both levels of sampling are essential in the development of an objective performance assessment; in this way the process becomes time and cost effective without undermining its credibility and purpose.

The same principle of sampling of areas of care is applicable in simulated testing. The faculty selects the potential array of possibilities (even at the conclusion of the first-level course) and students prepare to demonstrate competence in any and all of them. At the time of the examination students select a card on a random basis that specifies exactly which areas of care are to be performed. Students have no way of knowing in advance which areas actually will be tested and therefore must be competent in all of them—or risk resulting failure.

Depending on the type and placement of the examination, as many as 15 to 20 areas of care may be included in the potential array. Each patient situation, however, probably will not require more than five or six different areas to be explicitly tested. Expecting more than this is unrealistic, as the number of patients would be further limited, the time required would be excessive, and the patient probably would be too ill to be assigned for the purpose of an examination. Requiring more than one patient-care situation, however, expands the number of different areas available for testing because each patient's needs vary and the specific configuration is determined on that basis.

CRITERION 6

Areas of care are comparable in complexity and demands for integration of knowledge and skills. In selecting the array of areas of care to be used, it is essential that the committee apply the concept of comparability. As a matter of course, sampling limits the number of areas actually tested; therefore, they must be reasonably comparable. To the extent that this is possible, regardless of the configuration of area, students will be expected to demonstrate competence that is approximately equal in the degree of complexity required. While each patient's needs are different, the committee has the responsibility of giving reasonable assurance that each student will be subjected to equivalent demands on their ability to integrate knowledge and skill in clinical performance.

Some areas can be exactly the same in all patient-care situations and for all students. They occur frequently enough and are commonly expected of students or graduates: e.g., physical hygiene, use of fluids, or testing mobility and vital signs. By having several of these kinds of areas a certain degree of comparability is built into each testing episode. These *Required Areas of Care* (a term used by the Regents External Degree) provide a commonality of experience for all students. However, because patients' nursing needs vary considerably another dimension of flexibility must be added. This can be accomplished by creating a second list of areas, called *Selected Areas of Care,* from which a designated number can be drawn and added to the required areas. These selected areas include those that are frequently encountered, but are not necessarily required by all patients. For example, suctioning, oxygenation, irrigations, dressings, and medications are potential selected areas. Designating some areas as required and some as selected helps to ensure a higher degree of comparability of expectation for students, as well as to make the test sufficiently flexible in the actual setting. However, this is predicated on the idea that the selected areas are about equally demanding; if this is so, whichever configuration is necessary for the available patients, students will have reasonably equivalent opportunities to demonstrate their nursing ability.

An examination focusing on the students' ability to conduct a physical examination also might include required and selected areas for testing. For example, all students could be required to demonstrate competence in examining the abdomen, lungs, and heart at a level consistent with beginning baccalaureate nursing practice. Two to three other areas could be randomly chosen from a list of selected areas to increase in a controlled and objective manner the total number of areas to be examined—such as head and neck, breasts, cranial nerves, reflex functioning, circulatory status, etc. The sampling process is enhanced by designating some areas as required and some as selected, which allows for both consistency and flexibility in the examination.

One other category of areas of care involves those overall nursing skills that apply in every situation and all the time. The Regents External Degree Nursing faculty labeled these as *Overriding Areas of Concern* because regardless of whatever else is required during the examination, students always are evaluated on these points. If at anytime an overriding area is violated the student is failed for that portion of the test. These overall concerns provide a mechanism for testing a wide range of unanticipated events that emerge in the actual clinical setting. They test the application of some essential all-pervasive principles of nursing. Three of the major overrides are: physical jeopardy, emotional jeopardy, and asepsis. While physical and emotional jeopardy are somewhat subjective terms, they are necessary for coping with a potentially unlimited number of unacceptable nursing behaviors not already covered by specific critical elements. Because of this ambiguity other precautions must be taken to ensure their judicious and appropriate use. This will be discussed later in more detail. In general these areas can apply to examinations of technical bedside care, specialty simulations, or health-assessment examinations.

Overriding areas of concern also help to ensure comparability of the testing episodes. This category gives the evaluators the necessary authority to deal with unanticipated situations within a stated context and definition. It is a very useful way of exerting some control over some critically important student behaviors.

CRITERION 7

An area of care encompasses two or more specific activities that depend on the same essential principles. Areas of care (or dimensions of practice) are not procedures although procedures or techniques are inherent in most areas of care. Areas of care typically focus on a cluster of activities that require the application of common knowledge and principles. By designating areas of care rather than procedures, fewer discrete categories have to be developed and greater flexibility is allowed in the test, making it more functional in the actual clinical setting.

For example, the area of medications, as defined by the external degree faculty subcommittee, is broad enough to allow the student to administer any drugs by any route (oral, IM, IV, rectal, or any other way) ordered by the physician. The critical elements are written in such a way as to apply to all of these possibilities. Another example is irrigations. Any particular type of irrigation is acceptable so long as it fits within the definition. Some examples include enemas, douches, wound irrigations, etc. The knowledge required is basically the same and the clinical skills needed are comparable. While each of these procedures may not be readily found for testing, one or more probably will be required by patients on medical–surgical, pediatric, and other units.

Other clinical examples include dressings (which may include dry or wet, with or without packing or other special considerations); mobility (which may include ambulation, transfer activities, traction, or in-bed exercises and positioning). It is possible to list each particular nursing procedure or task instead of areas of care; however, this would require the development of explicit critical elements for every one. Such an approach is both time consuming and repetitious except for limited or simulated examinations given early in the program or used for special-focus content areas. Specific nursing techniques are quite appropriate for a simulated test, or for an actual performance examination given at the end of the introductory clinical nursing courses or at the conclusion of short-term or highly specialized areas (e.g., care of patients in premature nursery, recovery room, emergency room, etc.).

Once again, it is important to keep in mind the purpose of the performance examination, its placement in the program, and the type and level of students being tested. The scope of complexity of areas of care in licensed practical nurse programs will differ from those in associate and bachelor's programs, which will differ still from those necessary for practitioner or clinician programs or for short-term, staff-development programs.

When possible and appropriate, time and effort are conserved by identifying areas of care that encompass more than one specific activity. This approach also emphasizes the integration of principles related to several particular nursing activities, whether one is dealing with basic technical procedures, health assessment, or more complex areas such as leadership or collaboration. In actuality students will perform several particular nursing activities, simply because nursing care is provided through specific techniques; but in terms of developing an examination, the focus on critical elements can be directed to a somewhat broader scope. This allows for greater flexibility in selecting patients without the necessity of writing critical elements for scores of specific tasks.

CRITERION 8

Areas of care include those readily available and commonly required by patients in the setting to be used for the examination. After a tentative list of areas is drafted, it is very helpful for the committee to go to the clinical setting on any day and to count the number of patients actually available who require each of the areas of nursing care identified. Another aspect of the same problem, related both to examination content and process, is the potential availability of the specific areas of care at the time of day during which the examination is expected to be given. It is not enough that the areas are readily available sometime or cumulatively over several days; they must be needed by patients at the time students are assigned to take the examination. This is a matter for discussion in subsequent sections, but it is important here for preliminary consideration. If certain areas of care are not found with sufficient frequency or at the required times, it would be wasteful to develop critical elements for them. An exception can be made if the faculty wants to hold students accountable for such areas of care, even though the likelihood of their inclusion on the examination is limited. In this case they can be included in the total array of possibilities for which students should prepare.

Expecting every student to insert a Foley catheter is unrealistic if very few patients require such treatment, or if such catheters are inserted only for patients in the operating room, or if they are forbidden by medical practice in the particular agency. Similarly, one should not expect every student to administer intravenous medications if in fact such drugs are required only by a few patients and then are ordered once every 6 hours. Of course, all other criteria of appropriateness for the patient situation also must apply. Including areas of care rarely found on the patient units offers little payoff for the required investment of time and effort; therefore, unless some specific purpose is being served they probably should not be developed. Preliminary exploration of the availability of all areas, in the variety of potential settings, will help the committee to be realistic in finalizing the array of required areas and selected areas to be developed. The various stages of pilot-testing and working out procedural matters also will influence the final list to be adopted and used.

The availability and appropriateness of areas of care will vary considerably depending on the contextual variables mentioned. The kinds of nursing requirements for geriatric patients in a nursing-home setting obviously differ considerably from those expected on acute medical–surgical units, or the intensive-care nursery for newborns. The purpose, placement, setting, etc., all are essential factors that influence the selection of areas of care to be used.

CRITERION 9

Areas of care are observable and objectively measurable. All areas of nursing practice are not equally measurable or even discrete enough to be specifically defined and observed. Some aspects of nursing are too complex to sort out in the multidimensional context of the actual clinical setting and are less suitable to objective scrutiny and testing. Manipulative technical skills are most easily observed, while communication, interpersonal, and psychosocial skills are less measurable through direct observation in the uncontrolled environment. They are complex and usually involve multiple other variables that influence the behaviors being tested. Trying to test these more ambiguous and complex nursing competencies is very difficult in the actual client-care setting; they are more easily evaluated on written examinations and through simulated performance examinations in which all of the essential variables are programmed and controlled.

The very fact of testing areas of practice in a simulated setting subjects them to a certain artificiality: however, trying objectively to test them in the real clinical setting is remarkably frustrating and offers no guarantee that competence in the desired behaviors is actually being measured. It is a toss-up whether to control and limit the variables, which would enhance objective testing of essential behaviors, or to observe a complex interrelation of less controlled variables and hope that the test is at least somewhat more objective than otherwise would be true. This is one of the hard choices to be made by the faculty, particularily those in basic baccalaureate programs. It should be kept in mind that cognitive learning about these dimensions of practice can best be evaluated by objective written examinations, projects, nurse–client oriented papers, and other more conventional ways. The purpose of the performance examination is to document competencies that must be seen and cannot be tested in other ways.

The extent to which such areas as leadership, collaboration, and interpersonal relations can or should be tested in the actual clinical setting will undoubtedly require considerable faculty discussion and debate. The conflict between the desire for objective measurement and the nature of the behaviors to be tested is very real and not subject to quick and easy resolution. It will be helpful for the faculty to remember that objectivity is on a continuum, with subjectivity at the opposite end of the line. Not all areas of nursing care are equally measurable or extend to the same point on the scale. Some complex functions performed by the student may be measured ultimately somewhat less objectively than others. Every effort, however, is made to push for as much objectivity as possible. The faculty has to decide how much ambiguity and subjectivity will be tolerated on the examination per se. Regardless of the choices, a balance between the ideal and the acceptable must be reached, which means that a certain degree of compromise with reality is inevitable. Even so, all of the collective efforts to increase objectivity and to address these criteria to the extent possible will ensure the development of a more equitable and effective performance examination than otherwise would exist. The realities of life include the fact that not everything incorporated in the complex performance of professional nursing is amenable to objective clinical testing. The challenge is to persist in spite of these difficulties and to develop more effective and objective assessment tools while accepting the current state of the art.

Further Comments

A few other points might be helpful to faculties trying to resolve this nagging problem. Every effort should be made to improve the objective evaluation of the students' competence in these less observable areas through written examinations and other projects. The total evaluation also might include the circumscribed use of anecdotal notes that are written as objectively as possible, even though they are most useful for the purpose of providing feedback during the learning process. Many aspects of psychosocial, affective, and other complex dimensions of nursing practice are inherent in the comprehensive clinical examination even though they are not specifically identified or developed.

For example, in the Regents External Degree Clinical Performance Nursing Examination, candidates are evaluated on interpersonal relations in part through the "emotional jeopardy" overriding area of concern. The faculty committee struggled for nearly three years to develop explicit critical elements for communications and other psychosocial aspects of clinical performance. In the final analysis, they acknowledge that administering the examination in the actual patient-care setting restricted the possibility of objectively measuring these behaviors as specifically as other areas. It is essentially impossible to control the multiple variables or to ensure comparable patient situations; therefore a limited number of critical elements for communications were used in conjunction with the overriding area of emotional jeopardy. The committee decided that although idealistically they preferred a more specific and elaborate set of critical elements, they had little choice but to accept these broad perimeters in evaluating potentially unacceptable behavior of the students. This approach allows a broad circle to be drawn around the students' behavior throughout the patient-care situation so that any action or inaction on the part of the candidate that clearly interferes with the patient's emotional well-being is grounds for terminating that situation. However, for the protection of students and faculty the evaluator must document the manner and extent to which the patient was jeopardized. The broad circle of acceptability and the admittedly somewhat subjective nature of the documentation are not exactly the ideal, but they are ways of coping with the need to measure the students' general ability to communicate with patients in the context of an objective examination in the real clinical setting.

Clearly, as some areas of care are difficult to assess objectively in the actual setting, simulation testing may be preferred. For example, the Professional Performance Examination (PPE) required in the Bachelor of Science in Nursing External Degree Program is designed as a totally simulated test of the student's competencies in such dimensions of practice as relating with others, clinical decision-making, teaching, management of clients, leadership, collaboration, and research process. Because these abilities must be tested in regard to the whole range of major health problems, client-care settings, age groups, nursing process, etc. (as well as to individuals, families and groups), a simulated examination is most feasible. Nonetheless, the selection of areas (definitions and critical elements, etc.) still must relate to what is practical and possible given all of the contextual variables. Simulation helps to resolve a number of problems of variable control, but it introduces still others related to the mechanics and process of examining the competencies.

Regardless of the fervor, commitment, ability, and experience of the faculty, some areas of care may have to be deleted from the performance examination or modified according to the complex reality in which the examination is ensconced. A compromise between ideal and possible areas must be reached, but in doing so the examination itself is more fully understood and moves forward in the direction of acceptability and objectivity.

CRITERION 10

The number of areas of care varies with the objectives and context. There is no mystical number of areas that must be included in the examination. Other variables influencing the content and process of the test will help the faculty committee to determine how many areas should be included in the array of possibilities as well as how many should be required for each testing episode. Preliminary for specific exploration of the areas actually available in the clinical settings, obtaining feedback from colleagues, continued discussion by the panel of experts on the committee, and final pilot-testing will influence the number of areas to be included in the final array.

GENERAL COMMENTS

To summarize up to this point, major criteria are outlined that are useful in specifying the areas of care to be included in a performance examination. The process of identifying the areas is evolutionary and interrelates with the multiple variables related to the context and the conditions under which the examination will be administered. Content and process constantly interact throughout the developmental process. These criteria are guidelines to help faculty explore potential content areas for assessment.

CRITERIA FOR DEFINING AREAS OF CARE

The second step in specifying content for a performance examination is to define explicitly each area of practice to be included. Definitions are necessary to ensure comparability of testing episodes and consistency among evaluators in selecting patient care situations to assess the student's competence. They set the limits defined by the faculty and help students to understand what they are expected to know and do. They are essential for the faculty committee in writing related critical elements and evolving the process for the administration of the examination. Definitions are stated in operational, practical terms rather than academic and theoretical jargon. The following criteria are intended to help the faculty to write and/or refine definitions for the identified areas of care. Examples are drawn primarily from the performance examinations of the Regents External Degree Program.

CRITERION 1

Each area's definition specifies its precise meaning for purposes of the examination. Probably half a dozen definitions could be written for any particular nursing activity. One approach is the dictionary version, which focuses on an academic, pure, or global meaning of the term. While this is useful in helping the committee to clarify its thinking, it probably will not result in the most desirable definition for purposes of the examination. Based on the dictionary definition the committee can discuss a more specific meaning to clarify the area of practice as it will be applied during the examination.

The area of vital signs provides a simple example. In the CPNE it is defined as:

> *Vital signs:* The taking of temperature, pulse, respiration, blood pressure and weight.

Obviously, this differs considerably from an academic definition, but it clarifies exactly what will be included during the test. Other specific vital signs also might have been included, but for purposes of this examination only the taking of temperature, pulse, respirations, blood pressure, and weight are to be tested.

Collaboration, a dimension of practice in the Professional Performance Examination (PPE) provides another example. The dictionary states that collaboration is: "1) The act of working together, or 2) cooperation with the enemy." However, for purposes of the PPE, the committee defined collaboration as:

> *Collaboration:* Collaboration is the process of establishing a mutual exchange of expertise among members of the health care team, directed toward resolving client problems. The candidate will be expected to initiate a conference, to contribute from the professional nurse perspective and to make recommendations based on the outcomes of the conference.

This is a more complex area of practice than vital signs, but both examples specify what will be expected of the student during the examination and give direction to the faculty in specifying both the content and process to be evaluated.

Another example is taken from the Health Assessment Performance Examination (HAPE). In the health-history portion of that test, candidates are expected to explore the client's current health status, as defined below:

> *The Exploration of Current Health Status:* The exploration of current health is an in-depth statement of the client's perception of his current health status including an analysis of a symptom (if present), activities of daily living, personal-social history and environment.

This definition clarifies what the student is expected to do and what the faculty will be evaluating during the examination in this area of practice.

CRITERION 2

The definition is stated so as to specify direction for selecting clients to be assigned during the examination. The selection of patients/clients for assignment during the examination period has a fundamental influence on the potential outcomes for students. In an objective examination, comparable testing episodes must be assured; faculty also need direction in choosing patients to facilitate reasonably equivalent situations. The definition helps to accomplish both of these aspects. If certain kinds of patient care are necessary, this should be specified or included in the definitions; otherwise, evaluators who select patients could include any number of diverse testing situations, which would interfere with comparability and the intent of the examination.

Medications (from the CPNE) provides another example. For purposes of this examination the committee specified that the administration of any type of drugs by any means may be used to satisfy the critical elements. Therefore, so long as other criteria also are met, any patient with drugs ordered during the testing period may be used in testing the candidates's competence in providing this area of care.

> *Medications:* The administration of drugs by any route: by mouth, intramuscular, intravenous, subcutaneous, or other routes.

The definition gives directions to evaluators for choosing patients by identifying the acceptable elements necessary. It allows enough flexibility to select patients requiring the administration of any type of medication.

The area of sterile dressing provides another example.

> *Sterile Dressing:* The changing of a sterile covering on a wound.

This simple, straightforward definition also permits the selection of any patient requiring the changing of any type of sterile dressing, however large or small, simple or complex, wet or dry, with or without medication, etc.

Another example is taken from the physical examination of the HAPE guide: for purposes of this test, examination of the breasts is defined as:

> *Breasts:* An examination of both breasts and axilla in female clients.

In this case only female clients will be used in order to help assure comparability of testing episodes. Breast tissue of males also is usually examined but the committee decided that using only female clients would provide a comparable test of the students' competence. Therefore, even though in the real world both male and female clients would have their breasts examined during health assessments, for purposes of this performance test breast examinations were required only for female clients.

CRITERION 3

The definition establishes limits of inclusion and exclusion of particular aspects of care to be tested. Two examples from the CPNE illustrate this criterion: fluids and suctioning. In both cases the evaluator is given direction as to which specific aspects of the area will be used, and consequently which may not be included.

> *Fluids:* The administration, measurement and recording of fluid intake orally, parenterally or by gastric tube; when necessary, the measurement and recording of output.
>
> *Suctioning:* The removal of secretions from oral, nasopharyngeal or tracheobronchial areas by catheter.

Although other factors related to fluid administration and suctioning are important in the teaching and experiential phases of learning, for purposes of providing a reasonable sample of typical areas of care only certain aspects will be admissible during the examination. The area of suctioning also could have included thoracic closed chest suction or wound suction. However, to enhance comparability of the testing episodes they were deliberately omitted.

The definition of the examination of head and neck (from the HAPE) also specifies which aspects will be included in the test:

> *Head and neck:* An examination of the external structure of the head, and an examination of the neck including mobility, size and placement of internal structure, and presence of lymphadenopathy.

The definition of each area of practice, therefore, gives specific directions to both students and evaluators as to what will and will not be examined. This criterion helps to ensure comparability of testing episodes and objectivity in selecting patients.

CRITERION 4

The definition is worded in simple and precise language. Simple, clear wording is of utmost importance. In drafting the content of the examination, and the related study guide, the committee may need a reminder now and then that the document being written is not an erudite statement to be submitted for the scrutiny of the academic community; rather it is the clearest possible expression of the standard of expectations for students at a designated level. Using unnecessarily complex or obscure language only confuses students and leads to potential inconsistency among faculty in selecting testing episodes.

The definition of irrigations as an area of care in the CPNE provides an example:

> *Irrigation:* The introduction of fluid into and drainage from any wound, body orifice or cavity.

It sets the limits, allows flexibility, and specifies the aspects that are to be included. Yet the language is simple and clearly stated.

Research (PPE) is a decidedly more complex area of practice but the definitions need not be obfuscated.

> *Research Process in Clinical Practice:* The research process in clinical practice is the application of the scientific method in the investigation of a clinical nursing problem. The competencies include identifying a problem for investigation, outlining a plan for conducting the study, and suggesting potential applications of the findings.

From the HAPE tool another definition of an area of practice is included further to illustrate the intent of this criterion:

> *Review of Systems:* The review of systems is a comprehensive account of the past and present status of each body system, obtained by direct questioning during the history taking phase. This systematic fact-finding review prevents the omission of significant subjective data that relates to the present health status and that otherwise may have been overlooked.

This is a lengthy definition, but all particular aspects are itemized clearly to help students know exactly what is expected and to help evaluators be consistent in what they are testing.

CRITERION 5

The definition provides the basis for all associated critical elements. The definition sets the stage for the further elaboration of content—namely, the specific observable behaviors to be tested. Aspects of the areas, what is to be included and excluded, and the kinds of clients to be assigned all help in this process. However, in some situations clusters of critical elements are required. The groundwork for their development is laid in the definition.

For example, physical hygiene, tested in the Clinical Performance Nursing Examination, is described as the partial or complete assistance with the bath and includes care of the bed or patient's immediate environment. A cluster of critical elements is written for bath and another cluster is written for bed-making.

Mobility is another example in the Clinical Performance Nursing Examination. It is defined as follows, and requires several subclusters of critical elements:

> *Mobility:* The partial or complete assistance with movement which may include positioning, exercise, transfer activities, and ambulation. The patient may be in or out of bed, may or may not require supportive devices, but *must* require the nurse's assistance.

In summary, the words chosen to define the areas of practice included in the examination have significant implications for the exact content being tested, for the comparability of testing episodes, for the selection of patients and aspects of the areas of care to be used. Faculty evaluators and students must be able clearly to understand the meanings if the examination is to fulfill its purpose of providing a fair and objective opportunity for the student to demonstrate competence in performing designated areas of care. As with the listing of areas previously discussed, definitions should be shared with students, other faculty members, and those in nursing service to determine whether they are clearly and consistently understood. Sufficient time should be taken to draft and refine definitions before too much effort is devoted to subsequent aspects of development. However, refinement of the definition sometimes is expedited after the first draft of critical elements is written. These two aspects are mutually interactive and clarifying. Specifying the critical behaviors helps to crystalize the definition, just as a refined definition helps to focus and finalize the related critical elements.

CRITERIA FOR WRITING CRITICAL ELEMENTS

The third, and most difficult, step in specifying the content of the performance examination is identifying and writing the critical elements for each defined area of practice. Critical elements are the simple, discrete, observable behaviors of the nurse that are mandatory for the specified areas of care. They are the finite units of measurement in the examination; they are, with few exceptions, the collective basis on which students are passed or failed. They are the specific indicators that the student is competent to meet the standard of care established and expected by the faculty. In one sense critical elements are like the calibrations on a ruler or other measuring tool; collectively they establish the standard and individually they specify the essentials comprising the standard.

After listing the initial array of areas of care and defining them, the committee can then turn its attention to the arduous task of identifying and wording the critical elements. The process is difficult for at least three reasons. First, instructors typically think in terms of procedures and the multiple sequential steps necessary to perform them. Nursing has a long tradition of teaching by procedure manuals, which is not necessarily intended as a criticism. A procedure manual presents one way of doing things and is essential to ensure some degree of continuity of practice in a given agency or institution. Because of the perpetual inflow of personnel and students, a standard specifying the acceptable ways of performing certain procedures helps to assure desirable patient care. It is not unusual, therefore, that historically procedure manuals readily became the vehicle for teaching technical aspects of nursing care. However, the approach used to develop such manuals is deliberately to identify every specific action, listed in sequence, so that anyone may perform the procedure by following the steps exactly as written. Procedure manuals are like cookbooks, listing required ingredients (equipment) then describing how to use them to complete the recipe (procedure). This approach is useful to students (and staff) while they are learning how to perform a given task, but it differs considerably from the critical-elements approach, as the following section explains. Basically the faculty has to be reprogrammed away from the traditional "every-step" way of thinking to an approach of focusing only on behaviors essential for meeting the standard. It requires a new attitude of shifting priorities and recognizing the marked distinction between clinical teaching and clinical examination.

The second reason the critical elements approach is difficult is that it requires the writing of specific nursing behaviors, exactly as they will be observed, rather than using more general and global statements (such as clinical objectives) for evaluating the students' competence. Use of nonspecific and ambiguous general statements for clinical assessment is common practice, but it leaves an undesirable residue of uncertainty and subjectivity. The difficulty for faculty in changing to critical elements is in converting the previous penchant for generalization into precise statements of the expected, essential nursing behaviors. This requires an internal reprogramming and takes a period of guided transition if it is to be fully accomplished.

The third difficulty in using the critical-elements approach is that it requires the faculty to make hard decisions about exactly what are the essential nursing behaviors expected of students. The faculty ultimately is responsible for determining what they consider to be acceptable and expected competence for a designated area of nursing practice, regardless of what other groups have said or done. They will be held accountable for the standard they write. Such statements remove ambiguity but they also clearly express what a particular faculty regards as baseline for practice. In one sense writing such a document is intimidating because it puts the faculty on record and means that they will be subject to overt and covert criticisms from professional colleagues (both positive and negative). Some will understand and others will misread, misunderstand, and misapply the test. It is reasonable that such a possibility may be frightening (consciously or unconsciously) to some faculties and could block progress in committing to writing and finalizing the performance examination. This is a very real potential, and the committee will have to be sensitive to such feelings and deal with them directly rather than allowing insecurity and fear of rejection to lurk in the periphery. When assistance is needed—in content, in testing procedures, in process, or in dealing with emergent feelings—it should be obtained promptly to prevent paralysis of the committee in efficiently achieving its objectives.

Therefore, in addition to wanting an objective performance examination, the faculty committee must be willing to learn how to do it and be willing to take the risks of actually putting on paper the specific critical elements they believe can be used to document the student's clinical ability for a given area or program. The use of critical elements removes the haziness from clinical evaluation by focusing on the explicit observable behaviors mandatory for both students and evaluators. To do this means taking a risk, even though it also has the potential for markedly improving clinical assessment.

Writing critical elements requires the same brainstorming, discussion, and debate suggested in the other two phases of content development, only more so. The statements do not emerge automatically nor in wording that is immediately acceptable. They do emerge as ideas or suggestions that are ultimately transformed into potential critical elements. The wording will be picked over, rejected, debated, and modified before an acceptable statement is found. It is most helpful for the committee to think in terms of evolving one draft at a time. The first draft merely gets all of the ideas down on paper as clearly as possible, as a starting point and as a springboard for more objective analysis. The writing of subsequent drafts focuses on the behaviors to be included and the precision of the language used in each statement. Some critical elements originally considered absolutely essential are subsequently omitted, others are revised (many times over, in some cases), and still others are added to the list.

The evolution of a more precise document requires the continual efforts of the faculty, feedback from colleagues and students, and the application of a number of specific criteria useful in writing critical elements. While each criterion is written separately it is important to realize the complex interactions among them. While they are being written, critical elements should be tested against the criteria listed below. Not all critical elements meet all of the criteria, but all of the criteria should be considered in evaluating the acceptability of each critical element. Each criterion listed below will be illustrated by the work of the faculty committees of the Regents External Degree responsible for developing performance examinations.

CRITERION 1

Critical elements specify the performance behaviors to be judged and are not intended to test theory per se. Theory can be tested best on carefully constructed objective written examinations. A performance examination is designed to assess the learner's ability to demonstrate the application of theory in a clinical context. In most instances it requires a physical, observable action on behalf of clients and is tested without verbal collaboration or interaction. Critical elements test knowledge inherently, as students presumably cannot perform them satisfactorily without integrating the basic theory and psychomotor skills that are required.

For example, one of the critical elements for irrigations is: "Positions patient to facilitate flow." This and the other elements for this area of care are used for procedures such as giving an enema, irrigating a colostomy, or irrigating a gastric tube or Foley catheter. In order to position the patient correctly the student must know the inherent principles, related anatomy, and specific modifications for each particular procedure. The student's actions are assessed in relation to what has been taught or learned, the designated references, and, finally, the trained evaluator's judgment.

In conducting a health assessment the student is required to analyze a symptom. One of a series of critical elements to be met is: "Records exploration of the presence or absence of at least two commonly associated signs and/or symptoms." The student is held accountable for knowing an array of signs and symptoms potentially associated with the primary one identified by the client. Furthermore, the student must know how to elicit and document such associated symptoms.

In the physical examination one critical element demands that the student: "Examines at least one sensory or motor function for nine of the twelve cranial nerves to determine the presence or absence or normal function."

Students must know the anatomy and physiology of all cranial nerves as well as specific methods for determining sensory and motor function. The critical element also holds them accountable for determining deviations from normal function.

Without saying so explicitly, the critical elements inherently require integration of theory and the application of it in performing the designated areas of practice.

CRITERION 2

Critical elements establish realistic expectations for competence. This criterion probably cannot be fully met until the critical elements are completed and pilot-tested. During the developmental phase the faculty needs to ask questions of each critical element to satisfy this criterion: Is it too hard? Is it too easy? Is it enough? Is it too much? Ultimately all critical elements—as well as the entire examination—have to be defended as appropriate and realistic for the type and level of students involved.

Two critical elements from the baccalaureate-level health-assessment performance examination illustrate this criterion. In examining the chest and lungs the candidate is required to meet the following critical element, along with several others: "Describe adventitious respiratory sounds if present."

Rather than expecting students to diagnose and name all possible sounds, they are required to detect and describe adventitious sounds. The faculty believes this is consistent with the expected ability of new graduates of bachelor's nursing programs. Different expectations (and critical elements) would be required for those completing master's-level or practitioner programs.

In the examination of the heart (HAPE) one critical element is: "Identifies the presence of grade III or greater cardiac murmurs, describing placement in the cardiac cycle." The faculty believes graduates of BSN programs should be able to perform at this level. It establishes the level of competence and knowledge expected of all such graduates.

In testing the student's ability to demonstrate management of client care, one of a series of critical elements states: "Identifies at least one long term and one short term client-centered goal to be discussed with the client."

For a given patient assignment the student must be able to meet this critical element because the faculty has established it as a reasonable expectation for the student being tested. The level of difficulty and complexity is determined by several controlled variables such as the kinds of clients selected and the number of goals (or needs) to be identified.

CRITERION 3

Critical elements apply to all procedures or activities that may be included in a particular area of care. The critical elements for irrigations illustrate this criteria quite well. They apply regardless of the type of irrigation or the reason for its use.

1. Secures correct solution
2. Determines appropriate temperature of solution (approximate)
3. Positions patient to facilitate flow
4. Instills solution into correct area
5. Controls flow of solution
6. Provides receptacle for return flow

Another example is found in the critical elements for asepsis. Because this is designated as an overriding area of concern, the critical elements apply at all times throughout the entire examination, regardless of whatever else is happening. The wording of the critical elements is both specific and general. They identify the behaviors to be demonstrated without limiting the situations in which they will be met.

1. Protects self from contamination
2. Protects patient from contamination
3. Disposes of contaminated material in designated containers
4. Confines contaminated material to contaminated area
5. If a sterile field is required: Establishes and/or maintains a sterile field including instruments, equipment and working area

CRITERION 4

Critical elements must be specific and complete. Once the performance examination is finalized and implemented, individual instructors cannot add to or subtract from it on impulse to suit particular situations. Because the critical elements form the basis for judging the students' competence they must be as specific and as complete as possible before they are actually implemented. There is no desirable number of critical elements; some areas require two while others may require ten to fifteen. The examples of asepsis and irrigations presented above illustrate the present criterion. No other behaviors may be added during the test, nor may any of those stated be eliminated. For the purpose of the performance examination only the stated critical elements may be used to judge the students' clinical ability. Once the critical elements are approved, no individual faculty member has the right to abridge or modify that standard. Only the committee and/or total faculty has that prerogative.

CRITERION 5

Each critical element is essential to demonstrate competence in the related area of care. When the faculty committee begins to identify critical elements, one of the most common errors is to list the steps associated with the inherent procedures. Almost without fail they list the first critical element as: obtains necessary equipment. In preparing to bathe a patient it is important to gather the linen, the basin, soap, other articles for personal hygiene, etc.; however, the essential behavior is that student bathes the patient, which simply cannot be done without the "necessary equipment." Therefore three of the seven critical elements for that area in the Clinical Performance Nursing Examination are:

- Washes skin surface patient cannot wash
- Rinses skin surface patient cannot rinse
- Dries skin surface patient cannot dry

It sounds so simple, yet these elements are essential behaviors in providing personal hygiene to patients who need such assistance.

Obtaining the blood pressure apparatus is not a critical element for taking vital signs. The blood pressure reading cannot be obtained without appropriate, well-functioning equipment. The critical element for blood pressure (as one portion of vital signs) is: "Reads the instrument within a range of plus or minus 6 millimeters (of the evaluator's finding)."

Other kinds of competencies also are evaluated indirectly and therefore do not require specific statements. For example, in the Clinical Performance Nursing Examination, there are no critical elements for organization of work, time, planning, etc. However, the student who is disorganized and unknowledgeable will be unable to complete the total planning, implementation, and evaluation of patient care within the three-hour maximum period allowed for each patient-care situation. This also provides an example of the interaction between what is being tested and the process of testing it. The patients selected must require five or six areas of care; under ordinary circumstances the care requires one-and-a-half hours to complete. Therefore, students who do not complete all critical elements in the designated time period fail on that basis. A time limit is not prescribed for each area but rather for the total patient-care situation.

In some areas it is not essential that every aspect of the area be completed in order to determine the student's ability. Critical elements clarify this in the way they are stated. For example, in that part of the health history related to the client's "intrapersonal functioning," the critical element states: "Records the clients perceptions of and feeling about at least two of the following: current life style, usual pattern of adaptation to stress, usual mood, and strengths and weaknesses."

For purposes of the examination, exploring and recording the client's perceptions of any two of the areas is sufficient. The realities of time available for the examination as well as application of the basic concepts—as with sampling and the baseline of acceptability—help the faculty to determine which behaviors are essential and how many are enough.

CRITERION 6

Each critical element states a specific behavior that is observable or measurable. One of the keys to an objective examination is that the behaviors to be assessed are directly or indirectly observable. Those behaviors that test cognitive function are best included on paper-and-pencil tests or evaluated in other ways. A performance test requires that the evaluator must see the action, or the result of it, in order to judge the student's competence. Note the examples already given. Each one requires direct observation.

Other critical elements for vital signs include: "Counts within a range of plus or minus 2 respirations per minute" and "Counts within a range of plus or minus 5 beats per minute for pulse."

These and other specific findings are documented against those simultaneously obtained by the evaluator, and the results of comparison are instantly known. The evaluator can make the judgment then and there about the student's ability. In other situations the result is not known until later. For example, in conducting a physical examination when the technique of inspection is used, the evaluator can see the student "inspecting" but does not know until after the written record is submitted what the student observed on inspection. One of the critical elements for examination of the eyes offers an example: "Inspects alignment of the eyes for strabismus." That the student is "inspecting" can be observed, but the result will be evaluated on the written report submitted at the conclusion of the examination.

Each critical element must be written to preclude hunches or institutions' guesses or assumptions about the student's behavior. If the behavior is essential to performance during the examination it must be stated in observable terms. The following statement frequently is used but it is not an objectively observable behavior:

Evaluates level of consciousness.

It is important and it relates to nursing care, but how is it done? What behavior will the evaluator actually see while the student is "evaluating" the client's level of consciousness? To be more specific and to make the critical element observable, the statement could be rewritten as follows:

> Asks questions to elicit client's orientation to time, place and person
> [or]
> Asks patient to respond to simple demands.

CRITERION 7

Each critical element is stated as a single behavior to be performed. When two or more behaviors are included in a critical element it becomes more difficult to evaluate. If one part is failed, a question automatically is raised: Is the entire critical element failed even though 50 to 75 percent of it was passed? Was the behavior more acceptable or more unacceptable? Rather than inviting such potential conflicts, each behavior mandatory in establishing basic minimum acceptable performance should be written as a separate critical element—a single discrete observable behavior.

If the skill being observed is: "takes vital signs correctly" and the student accurately takes the temperature, pulse, and blood pressure but fails to get a correct count of respirations should it constitute a pass or fail? As indicated in previous examples if such subpart of vital signs is identified along with the acceptable range, the problem is avoided. However, with this statement the evaluator is still left with the problem of consistently defining "correct." Similarly, in providing for oxygenation procedures, the statement: "set liter flow and humidifies the air" contains two essential and different behaviors. The examination would be more objective if each activity is listed and tested as two specific critical elements.

The examples given above concerning bathing and irrigations also illustrate the need for each essential behavior to be written as a critical element.

CRITERION 8

Each critical element specifies a discrete behavior in unambiguous terms. The objective of this criterion is to get rid of as much ambiguity as possible from the wording of the critical elements, in an effort to minimize bias and personal interpretations by evaluators. Words such as "appropriate," "correct," "proper," or similar terms are subject to various interpretations depending on the evaluator, the student, the situation, and the psychodynamics of the situation. What is correct for one teacher may be totally unacceptable for another.

The statement "correctly administers medications" is subject to any one of several evaluations, as no specific behavior is mentioned. This overall skill should be divided into its specific observable behaviors. Five of the seven critical elements for medications used in the Clinical Performance Examination are:

- Secures correct medication
- Measures correct dosage
- Administers the correct drug to the correct patient
- Uses the correct route and/or site for administering the medication
- Administers the medication within ½ hour of scheduled time

Notice the word "correct" appears in four of the critical elements. In this case, there is no possibility of varying opinions about what is correct, as the drug dosage and route are prescribed by the physician for a designated patient. There is no ambiguity here, as there would be for a critical element stated as: "uses correct technique to change a sterile dressing."

In obtaining a health history one of the critical elements related to exploration of a symptom might be: "Records time since onset." But how? Does it matter what terminology or time frame is used? Maybe yes and maybe no. To avoid ambiguity and possible confusion, the phrase could be reworded as: "Records length of time since onset by noting either the approximate date of onset or length of time since onset."

Another nuance of ambiguity related to health assessment is addressed by the following critical element: "Describes presence of all precipitating factors recalled by the client or records absence of such factors." Without the last portion of the statement, the evaluator would have no way to judge whether the student explored the topic or whether the client had nothing to say. The critical element requires a written statement indicating that precipitating factors had been explored, regardless of the results.

CRITERION 9

Critical elements specify the range of acceptable behaviors. Sometimes critical elements can be stated as very precise, direct behaviors, such as:

- Describes whether onset of symptom was abrupt or gradual (for health history)

- Clears air from tubing before initiating flow for (IV fluids or IV medications)

Other critical elements allow some flexibility but establish the limits of acceptability:

- Describes at least one temporal aspect of the symptom (health history)
- Inspects breasts for dimpling and retraction while client performs one of three accepted maneuvers (physical examination). Directs client to move four of the following major joints through functional range of motion, bilaterally, noting function: shoulders, elbows, wrists, hands, hips, knees and ankles
- Reads thermometer within plus or minus 0.2 degrees (F)
- Records presence or absence of those immunizations listed on the recording form

For purposes of the examination some flexibility can be—and perhaps should be—built into the critical elements or the recording form. The level of tolerance from the theoretically correct or perfect behavior can be dealt with in one of several ways, as illustrated above. Because it is an examination, time is an important factor. When the student is learning, or writing a detailed paper, or reading a text, all possible factors can be considered. Time is less critical during the learning phase. Furthermore, the examination is designed objectively to test a representative sample of behaviors in as controlled a situation as possible to ensure comparability.

Therefore, in developing critical elements, the faculty can build in the sampling of minute subbehaviors, as well as restrict the number of behaviors that will be tested. Critical elements also control the degree of tolerance (deviation from ideal) that will be accepted. During the developmental phase all critical elements should be reviewed over and over with this criterion in mind. As the entire examination begins to be finalized, additional areas for flexibility and tolerance can be founded to help balance stringency with acceptability.

CRITERION 10

Critical elements may state a precise method or technique or required conditions. As with the previous criteria, either precision or flexibility can be incorporated in the critical element depending on the decisions of the faculty as to exactly what is essential. When more than one method of achieving the desired behavior is acceptable the critical element should allow for variations as illustrated in the examples below, taken from the HAPE and PPE:

- Palpates for enlargement of the thyroid gland using one of two approved techniques
- Palpates both breasts and axilla systematically for masses and tenderness, using palmer surface of fingers and using one of two patterns of examination, with patient in a sitting position

When several techniques are allowed, they are contained in the references provided in the examination study guide or course outline. Students are free to select the particular method that seems most suitable, but they must perform it correctly as described in the resources.

Another way of allowing variations in the action to be evaluated is illustrated by a critical element related to clinical decision making:

> Writes a rationale for the decision (just made) based on logic, scientifically based principles and/or published literature

Another example is found in the dimension of applying the research process:

> Lists at least one possible method to analyze the data (related to a researchable problem)

Sometimes there is only a single precise method that is accepted for fulfilling the critical element. If this is so, that method should be incorporated in the statement so that students and faculty evaluators are uniformly clear about expectations.

- Auscultates breath sounds over each lobe of the lungs moving the stethoscope systematically from side to side and top to bottom, over anterior and posterior surfaces while client breathes deeply through the mouth
- Palpates for symmetry of respiratory excursion by placing hands on back at the inferior border of the rib cage with thumbs proximal to spinal column
- Inspects movement of uvula while client says "aah."
- Stimulates the tendon associated with the required reflexes, using a documented technique

In the examination of the eyes one specific technique may be required:

> Uses Snellen chart to determine client's visual acuity (using glasses if glasses are worn)

In developing the area of care related to sterile dressing (CPNE), the committee was involved in considerable debate as to the best and/or most appropriate method for changing a dressing. Some thought sterile gloves were required, some thought instruments should be used, some thought both should be used, and some thought a dry sterile dressing could be changed carefully by using clean hands and a particular handling-of-the-edges technique. Ultimately the critical elements were left open to the judgment of the student so long as the stated essentials were met:

1. Removes soiled dressing without contaminating the wound or self
2. Disposes of soiled dressing in appropriate container
3. Applies sterile dressing without contaminating the wound
4. Fastens new dressing

CRITERION 11

The wording of each critical element begins with an action verb. Beginning each critical element with the essential action to be observed helps to make the statement simpler and more direct. Rather than confusing the statement with parenthetical or introductory clauses, one should begin it directly with the verb identifying exactly what action will be seen, heard, observed, measured, or otherwise evaluated. The relevant phrases can be attached after the key behavior has been identified.

For example, the following statement pertains to the physical examination of the heart: "Using both the bell and diaphragm of the stethoscope, listens to cardiac sounds over the 4 valvular areas." By changing this statement and beginning it with the action verb it becomes more direct without losing any of its specificity: "Listens to cardiac sounds over the 4 valvular areas, using both the bell and diaphragm of the stethoscope for each area." In the area of special skin care, an initial idea about improving circulation might be stated as follows: "Unless contraindicated specific areas should be rubbed with a lubricant." This critical new element is improved by beginning with the action to be observed and evaluated: "Stimulates circulation by rubbing specified areas, unless otherwise contraindicated."

In the area of postural drainage a preferred statement would be: "Positions patient so that the affected area of chest is in the superior position to facilitate gravity flow." A less helpful way of stating this critical element might be: "In order to facilitate gravity flow of mucus from the affected part, positions patient properly." The second version is confusing and less clear. Whatever action the student is expected to perform and the evaluator is expected to judge should be stated at the outset by a present-tense verb related to the student's behavior. Some initiating verbs include the following: lists, writes, asks, counts, places, positions, washes, uses, maintains, initiates, applies, injects, selects, inspects, palpates, percusses, performs, observes, records.

While this criterion may seem unimportant, if it is consistently used it will help the critical elements to be more clearly understood by students and evaluators. To the extent that this is true, the examination will be a more valid test of the student's actual competence to meet the standard desired by the faculty.

CRITERION 12

Critical elements are worded to focus on the student's behavior in relation to the client's *needs*. There is a tendency to include statements pertaining to the student rather than to the patient. Sometimes such concerns slip in because teachers are so used to helping students with their practice behaviors as a part of the learning process. Some of the favorite topics include organization, outlining care, and the student's use of body mechanics. As indicated earlier, organizational ability is measured indirectly, but no less surely, through the structure and process of the examination. The emphasis of the performance test is to determine the students' competence to meet the designated needs of clients for nursing care.

In the area of mobility, faculties often are tempted to write critical elements directed at the student's use of body mechanics to protect himself. This is an important area for teaching–learning, for inclusion in cognitive examinations, and ultimately in practice—but it is not a critical element in determining the student's ability to meet the *patients'* need for mobility. If the student uses poor body mechanics and thereby endangers the patient, it is grounds for failure (because of the physical jeopardy overriding area of concern). If the student is practicing in such a way that could potentially endanger his own future health he should be counseled about this after the examination. The behaviors being judged, however, are in reference to the client's needs and the student's ability to meet the critical elements that ensure the client's well-being. When the student does something not in the best interest of his own health he should be advised accordingly, but not necessarily failed. Otherwise, behaviors such as smoking, overeating, and inactivity also might have to be included for evaluation.

SUMMARY

In summary, this chapter has focused on how to identify, specify, and precisely word the content of the performance examination. Before the actual work can begin certain preliminary considerations have to be discussed and decided, related to the probable scope and context of the examination. The first major step is to brainstorm into existence an initial list of potential areas of practice to be examined. Drafting the list is based on course and program objectives and specific objectives of the examination. Feedback from students and colleagues will be helpful in refining the list throughout the developmental phase.

The second step, and one that also helps to shape the list, is to set forth in operational terms the definition of the areas of practice for purposes of this examination. Indirectly the areas and definitions establish the kinds of patient situations to be used during the examination and consequently draw the lines around the scope and type of behaviors to be assessed.

The third and most difficult step is the writing of simple, discrete, observable behaviors essential for the acceptable performance of the area of practice. Great care must be taken in the wording, focus, intent, scope, and flexibility of the critical elements for with a few exceptions they serve as the indicators of the students' success or failure. Evaluators must use the critical elements to decide whether the student has met the standard of care expected by the faculty. If the statements are vague, ambiguous, confusing, complex, subjective, or inappropriate, the final evaluation reached by the examiner will reflect these shortcomings. Therefore, rather than prematurely introducing a "good draft" of the performance examination, students, teachers and all others involved would be better served if sufficient time were taken to develop the instrument thoroughly, seek validation through pilot-tests, and make modifications before the examination is used for actual evaluation purposes.

Several other major aspects have yet to be discussed but which require equal concern and development. These factors relate primarily to deciding on the conditions under which the examination will be administered, the structure and process of administering it, preparation and supervision of evaluators, and the transition for students, faculty, and staff. These subjects will be discussed in subsequent chapters.

For convenience the criteria for developing content are summarized below as they relate to designating areas of practice, defining areas, and writing critical elements.

SUMMARY OF CRITERIA FOR SPECIFYING CONTENT

A. Identifying Areas of Care

1. The areas of care selected for inclusion in the examination emanate from stated objectives.
2. Areas of care are appropriate to the student (or graduate) of the particular type of program.

3. Areas of care are consistent with the student's level in the program.
4. Areas of care are typical and commonly expected in the practice of beginning graduates.
5. The total array of areas provides a reasonable sampling of all that are possible to select from the universe of nursing concerns.
6. Areas of care are reasonably comparable in complexity and demands for integration of knowledge and skills.
7. Each area of care usually is broad enough in scope to encompass two or more specific tasks or activities.
8. Areas of care to be used include those readily available and commonly required by patients (or clients) in the setting to be used for the examination.
9. Areas of care selected are observable and objectively measurable.
10. The number of areas of care to be included varies with the objectives and context of the examination.

B. Defining Areas of Care

1. The definition of each area of practice specifies its precise meaning for purposes of the performance examination.
2. The definition is stated in such a way as to specify direction for selecting patients to be assigned during the examination.
3. The definition establishes the limits of inclusion and exclusion of particular aspects of the area of care to be used in the examination.
4. The definition is worded as simply and precisely as possible, using language that is understandable to both students and evaluators.
5. The definition provides the basis from which all associated critical elements will emerge.

C. Writing Critical Elements

1. Critical elements specify the performance behaviors to be judged and are not intended to test theory *per se*.
2. Critical elements establish realistic expectations for competence, depending on the type and level of students being tested.
3. Many critical elements may cut across the lines of specific procedures and apply to several activities including under the area of care; some may even apply to the entire examination.
4. Critical elements form the basis for judging the students' practice competence; therefore, they must be specific and complete.
5. Each critical element is essential for the demonstration of competence for the related area of care.

6. Each critical element states a specific behavior that is observable or measurable.
7. Each critical element is stated as a single behavior to be performed by the student.
8. Each critical element is a discrete entity, stated as precisely and free of ambiguity as possible.
9. The critical element specifies the range of acceptability of behavior to be evaluated.
10. The critical element may state a precise method or technique when essential and any conditions required for carrying out the behavior to be assessed.
11. The wording of each critical element begins with the action verb that designates the specific behavior to be tested.
12. The critical element is worded to focus on the student's behavior in reference to the *client's* needs, not in terms of the student's needs.

CHAPTER 6

Specifying Conditions and Context for Implementation

While the faculty committee is discussing the broad range of topics related to content identification, many aspects concerning the mechanics of administering the performance examination also will emerge. These two major sections for development are separated for discussion in this text, but in reality they are parts of an integral whole and frequently must be discussed together. Each one clearly influences the other. During the content-development phase all ideas, problems, possible approaches, and other aspects related to process should be noted in the minutes of each meeting to be retrieved later for full development. It probably would be helpful to have a designated section of the minutes for this purpose, which will make it easier to find these points when it comes time to describe the conditions and context for implementation.

Specifying the manner in which the performance examination will be organized and implemented is as much an evolutionary process as is identifying the content to be included. Brainstorming is one way to generate the list of potential administration areas that will require discussion; it should include topics such as: how many PCSs are needed, how many areas of care to test, which and how many agency units to use, scheduling and other time factors, selection of evaluators, and forms to use. Once these areas have been identified, the committee debates the pros and cons and finally identifies what seems to be the most useful suggestions. Once these initial ideas are organized they can be "tried out" in minipilot-tests to determine whether they actually are functional. The process of brainstorming, discussing, testing out, and then revising each aspect of implementation results in a series of draft document, each one more complete, more realistic, and more functional than the previous one. This evolutionary approach ultimately results in the most appropriate and most specific statements describing the conditions under which the examination will be administered, along with all of the necessary statements related to testing procedures.

Neither the content nor the procedural conditions is easily or automatically discerned. As with aspects previously presented, they usually emerge from the deliberate and concentrated efforts of the committee, the feedback sought from colleagues and students, and the experience of trying out each and every subpart in the clinical settings. The committee that realizes this process from the outset is less apt to get discouraged when several hours of any particular meeting have resulted only in diverging views, an excessive decibel level, and a collective headache. Difficult as it is, this process is essential in the evolution of both the content and procedures of the performance examination. It is more than probable that the intensity of individual involvement in the process contributes to the ultimate success of the examination. When faculty members struggle together and have direct input in resolving a complex problem, they are likely to endorse and support the outcomes. Building this kind of commitment is an essential part of integrating an objective performance examination into the evaluation process for an entire program. Thus specifying the procedures, conditions, and context for the test should be considered with the same degree of serious concern as the identification of specific behaviors that comprise the content.

CONTROL OF VARIABLES

One of the primary tasks in developing a performance examination is to isolate the multiple variables that impinge on it and to design ways to exert control over them. This is true for both actual and simulated examinations but it is particularly critical in the actual clinical setting, in which the variables are maximal and the possibilities of substantially altering them is minimal. By identifying and discussing those variables that potentially could influence the conduct of the examination, the committee can develop ways to control them—at least to some degree. Specific written statements help to ensure consistency and a more functional examination.

Finding ways to exert maximum control over both content and conditions is a major factor in moving the evaluation process farther along the continuum of objectivity and uniformity. This does not preclude faculty judgment based on knowledge and experience, but it does require that their decisions be made consistently and within the same context for all students. When the procedures and conditions as well as content are established and mutually agreeable to faculty and others directly involved in the examination, chances are improved considerably for determining the students' actual competence in the designated areas of practice. The basic concepts presented earlier are equally applicable to this phase of developing the examination because the conditions and procedures directly influence its outcome.

Statements regarding the expected behaviors of students, evaluators, and staff, as well as the explicit conditions under which the examination will be administered are mandatory and are derived from the deliberations of the faculty committee. These statements form the second major section of the examination study guide used by students, faculty, and agency staff. They complete the expression of expectations during the preparation and implementation phases of testing.

The examination study guide, then, outlines the standard against which students will be measured and the manner in which objectivity, comparability, acceptability, consistency, sampling, flexibility, and the other concepts will be assured. It specifically and systematically outlines all potential areas of care, their definitions, and critical elements as well as all procedures, conditions, and any other aspects essential for the conduct of the test. Essentially, everything about content and process is included. It, therefore, is envisioned as the "master document" that guides both students and evaluators for all aspects of the examination.

The following discussion will focus on criteria helpful in specifying the conditions and context of the examination. The criteria are clustered around those concerns that focus on students, on the examination process, and on the context of the clinical setting. The criteria will be discussed and illustrated to show their influence both positive and negative on the outcomes of the entire examination process.

Figures 6.1 and 6.2 illustrate the interrelationships that exist between and among students, the content, the examination process, the conditions, and the context within which the test is given. Each of these aspects is important in and of itself but also should be described in terms of mutual effects.

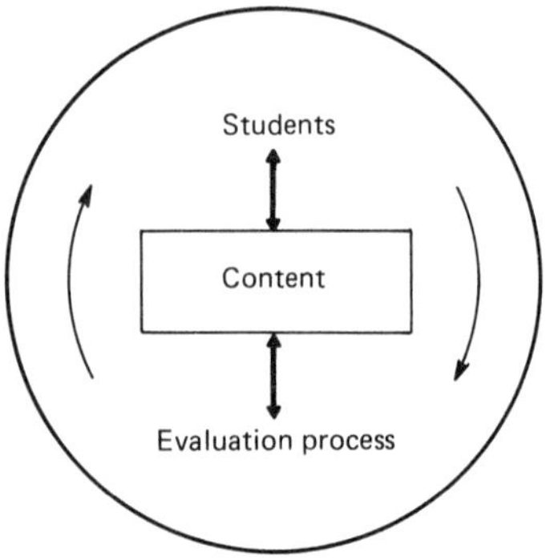

Fig. 6.1. Interaction among content, expectations for students, and evaluation process.

CONDITIONS THAT FOCUS ON STUDENTS

CRITERION 1

All aspects of the examination are clearly stated in the study guide given to students in advance. As the performance examination is a criterion-referenced test, it is essential that students know the standard against which they will be measured sufficiently in advance to allow the learning process to follow the direction of desired expectations. In this instance students are not in competition with each other as they are with norm-referenced tests, but rather are competing against the standard of performance prescribed by the faculty and outlined in the examination study guide. Because the performance examination (along with course and program objectives, etc.) helps the student to focus attention on the competencies to be achieved, the study guide is an important document both for long-term learning as well as short-term preparation immediately before the examination is to be taken. The earlier students obtain the study guide the more time they will have to discover individual strengths and weaknesses, to focus time and effort where it is most needed, and to learn the whole of the expected standard. Depending on the comprehensiveness of the examination, students probably would benefit from using the study guide for at least one full semester. Even if the examination is to take place in a simulated situation it is desirable for students to have two to three months to practice the potential areas of care and critical behaviors under circumstances similar to those expected during the testing period. Students obviously also would benefit from having the performance examination study guide early in the program.

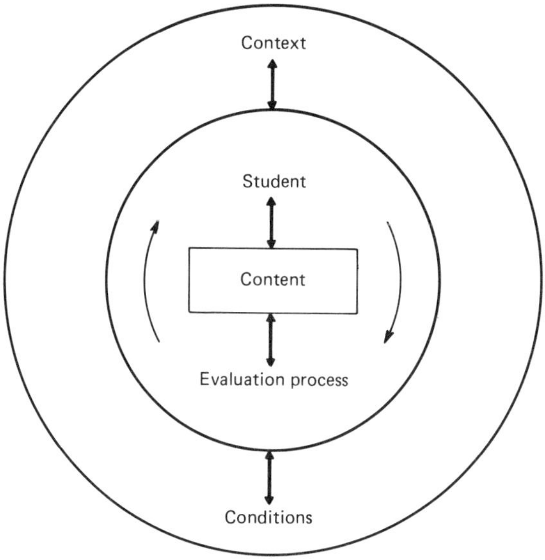

Fig. 6.2. Further interaction involves additional conditions and the context of the examination.

This suggestion should not be misconstrued to indicate that students are expected to learn only that which is included in the examination study guide. On the contrary, the overall course or program objectives and other teacher–learner activities establish the broader scope of knowledge and clinical competencies to be achieved. The higher goals of idealism and comprehensive achievement are still present and to be vigorously pursued. However, the examination guide establishes the baseline of acceptable performance of appropriate clinical skills and removes any doubt of expectations. When teachers and students alike are fully informed—in writing, in advance—misunderstanding and inconsistencies are reduced to a minimum. Students cannot claim: "I didn't know I'd have to do that" and faculty no longer will be frustrated with diverse and subjective evaluation techniques. The stimulus of teaching–learning activities direct the students' attention to comprehensive and ideal performance; the examination itself established the baseline of acceptability for passing during the testing period. This is the most important point for both teachers and students to understand clearly. The examination study guide includes all potential areas of practice and critical elements to be tested that comprise the standard of measurement. Unlike the total course study guide, it does not establish the upper limits of learning and does not include all topics covered during the course (or program). Rather, it is designed for the single purpose of specifying all details pertaining only to the preparation and administration of the clinical performance examination.

The study guide describes all aspects of the organization and structure as well as content. Students need to know the array of potential areas of practice and their related critical elements; the criteria for passing; how they will be evaluated; who will do it; and the where, when, and any other special consideration pertaining to the test. They also need to know how to prepare for the examination and what kind of resources could be used and where to find them. Furthermore, they need to know how to appeal a faculty decision if they believe an unfair judgment has been rendered. All of these and other related factors are appropriate to include in the examination study guide, because they inform the students of the essential conditions for which they will be held accountable.

CRITERION 2

The nature of acceptable relationships among those involved in the test is explicitly described. The behavior expected of students during a performance examination is considerably different from that expected during the learning phase of clinical experience. Clarifying these relationships in writing before the examination promotes objectivity and consistency. For example, while learning, students are expected to validate and discuss their clinical decisions and nursing-care plan with the instructor prior to and during the implementation of care; however, during the examination they are expected to make decisions and implement them without the benefit of faculty consultation. As this is a test of the students' ability to administer designated areas of practice, the instructor is present only as a neutral observer to document achievement in relation to the standard of expectations. During performance testing the instructor, who now is functioning as an evaluator, does not interrogate the student regarding what is being done and why, or the relationship to theory. Those are cognitive areas and are tested by theory examinations. Except for social amenities and certain directions that must be given at the outset, students and evaluators do not exchange conversation during the performance examination. There is no need for dialogue as the evaluator is present only to observe, not to teach or to assist.

Students usually need help in realizing that rather than being rude, they are performing as expected when they ignore the presence of the evaluator during the testing period. In fact, it will be essentially impossible to obtain an accurate measurement of the student's clinical competence unless both evaluator and student clearly understand this different student–teacher relationship that must be exercised during the examination. Students are expected to demonstrate clinical skills according to the specifics in the study guide while evaluators are expected to observe them in relation to the examination protocol and to make a decision about their clinical competence. Actually a minimum amount of communication is necessary to accomplish the goal. The problem is changing from the long-established custom of exchanging verbal and nonverbal communication during any "clinical experience." Both students and teachers need help in negotiating this change. Clarifying the expectations in the study guide is the first step.

The relationship between the student and patient also is somewhat different during the examination, and therefore needs to be described in the study guide. In a comprehensive clinical test, the student probably will be responsible for the complete care of the patient during a specified period of time, without instructional assistance. Except for incidentals, the student is expected to obtain any necessary consultation or physical assistance from the staff, rather than from the evaluator. The evaluator must remain uninvolved in order to fulfill the principal role of neutral observer. Obviously, if the student is performing some aspect of care and the evaluator is on the opposite side of the patient, or down the hall in the utility room, or is otherwise prevented from direct observation of the student, critical elements cannot be accurately documented. Both students and evaluators must fulfill their roles within this frame of reference, otherwise patients could misunderstand what is happening and become unnecessarily concerned. It is the student alone who assumes the active nursing role, and who keeps the interaction focused on the patient and his needs.

Examination and the Patient

Another essential point should be raised for discussion concerning the student and patient relationship. Patients are not usually told they are participating in the clinical examination of the student. Two basic problems are likely to occur when the patient is advised that an examination is being conducted. Some patients, because of their natural anxiety, misunderstand and assume that they (patients) are scheduled for another examination. Their hearing of the word conjures up very different images, which usually are associated with anxiety. Obviously, this is not in the patient's best interest. Another problem that is even more likely to occur when patients are told about the examination is that consciously or unconsciously they will influence the conduct of the test either positively or negatively. Some will try to help the student pass, others will refuse to be "used as a guinea pig," and still others may attempt to make it difficult for the student. In any event, probably the best course of action is to try to maintain a neutral approach and to obtain the patient's permission in the customary manner and to treat this as a "usual clinical experience," in which the student is being supervised closely. Students, evaluators, and staff all must cooperate in this effort to maintain neutrality if the test is to be comparable and objective for all students. This is not an easy task.

In most situations patients in the examination setting are accustomed to having students care for them; keeping the situation as neutral as possible helps to control at least one undesirable variable that could skew the outcome of the examination. Therefore, students have a responsibility to consider these possible reactions by patients and to refrain from discussing with patients the fact that a final examination is being conducted in which they are required to demonstrate clinical skills. Some students need more assistance with this—and more supervision—than others. Others may look for the advantage of having the patient know exactly what is happening—hoping for some positive assistance. For comparability, however, students are expected to establish a nursing relationship with patients that excludes the direct disclosure that an examination is being conducted. The patient will be aware that the student is being closely observed because the "teacher" is present throughout all phases, which is different from the usual situation of care. The evaluators have the initial responsibility of setting the stage at the time patients are selected, but they and the students (as well as the staff) share the continuing responsibility of ensuring that the experience is kept as neutral as possible.

Establishing such a student–patient relationship is difficult to control in the actual clinical setting and therefore it has the potential of significantly altering the outcome of the examination. Because students, evaluators, and staff must use a commonly accepted frame of reference in approaching patients during the testing period, it is essential that these relationships be discussed in the study guide. Some students—and even some evaluators—may think they are being dishonest if they do not fully disclose exactly what is going on; others want to share a "little but not enough to really make a difference." If

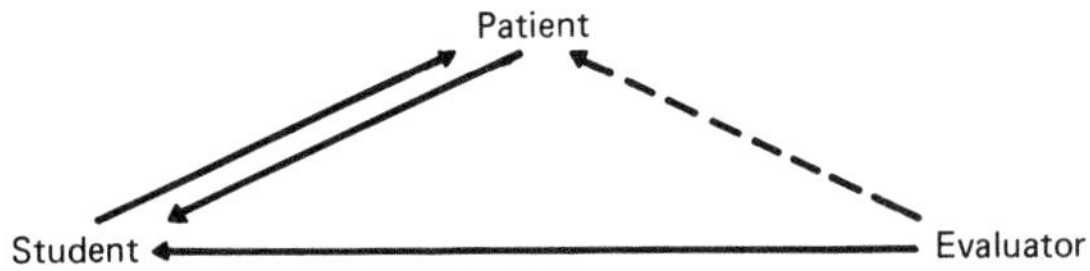

Fig. 6.3. The evaluator directly observes the student who is responsible for administering care to the patient; the evaluator also ensures the well-being of the patient.

either of these attitudes is implemented, chances are the examination outcomes will be contaminated. The objective of the test is to determine whether the student has achieved the clinical standard; clearly, this goal will be frustrated if extraneous variables are not controlled to the extent possible. The stated purpose for the student and evaluator being with the patient and the resulting relationships that develop are two factors that need to be identified, described, and ultimately controlled in a consistent and systematic fashion.

Figure 6.3 illustrates the desirable relationships in which the student is fully responsible for the patient's care during the examination and the evaluator is responsible for directly evaluating the student while indirectly ensuring the safety and well-being of the patient. Deviations from this model will influence the outcome of the examination.

Examination and the Nurse

The study guide also outlines the relationship between the students and the nursing staff as another one of the conditions under which they will be tested. If the performance examination is a comprehensive one given in the clinical setting then students need to know what is expected of them in terms of their relationships with other personnel in that setting. Exactly what kind of assistance can they obtain? To whom do they report? What do they do when unexpected demands arise? The study guide explains the evaluators' as well as the students' responsibility to the staff in an effort to control these potentially influencing variables.

The evaluator has a responsibility to communicate directly with the staff regarding patient selection and any other matters that need discussion prior to the examination period. During the test itself, however, the student is expected to be responsible for any direct communication with the staff on behalf of the patient. The staff is likewise

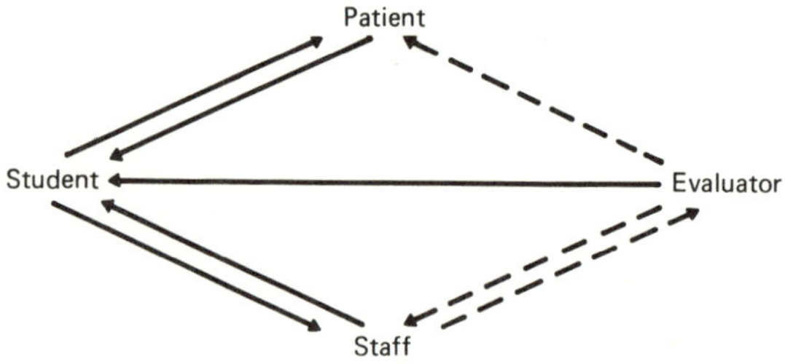

Fig. 6.4. The student maintains direct communications with the staff while caring for the patient; the evaluator maintains indirect communications with the staff to ensure the patient's well-being.

responsible directly to the student, but also must keep the evaluator informed to ensure safety of the patient and help preserve the integrity of the examination.

Figure 6.4 illustrates the relationships among the four categories of individuals (or groups) involved during the examination. Students, evaluators, and staff all must be held accountable for the behaviors expected of each during the examination in order to provide consistency and comparability. If some evaluators become intermediaries between the staff and students while others require students to function independently, the conditions will not be comparable. If some students are allowed to engage the evaluator directly in patient care while other evaluators remain appropriately uninvolved, the conditions are not comparable. The evaluator who directly participates in repeated conversation with the patient during the examination—either with or without coparticipation by the student—is deviating from the established model of relationships (Figure 6.4) and is altering the testing conditions. This kind of influence is partially controlled by repeatedly informing all parties involved of the conditions under which the examination will be administered, and by gaining cooperation with these protocols each time. Supervision also is necessary, especially during the transition period. These points require comprehensive discussion both in the examination study guide and during the orientation sessions with all groups involved.

CRITERION 3

Type of clothing to be worn and equipment to be brought to the test are specified. If one of the conditions for taking the examination is that students arrive on time and wear white uniform, shoes, and cap this should be so stated in the study guide. If they should wear some other attire, that should be specified. If students are expected to bring any equipment with them (watch, scissors, pen, etc.) that also should be described in sufficient detail to prevent any confusion. Once these expectations are clearly stated in writing and in the orientation session, students are held accountable for meeting them just as they are for other conditions associated with the examination.

CONDITIONS FOCUSING ON THE EXAMINATION PROCESS

CRITERION 1

All conditions related to the examination process are included. As explained previously, the only way to ensure that students and faculty hold a common understanding of the expectations for each during the test is to specify these criteria in writing in the examination study guide, to be used by everyone involved. Expectations related to what the student shall wear, the kinds of interrelationships to be developed, and the responsibilities for students, evaluators, and staff already have been discussed. Various ways in which these conditions can influence the examination outcome have been suggested. Similarly, it is essential that all conditions pertaining to the examination process itself be specified clearly and comprehensively. The structure, specific procedures for randomizing patient selection and choosing areas of care, the time constraints for completing parts or the whole of the test, the criteria for passing, and all other associated conditions are systemically outlined and explained. These criteria focus on the many aspects of the examination process rather than on the content, but they are equally important.

CRITERION 2

The time allowed for each segment and the total test are specified. Designating the time allowed for all subsections and the total examinations helps to ensure consistency and comparability. Students and faculty are held accountable for a common frame of reference and neither is permitted to deviate from this condition. The committee also determines any possible exceptions to the rule and specifies them as well.

Regardless of how the examination is organized, whether comprehensive patient-care situations (PCS) or smaller units, an overall time limit is designated. The amount of time allowed is based on such factors as the number of areas of care the student is expected to perform and the complexity of patient care. If comprehensive care is to be given, as with the External Degree CPNE, general guidelines for time are designated for each phase of the nursing process with an overall time limit for the entire PCS. This allows some flexibility for the student, depending on the particular demands of the PCS. For example, if two-and-a-half hours are allowed for the total PCS, it is suggested that the first 25 to 30 minutes be used for assessment and planning, about 90 minutes for the implementation phase, and the remaining 30 minutes for the evaluation, recording, and reporting phase. However, the only time periods that is mandatory is for completion of the entire PCS. Students may use a longer time for planning or a shorter time for evaluation or for implementation. In either case, all requirements for the PCS must be met within the designated time frame. Once such conditions are approved for the test, the evaluators are not permitted to deviate by insisting that each segment actually must be completed in a specific time. During the test they can remind students that all aspects of the PCS must be completed within the allotted time and help them be aware of the amount of time remaining. Some students begin more slowly and take more time to organize their work and decide on nursing-care priorities and actions but are able to make up for it by efficiently completing the implementation phase.

Furthermore, evaluators are not allowed to extend the time period for the entire PCS except for those conditions identified in the examination guide (e.g., interruptions in patient care beyond their control). Because the test is administered in an actual clinical setting with real patients, it is not possible to control all of the potential interruptions that may occur on behalf of the patient. Consequently some "cushion time" is needed between each PCS to ensure that each student has equivalent opportunity to complete all aspects of care. A period of 30 minutes between PCSs probably is sufficient for situations in which minor interruptions have occurred. PCSs that involve comprehensive care, therefore, may be scheduled for a maximum of three hours, and unless an unpredicted event interferes, the student is expected to complete all requirements in a 2½ hour period but with an additional 30 minutes to accommodate interruptions.

A second reason for the half-hour cushion time between PCSs is to allow both students and evaluators a much-needed break, to attend to normal physiologic needs, and to move from one patient unit to another when this is necessary.

Scheduling each PCS for two-and-a-half hours is probably equitable only when the comprehensive nursing care required usually can be accomplished by regular staff nurses in approximately one-and-a-half hours. If it takes longer for practicing graduates to give the same care, it is unrealistic to expect that the student can assess the patient's needs, write the nursing care plan (NCP), make essential decisions, implement the care, evaluate the patient's status, revise the NCP, record progress notes, and report to the responsible staff number all in the designated period. This consideration is integral to the conditions of time and should be dealt with uniformly. Patient selection, therefore, has a direct relationship to the time allowed as well as the content to be tested (see Figure 6.2). Statements about the condition of time and allowable modifications should be clearly outlined in the study guide.

Functions of Control

Controlling the variable of time for each patient situation serves several important functions. First of all, it imposes a carefully determined degree of reality on the situation. In an examination at the conclusion of a specific education program, students are expected to be able to administer care within a reasonable time frame; if other factors are controlled—such as number of areas of care, number of interruptions, etc.—students, knowing in advance how much time will be allowed, can practice and prepare for that imposed condition. The time allowed during the examination should reflect the expectations in the actual setting, at least to a reasonable degree.

Also by controlling the time factor, certain other competencies of the student can be tested indirectly. For instance, without writing critical elements for ability to organize work, that competence can be tested by controlling content and time requirements. Students who are unable to design a plan of care and implement it in an organized fashion simply will not be able to complete all required aspects of the PCS within the designated time. Those who run back and forth to obtain equipment, look things up in the procedure manual, or who are disorganized in administering each aspect of care will have insufficient time to complete the assignment. The carefully determined content, time allotment, and patient selection inherently provide the opportunity for simultaneously testing organization.

Similarly, controlling time as a condition of the examination process also helps to assess the student's ability to make logical and correct decisions and to apply theory in the practice of nursing. Students who do not really comprehend the needs of the patient or how to meet them, who constantly seek clarification from the staff or from references on the unit, or who require excessive time to think through what should be done will not be able to pass the examination. The allotted time will expire before they can recall and integrate the essential theory and implement it. The requirements of the PCS inherently test the application and integration of nursing theory, organization, management, and nursing process; controlling the variable of time imposes its own test of these factors and the student's ability to cope with realistic and reasonable clinical demands.

In addition to specifying time allocation for subsections, controls also are necessary for the entire examination, which may consist of one or several patient-care situations administered during one day or even two days. The number of PCSs depends entirely on the decisions made regarding such factors as required behaviors for the placement of the test in the program, the kind of program, the reason for the test, other performance tests being used, etc. (as discussed in a previous chapter). If more than one PCS or simulated segment is to be tested, the time allowed for the total test is specified to ensure comparability and consistency. In some situations two to three PCSs are required. It is possible to arrange for them to be completed in a single day, or to spread them over a two-day period. It may even be possible to assign the first PCS at midterm and another just before the conclusion of the semester, with one makeup period individually arranged in case of failure. Regardless of how the test is divided or how extensive or restricted it is, the total time frame should be specified in the examination guide. Other aspects related to scheduling the test and mechanics about how it can be accomplished given the full schedules of faculty and students will be discussed in a subsequent chapter.

The time frame for the CPNE of the New York Regents External Degree Program illustrates the criterion related to time. The entire examination takes place over a two-and-a-half-day period, beginning on Friday afternoon and extending through Sunday afternoon. The orientation and first of two simulated laboratory situations is given between 4:30 and 7:30 p.m. on Friday. The first two PCSs are administered on Saturday, from 7:30 a.m. to 2:00 p.m.; and the second simulated laboratory segment is given from 2:30 to 3:30 p.m. on the same day for those who failed the first one. On Sunday, the third PCS is assigned between 7:30 and 11:30 a.m. Passing one laboratory and three PCSs meets the requirements and candidates are finished with the examination approximately at 11:30 a.m. on Sunday; those who failed one adult and/or one child PCS have the opportunity to repeat them between 11:30 a.m. and 5:00 p.m. on Sunday. Pass–fail decisions about all candidates, therefore, are made by late Sunday afternoon. No one may extend the time longer or consolidate it into a briefer period. This practice ensures that all candidates are examined under the same conditions of time, for each PCS as well as for the total examination.

Potential deviations from the specified time allotment that are predictable can be outlined in the examination guide from the outset to avoid confusion and inconsistency during the test. As suggested earlier, it is essential that the patients who are selected be expected to remain in their rooms during the test period. This is one reason weekends are desirable. However, sometimes the patient may be called away to X-ray, or to physical therapy, or for another special purpose. When this occurs during a PCS the evaluator must have some guidelines to follow regarding what actions to take. Every effort should be made to allow the student to complete the care if more than half of it already is finished. If the student is just getting started, another PCS should be selected even though this means the time and rotation schedule will be offset and must be adjusted. Evaluators have a major responsibility to anticipate such problems by discussing assignments with the staff and requesting that, when possible, interruptions be deferred until the completion of the PCS.

It is clear that patient selection and time allowed for the test are two highly interrelated conditions that require meticulous attention by the committee that is developing the performance examination and by the evaluators who administer it to students. Other factors related to patient selection will be discussed subsequently. The essential point to be made here relating to the condition of time is that the committee should anticipate most of the problems that might interfere with the time schedule and can decide in advance how evaluators are expected to respond to such situations. This will facilitate consistency and therefore assure a more equitable test for students.

CRITERION 3

Characteristics of the patient to be selected are clearly specified. As suggested earlier, the type of patients selected for the performance test is one of the most important conditions of the test because it is so interrelated with content and has such potential for influencing the outcome, irrespective of the student's actual competence. Exercising complete control over patients' behavior and needs for nursing care is essentially impossible, but determining which areas of care will be selected is not only possible it is essential in administering an actual clinical test. The primary criterion used to select patients is that they must currently need the areas of nursing care designated for inclusion by the faculty committee as the vehicle for testing the student's competence. Patients also must agree to allow the student to provide care.

If the patients' needs change during the hours between the time of selection and the administration of the test, problems can be expected to result both for the student and the evaluator. Primarily, the time schedule will be altered because another patient will have to be selected in order to meet the specific criteria. On the other hand, if the evaluator persists in using that patient even though he does not meet all requirements, the student will be tested on conditions that deviate from those specified in the examination protocol. This violates the concepts of comparability and consistency as this particular student will be tested on areas of care not developed or on too few areas of care in relation to other students.

To control the condition of which competencies will be measured, it is imperative that criteria for the selection of patients be specified in the examination guide and be conscientiously implemented by evaluators. The criteria listing the kinds of patients to be included or excluded should be sufficiently comprehensive to allow for a variety of customary patient situations.

If only those patients of a certain age or status of psychological functioning are appropriate, such criteria must be itemized. Consideration should be given to both patients and students to protect their mutual interests. The committee that develops the examination and the evaluators who implement it have to fully acknowledge that they are concerned with rendering an objective examination of the students' clinical competence, not providing another clinical–learning experience. The kinds of patients selected should provide the best opportunity to test competence at the level appropriate for the student.

The criteria for excluding patients are equally as important as those related to inclusion; some patients may be excluded because they are too ill (near death), too vulnerable (require reverse isolation), too mentally deranged (thus preventing administration of care), or do not speak the language of the student and evaluator. Others may be excluded because they endanger the student (e.g., radium implantation, rubella). All of these factors suggest variables that can and should be controlled during this already complex anxiety-ridden examination situation. Controlling the selection of patients helps to minimize the potential variations in a complex test and to assure some degree of comparability of the demands expected of all students during the examination.

The faculty committee developing the test is responsible for thinking through the potential problems, selecting or excluding different kinds of patients, and for specifying the final list of criteria. Thcsc criteria guide the evaluators in choosing patients, and help to exert some control over the natural tendency of teachers to choose testing episodes that are inappropriate for the clinical examination. The criteria also help students to be aware of those situations that may or may not be imposed on them during the test period, which should help to allay unnecessary stress, as there already is more than enough anxiety inherent in the situation. They also exert some control over the instructor who looks for the most difficult, unusual, or "interesting" patient experiences to ensure that students really are prepared and put to a sufficiently difficult test. Thus specific criteria are essential to move the assessment process along the continuum toward more objectivity, comparability, and consistency. Without such controls over the kinds of patients to be selected, it would be essentially impossible to administer an objective examination regardless of all the time and attention given to specifying the content to be tested.

CRITERION 4

The number and kinds of areas of care and potential combinations are predetermined. While the specific array of defined areas of care and their related critical elements outline the content to be tested, the number of areas required exerts control over the complexity and extent of the demands placed on students. Establishing a number, or range of numbers, also controls the comparability of testing episodes. If such controls are not specified and enforced, individual evaluators will be free to decide their own limits, thereby nullifying other attempts to make the examination fair and objective.

The particular configuration of testing episodes is dependent in part on the kinds of nursing needs the available patients manifest at the time of the examination. It also depends on the prespecified directions to evaluators regarding the potential combinations of areas. For example, as previously mentioned, one approach suggests that the total list of areas of care can be divided into two main categories: required areas and selected areas. The required areas are those most commonly expected to be practiced, most frequently needed by patients, and therefore most readily available in patient-care situations. All students will be expected to perform these areas for each PCS. In addition, however, patients have a variety of other nursing-care needs that are encountered less often, but which occur frequently enough to be included in the clinical examination. These areas are included in the list of selected areas, from which a specified number (in any combination) can be added to the required areas to round out the particular configuration for each PCS.

The committee developing the performance examination decides which nursing care will be listed in each category and then determines how many of each will be included in a total patient-care testing episode. Evaluators then choose patients whose nursing care includes the required areas and designated number of selected areas. This ensures comparability of testing episodes and incorporates the concepts of sampling and flexibility so that the examination is both realistic and functional in the actual clinical setting.

For example, suppose the following two lists represent a few required and selected areas of care in a hospital-based clinical examination:

Required

- Personal hygiene
- Vital signs
- Mobility
- Fluids

Selected

- Medications
- Sterile dressings
- Irrigations
- Drainage

Also suppose that the committee decided that students should perform five to six areas of care during each PCS. Furthermore, the number of required and selected areas is also designated, depending on the time of day the test is being given. For example, it might be decided that evaluators could choose any patient whose nursing care included 4 required areas (e.g., personal hygiene, vital signs, mobility, and fluids) and any one to two of the selected areas (say, medications and drainage) for a maximum total of six areas. Given the same rule, another patient could be chosen who needed all of the required areas and also needed the change of a sterile dressing and an irrigation, making a total of six areas. Still another patient might be chosen who needed all required areas plus medications and sterile dressing change as the two selected areas.

These patient situations are not *exactly* the same but they are comparable in the number of areas of care the students are to provide. By requiring certain areas in every PCS, students can be compared directly, but the reality of the clinical setting mandates some flexibility in the exact areas to be demonstrated. By design, the selected areas are reasonably comparable to one another in complexity and demands placed on students. The number of areas, the kinds of areas, and the potential combinations are determined and specified in the study guide in order to ensure comparability of testing episodes while still assuring that the test is realistic and functional.

If the entire testing day extends over several hours from morning through afternoon, other specifications related to kinds of areas to be used have to be clarified. For instance, it is quite customary to provide personal hygiene (bath and care of bed and immediate environment) in the early morning; therefore, in most situations it is problematic to require that area of performance at midday or in the afternoon. Patients and staff alike prefer that this kind of nursing care be completed before lunchtime. In most instances, forcing the issue only results in problems on general medical–surgical units. Therefore, that area could be required only for the early-morning PCS, and another selected area could be added to later PCSs. In these situations, for example, vital signs, mobility, and fluids could be combined with medications, sterile dressing, and drainage for a total of six areas of care. For these later PCSs a more appropriate area would be afternoon (p.m.) care, to refresh the patient without giving a complete bath and changing the bed linen. It is appropriate, functional, and tests most of the same basic nursing principles.

Patients who require only five areas of care also are appropriate for selection, as there is reason to assume that six areas discriminate more satisfactorily than five areas. Furthermore, the needs of patients do not always comply with such a demand. Establishing a range of numbers of areas—for example five to six, or four to five—ensures a reasonably comprehensive patient situation for testing but does not mandate that every patient must have only that specific number of areas of need. This condition allows greater flexibility and also helps to increase the functionability of the performance examination in the actual setting.

Predetermining the number of areas, the categories or areas, and the potential combinations for given testing situations are essential in controlling some of the conditions that influence the examination and the resulting outcomes for students. Statements governing these conditions are particularly important in relation to the concepts of objectivity, comparability, sampling, and flexibility.

CRITERION 5

Guidelines for assigning patients are predetermined and specifically outlined. Another condition that could have a direct influence on the objectivity of the examination is the manner in which students are assigned to patients during the test. Some mechanism has to be used in this pairing process in order to control potential evaluator bias (conscious or unconscious). A technically pure random selection would be difficult in most circumstances; however, a close facsimile can be used. The fundamental idea is that students should not be deliberately assigned to certain patient situations because of known characteristics, needs, or preferences of any of the parties involved. Any one of several approaches could be used to ensure a reasonable objective assignment. For instance, students could sign up for an examination appointment and location without knowing which instructor will be the evaluator for that time and place. In the same example, the evaluators would select patients for the potential appointment times without knowing which students had selected the given examination periods. Only after these decisions have been made would students and evaluators know the results.

Another approach is to use a random card-selection process. Students draw a card at random on which is written a designated rotation pattern, indicating the units, patients, and/or evaluators to be used in a particular sequence. For instance, if three PCSs are to be used, each on a different unit and with different evaluators and patients, the cards might indicate pattern I, pattern II, or pattern III. Each pattern designates a prearranged nursing unit and evaluator; the evaluator on the particular unit selects patients who meet the criteria, without knowing which students will be coming at a particular time. Table 6.1 illustrates a rotation pattern for 3 time periods. For example, student A begins with evaluator 1, goes to evaluator 3, then rotates to evaluator 2. The student who randomly selects pattern III begins the examination by going to pediatrics and evaluator 3 for the 7:30 to 10:00 period, then rotates to West Wing and evaluator 2 at 10:30, and finally, goes to East Wing and evaluator 1 at 1:30. In this way, neither students nor evaluators know ahead of time who will be paired with whom, leaving the results to chance by the random selection of a card. The process is

TABLE 6-1
An Example of a Simple Rotation Pattern

PCS Testing Periods	Rotation Patterns* I	II	III
7:30–10:00 a.m.	A	B	C
10:30– 1:00 p.m.	B	C	A
1:30– 4:00 p.m.	C	A	B

*I, West Wing, evaluator 1; II, East Wing, evaluator 2; III, Pediatrics, evaluator 3.

further safeguarded by having someone other than one of the evaluators supervise the card selection and other aspects of the examination process. A clinical associate (the title given to someone designated to coordinate and monitor the entire examination without having direct responsibility for student evaluation)* is the natural choice to conduct this random assignment process.

Regardless of which mechanism is used, the committee is responsible for writing a clear description of the procedures to be followed. This is necessary in order to control the tendency toward biased assignments that results in subjective evaluation. Students and evaluators need to know the procedures related to the selection process prior to the examination; ideally these procedures should be outlined in the examination study guide along with all other pertinent conditions. This random selection process is another way in which the concepts of objectivity, comparability, samplings, consistency, flexibility, and systematized conditions are integrated into the development and implementation of the performance examination.

CRITERION 6

The role and responsibilities of the clinical associate are specified. It is recommended that wherever possible a faculty member (or some other responsible person) should assume the role of coordinator to ensure that all aspects of the examination are administered as specified. The title of "clinical associate" is used by the New York Regents External Degree Program for the performance examinations: however, regardless of the title used, the position is a critical one. Ascribing a different title to the new role helps to separate the person

*See next section.

from the inculcated stereotype of the clinical-instructor role. The change to a new role almost mandates a change in title to facilitate the transition toward objective examinations of clinical competence. The same principle, of course, is the reason for retitling instructors as evaluators during the examination period. Other names—such as proctors, testers, examiners, or the like also could be used—depending on the preference of the faculty committee.

Figure 6.5 shows the coordinating function of the clinical associate and relationships among all those involved in the examination. The person in this position helps to increase objectivity, comparability, and consistency by remaining uninvolved in direct observation responsibilities while ensuring that evaluators function as prescribed.

The role of the clinical associate is to coordinate all aspects of the examination and to be responsive to the needs of the evaluators, students, staff (and sometimes the patients) as they occur during the examination. With rare exceptions the associate does not engage in evaluation of students, although she or he does provide a neutral perspective and sounding board when a second opinion is needed to make a judgment about the students' performance. The associate continually supervises the administration of the test and makes certain that evaluators are performing their role of objective observer, that students have someone to come to for certain kinds of information, and that staff have someone to consult regarding the overall process.

The associate also has a variety of other responsibilities, such as the following:

- Orienting students just prior to the examination to be sure they understand the process and procedures.
- Implementing the random procedures to determine patient assignments.

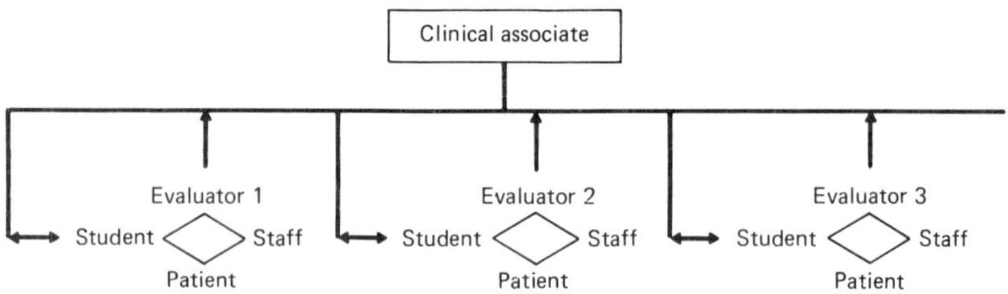

Fig.6.5. Coordination responsibilities of clinical associate and relationship to evaluators, students, staff, and patients.

- Monitoring evaluators to be sure they comply with the nonteaching observer role.
- Reviewing selection of patients to confirm that they meet the established criteria.
- Working with staff to gain and maintain cooperation.
- Helping to minimize student anxiety during the examination.
- Assisting evaluators with rapid selection of new patients when the situation changes during the examination (major and minor procedural crises).
- Assisting with questions and/or problems that arise during the test from staff, physicians, family members, etc.
- Assisting evaluators to make clinical decisions about "gray" areas, when there is some doubt about the student's performance vis-à-vis the critical elements or overriding areas of concern.
- Ensuring that all examination forms are completed and processed as required.
- Serving as liaison between administration and faculty.

As illustrated in Figure 6.5, all persons involved in the examination process have access to the clinical associate; the evaluator is directly responsible for examining the student interacting with the staff and ensuring the patient's well-being. The associate also may interact with these individuals as necessary for the proper administration of the performance examination. The role of clinical associate is essential, especially in relation to minimizing evaluator bias and ensuring objectivity; reducing student anxiety; maintaining positive relations with the agency staff; ensuring consistency of procedures and comparability of testing episodes; as well as a variety of other functions.

CRITERION 7

The role and responsibilities of clinical evaluators are specified. The behavior of the evaluator is crucial in conducting an objective, equitable performance examination. Knowingly or unknowingly, the evaluator can singlehandedly sabotage the effectiveness of everything the faculty committee has designed. The purpose of objective assessment can be defeated in dozens of ways by careless, stubborn, timid, disgruntled, or hostile instructors who rigidly cling to personal preferences or old habits instead of cooperating in the transition toward more valid and uniform clinical evaluation.

There are two paramount roles to be fulfilled by the evaluators during examinations in the actual clinical setting:

1. To administer the examination according to the predetermined protocol regarding content and conditions.
2. To assure the safety and well-being of patients during the process.

In the first instance, evaluators are neutral observers of the students' behavior on behalf of patients in terms of the specific content and conditions outlined in the study guide. Evaluators are obliged to observe all nursing-care actions and to judge them in reference to the stated critical elements applicable to the areas of care identified for the particular PCS, or the overriding areas of concern (asepsis and physical or emotional jeopardy). They are responsible for testing only for designated areas and their related critical elements (or, in some instances, the stated conditions).

The second major role of the evaluator is to protect the patient against unsafe practice by the student during the PCS. If it appears that commission of an error is imminent, the evaluator is obliged to allow the student the opportunity to proceed with nursing care up to the point immediately before an actual jeopardizing error is committed. Only then should the evaluator interrupt the student to protect the patient. If, however, the student makes an error of the sort that does not cause harm to the patient, or is about to make an error, but immediately recognizes the error, she or he has a right to acknowledge and correct it. For example, if a student is about to give an incorrect medication, but does not recognize the error, he is stopped at the point just before administering it to the patient. However, if the error is perceived any time up to that point the candidate has an opportunity to correct it. If a piece of sterile equipment is contaminated while preparing to use it and the student recognizes the error, she or he may correct the situation and proceed without penalty.

This entire topic of the evaluator's role will be discussed in detail in a subsequent chapter; however, it should be clear that to maintain the concept of an examination that is objectively administered, the evaluator plays a most significant part. In these major overall roles, evaluators are also responsible for the following:

- Selecting patient care situations that meet the established criteria and that meet the approval of the service staff.
- Observing the student objectively and recording judgments for each critical element, at the time each is carried out.
- Maintaining an uninvolved, neutral, nonteaching stance during the examination, both with students and with patients.

- Completing all required assessment forms, related to patient assignments, student performance, explanations of failures, etc.
- Assuring that patients receive all care required during the testing period, either by the student or by a staff member.
- Communicating with the nursing staff regarding the care to be performed by the student and any care being omitted from the examination that is expected to be provided by the assigned staff nurse.
- Cooperating with the clinical associate in all matters pertaining to the examination and content and procedures.
- Seeking clarification from the clinical associate whenever necessary regarding students' compliance with critical elements.
- Interacting briefly with the students, after all aspects of the PCS have been completed, regarding either positive or negative performance, for the further benefit of the students' learning.

Each of these activities, and many other aspects pertaining to evaluators, will be discussed later; however, it is important to mention them here as conditions under which the examination will be administered. Both students and faculty have a major obligation to shift from the traditional imagery of role relationships during clinical instruction to the different expectations required during the clinical examination. As with all of the other conditions, when this criterion is not met, the fundamental purpose of the examination is jeopardized because the basic concepts are ignored or deliberately bypassed.

CRITERION 8

Mechanisms to control evaluator bias are preestablished and declared. As already discussed, the personal preferences and biases of evaluators can creep into the examination process at almost any point unless steps are taken deliberately to curtail them. Details will be discussed later, but it is essential to include here statements regarding the need for control over this potentially influencing variable. The faculty committee must consider multiple ways to minimize bias and state those that are applicable in the examination study guide. The specificity of the critical elements, criteria for selection of PCSs, supervision by the clinical association, and all of the other conditions help to limit the negative influence of overt or covert bias. This is a major area to be covered during the transition period, when clinical instructors are reprogrammed into another role—that of neutral, objective observer of the student's behavior measured against a predetermined standard of expected performance.

CRITERION 9

The basis for pass or fail is specified. Another condition that requires discussion and decision by the faculty committee prior to implementing the examination is the basis for pass/fail grades. On objective written tests the correct answers and the number of correct answers required for passing are predetermined. Students know in advance the criteria that must be met to pass, and they also know the consequences of failing to achieve the criteria. Similarly, there should be established criteria for passing the performance examination, known in advance by students and faculty alike.

Such criteria exert considerable control over the natural tendency of instructors to interpret performance subjectively, depending on prior knowledge of and experience with the particular student. Because of the tradition of basing clinical evaluation on accumulated anecdotal notes, many evaluators will be inclined to recall the students' clinical experiences during the learning phase and be influenced in one of three directions:

1. Because of positive past clinical experiences, lean in the direction of passing the student.
2. Because of negative past clinical experiences, lean in the direction of failing the student.
3. Because of ambiguous or unknown past clinical experiences, pass or fail the student on perceived performance during the examination.

Here again, the need for control of evaluator bias is obvious, even when criteria for passing/failing are clearly established. It also points out the need for overseeing the conduct of evaluators, especially during the transition period, to help them become sensitive to their conscious and/or unconscious tendencies toward subjectivity.

Establishing the rules for passing also helps students to understand in advance exactly what will be expected of them. It also clarifies that neither they nor the faculty can change the criteria depending on some personal idiosyncracy or peculiar happenings during the examination. Once the rules are determined and mutually agreeable to the faculty, evaluators have an obligation to make all decisions accordingly. If some evaluators rigidly enforce the criteria and others do not, the desired goal of an objective and equitable performance examination is nullified. Even some students whom the faculty thought would pass might fail because the criteria must be enforced equally; this is another reminder that the faculty committee has an obligation to be sure the examination is appropriate and at the acceptable level for the students taking it. Pilot-testing also is imperative to be sure the test is fair, because once it is implemented all aspects of it are applicable without individual modifications—which includes the criteria for passing or failing the examination, and the resulting consequences of such decisions.

Specific Requirements

In the Regents External Degree Program, criteria for passing the clinical performance examination include: successful demonstration of all critical elements related to a particular PCS with 100 percent accuracy; successful completion of three of five PCSs; and successful completion of one of two simulated laboratory sessions; all with 100 percent accuracy. These three subexaminations must include two adult and one child PCS. These are stringent criteria, but one must recall that the emphasis is placed on critical elements and not on a multitude of steps in procedures, and that students know the expected standard well in advance and can use it in preparation for the examination. Furthermore, the standard is based on what has been designated as an acceptable level of performance, which is confirmed by pilot-testing.

Regardless of how precisely the critical elements and conditions are identified, some situations will be difficult to judge. Because the examination deals with a human triad (as a bare minimum) involving patient, student, and evaluator, some subjectivity will intrude in most situations. This is inevitable, but it should be recognized openly and resolved in the most equitable manner that seems appropriate. The committee is responsible for establishing in advance a mechanism for dealing with these "gray" areas because they very much influence the decision for passing or failing students. For example, when an evaluator has difficulty deciding whether or not the student met the critical element with 100 percent accuracy, or whether principles of asepsis were violated, or whether the patient was emotionally jeopardized, the situation should be discussed with the clinical associate who helps to interpret the behavior and to make the ultimate decision. This removes the onus of "different but significant" decisions from a single evaluator.

Many gray areas involve asepsis, and the committee is responsible for being as clear as possible in outlining how such situations will be handled by evaluators. For example, asepsis in a hospital environment is vitally important, but expectations can be set so high as to be totally unrealistic. Only in the operating room or similar special environments is true asepsis enforced. The question here is: To what extent should asepsis be followed in the care of patients on general units as a baseline of acceptability, rather than the ideal or epitome? One must remember that this is an examination rather than a teaching–learning situation, and failure to meet any one critical element requires the failure of the total patient-care situation regardless of what other behaviors were satisfactorily passed. Careful consideration needs to be given to these possibilities before final decisions are made during the planning phase.

With these reminders it is easy to understand the stress placed both on students and evaluators. When the evaluator rules that critical elements for asepsis have been violated, she or he must be able to document that the patient was subjected to immediate or actual danger before a student can be failed for violation of asepsis. For example, if the student contaminates the top cuff of a sterile glove while changing a dry sterile dressing it is not grounds for failure because the wound was not contaminated. Precise wording of critical elements is essential, as this situation illustrates.

Other examples will be discussed in the chapter related to preparation of evaluators. The purpose here is to point out that all of the conditions for passing or failing the examination should be clarified ahead of time by the committee. Some of the conditions are ambiguous and require special consideration and procedures. Such situations should be described in the study guide along with the protocol for resolving inherent conflict or discrepancies. As much as anything else, objectivity of the examination depends upon clarification of the criteria for passing or failing the student.

CRITERION 10

The consequences of failure are specified. Another procedural matter that needs to be clarified prior to implementation relates to the consequences of failure of a part or the total examination. Students and faculty both need to know what is expected of them. For example, the criteria for passing may allow the failure of one PCS so long as a repeat PCS is passed. In the New York Regents External Degree Program two of three adult PCSs and one of two child PCSs must be passed with 100 percent accuracy. This means, of course, that one adult and one child situation could be failed but if the student passed the repeat situation, she or he still passes the total examination. Whatever the faculty committee decides, it should be clearly outlined for all those involved.

The same is true for failing the total examination. What happens then? Does the student have an opportunity to repeat the test at another time? Does it mean the student has failed the entire program or the course? May the student return to repeat the course—or just the performance examination—or only a part of the performance test?

Answers to these questions are determined by the faculty committee during the developmental phase. Students who clearly understand the consequence of failure undoubtedly will make every effort to achieve the expected standard prior to being tested—and that, of course, is the objective. Naturally, the consequences will vary depending on the type of test, when it is administered, how comprehensive and terminal it is, and other factors; regardless, the meaning of the failure is outlined in the study guide.

Another aspect of the problem is what to do about "patient care" when a student fails while in the midst of providing patient care. It is possible for failure to occur at any time during the PCS: within five minutes, after one hour, or even during the evaluation phase after all direct care has been provided. The problem is what to do about completing patient care when a critical element is failed. Should the student finish it anyhow? Should the evaluator be responsible? Or should the staff nurse be called in to complete the care?

Any of these actions is a possible solution. However, the true meaning of a critical element is that it is behavior that is essential to the patient. If the student ignores or misperforms it, clinical competence is in doubt and the patient is endangered. Technically, then, the student is failed and there is no reason to allow her or him to remain with the patient. During the Regents clinical examination students are removed from the PCS whenever a critical element is failed and must wait for the next scheduled PCS, unless they already have failed the maximum number allowed. As itemized in the agency contract, students are removed from the PCS at the point of failure and the regularly assigned staff nurse is immediately informed and continues the patient's care. However, if the student fails while literally in the midst of applying a sterile dressing or performing some other procedure, the evaluator either finishes that particular activity or assists the student to finish it in order to facilitate the smooth completion of the patient's care. The remaining aspects of care are then turned over to the assigned staff nurse.

Details about the implications for the nursing staff will be discussed in the next chapter; however, it is essential here to realize the importance of specifying this as a condition under which the examination is administered. As with all other conditions related to the process of conducting the examination, the consequence of partial or total failure should be identified and described in writing to ensure objectivity and consistency.

CRITERION 11

An appeal mechanism is identified. When the performance test is comprehensive and administered in the actual clinical setting, the impinging variables are numerous and the opportunity for misunderstanding and evaluator subjectivity is greater than in a more circumscribed, simulated situation. Consequently, it is possible for even well-prepared evaluators to make an error in judgment when failing a student. Because of this possibility an appeal process is a good idea. The requirements and limitations within which it functions should be outlined in the study guide. For example, it is important to clarify how long after the failure the appeal is acceptable, the exact process to be followed by the student, the composition of the panel that is responsible for reviewing the case, the possible outcomes, and other aspects.

It probably is desirable to require that the appeal be submitted within a few weeks following the examination, as details become more ambiguous and distorted with the passing of time. Students who appeal should describe in writing their perception of the details of the failure as clearly and fully as possible. The evaluator already will have described the failure on the examination form at the time the PCS was terminated. For legal purposes both evaluator and student sign that descriptive statement at the time the failure is declared. The appeal panel reviews the evaluator's comments and the student's letter of appeal and then makes a judgment. Sometimes, when it appears that the evaluator may have acted hastily or in error and that the competence of the student is unclear, the examination may be repeated. In other instances the evaluator's decision may be declared in error and reversed; in other situations the student may be shown to have been clearly in error and therefore the failure is upheld.

The panel—composed of faculty members who are not directly involved as evaluators (or evaluators for the student involved)—probably will be more objective in reaching a decision. Therefore, the panel should be selected with this in mind. Experience with several cases will help to clarify the types of problems and reasonable reactions to them. This review panel also serves the purpose of inherently monitoring the examination process. Through the kinds of complaints from students, the panel can detect potential problems that need investigation before they become widespread. Some of the most common complaints involve premature termination of the PCS (without allowing the student time to correct detected errors within the time frame), evaluators' assuming the role of teacher, selection of patients who do not meet the criteria, and excessive stringency in interpreting the critical elements (especially related to asepsis).

Specifying the appeal process can clearly help to increase the objectivity and consistency of the examination.

CRITERION 12

Required forms are developed, described, and illustrated. To promote consistency and objectivity, various paper forms are developed for use during the examination.* The most important one, of course, is the list of areas of care and their related critical elements, with space by each one to indicate pass or fail. This form is to be used continuously while the student is taking the test; it is not to be used retrospectively (based on memory). Therefore the format should be conducive to quick access and noting results for each critical element. By listing the critical elements under the related area of care, the evaluator merely has to locate the area when the student begins that section and check each critical element as it is performed. Final check marks are placed at the conclusion of the PCS when all aspects of total care have been completed. Space is provided at the beginning of the form for identifying data for both the student and the patient; space also is provided for the pass/fail results of the PCS and a detailed description of any failure. A similar form is used for the simulated laboratory.

Another important form is the nursing-care plan to be used during the examination. This form may be identical to the one used in the clinical agency so long as it provides sufficient space for notations required by the examination; otherwise, a modified version can be developed by the faculty committee. Certain basic information is identified by the evaluator when patients are chosen and the specified number of required and selected areas of care are indicated. These aspects typically are on the front of the Kardex-like folded paper. The inside is reserved for the list of patient-care needs and related actions,

---

*Forms used in the CPNE are included in the monograph on nursing that is available through the Regents External Degree Office.

both to be outlined by the student during the planning phase of the PCS. The student also identifies priorities of patient care with related rationale. On the back page, space is provided for the evaluation phase to be completed after all other aspects of the PCS are completed. Here the student revises the nursing-care plan and identifies continuing patient-care needs, in keeping with the guidelines for evaluation described in the study guide.

A third essential form is used to communicate to the patient assignments to be used during the examination. This form lists the patients, the time period the patient will be cared for by the student, and any nursing care that will not be carried out by the student (i.e., that is expected to be performed by the staff). This form is completed by the evaluator the day before (or morning of) the examination and reviewed with the head nurse or team leader before it is posted. Specific communication with the staff is essential to ensure that the patient is not neglected and that all areas of care needed for the examination are left for the assigned student (unless otherwise specified).

These forms and any others to be used during the examination should be described and illustrated in the study guide to ensure that students know what is expected of them. They also are reviewed during the orientation period (as described in the next chapter). These forms are legal and permanent records and therefore must be consistently and appropriately completed by evaluators and signed by both students and evaluators, as indicated. The clinical associate is responsible for overseeing evaluators in this task, to be sure the records are complete and submitted after the examination. The importance of such records is obvious, but nonetheless evaluators seem to need assistance in remembering to complete each form thoroughly, objectively, and legibly.

SUMMARY

The above-described criteria help to identify some of the conditions related to the examination process. Some degree of control needs to be exerted for each of them in order to ensure objectivity, comparability, consistency, acceptability, flexibility, and systematized conditions. The description of each is brief but suggests the kind of consideration that needs to be given to the multiple variables that potentially can influence the outcome of the examination. As indicated earlier, if an objective clinical examination is to be administered, these conditions require as much careful deliberation as specifying the content to be tested.

THE PHYSICAL CONTEXT

An additional condition also needs clarification: the context within which the examination is administered. Just as the previously mentioned conditions create impact on the process and the outcome of the clinical assessment of students, variables related to testing environment (or context) also can exert a major influence on the examination. Whether the test takes place in a simulated or actual situation, the committee needs to consider the relationship of the context to the examination. Naturally, a comprehensive test given in the actual clinical-care units presents a more challenging environment, thus the discussion here will focus on considerations applicable there. (The reader can extrapolate from the criteria presented below those aspects suitable for the more limited or simulated examination.)

CRITERION 1

The clinical units to be used must have sufficient patients requiring the specified care. The entire examination effort can be frustrated unless enough patients are available to meet the criteria for selection. Consequently great care should be taken in deciding which hospital units to use. This seems obvious but the point is important enough to be made explicitly. Frequently when the units are used by other groups of nursing students, medical students, or others for clinical experience, it may be difficult to find enough patients who meet the criteria for selection. When more than one instructor is vying for the same patient the competition can result in frustration as well as frazzled relationships and inadequate experiences for all students involved. In order to protect the consistency, comparability, and objectivity of the examination, the committee responsible for designing and implementing it probably will have to consider these other groups and negotiate mutually compatible terms. The days of the week and/or times of day may be determined in part by such negotiation. Of course, these criteria pertain only to the scheduled examination times, but then they are essential. Clearly, fewer problems will be encountered if this contextual variable is considered before the examination is actually administered.

Another factor related to the availability of patients concerns their degree of illness and, consequently, the type of nursing care they require. Generally speaking, if patients are critically ill they need care from thoroughly competent practitioners, not anxious students taking a test. Assigning such patients for examination purposes (except in special circumstances) is unreasonable from the point of view of their physical and emotional well-being. It also is unreasonable from the student's perspective because of the unpredictable and serious nature of the patient's condition. This only introduces other potentially uncontrollable variables that contradict the intent of providing consistent, comparable, and objective opportunities for making judgments about the basic competence of students. Critically ill patients—or those on specialty units—are appropriate only if the examination is designed explicitly to test the students' abilities to function in such situations. However, the potential dangers, complexities, and legal problems should be realized from the outset.

CRITERION 2

Characteristics of the patient units must be conducive to an objective examination. In addition to the availability of the right kinds of patients, other variables in the context must be supportive of the examination process. Some of the characteristics that deserve consideration include the stability of the nursing staff, their support of the testing process itself, space, and the availability of necessary supplies and equipment. Units on which the nursing staff is constantly changing, or on which most nurses are inexperienced or new to the institution will present additional (but predictable) problems. The understanding, cooperation, and support of the entire nursing staff (from supervisor to aide levels) is essential if unnecessary problems are to be prevented. To a large extent this depends on the professional ability, personal security, and assignment stability of staff members. All patient units periodically have staff changes, but an unusually high turnover rate requires repeated orientations and constant supervision to ensure compliance with the predetermined conditions under which the examination is to be administered. The role of the nursing staff cannot be underestimated or taken for granted. To implement the examination process as designed, the nursing staff must understand the distinctions between clinical experiences and a clinical examination; new and inexperienced nurses may have more difficulty adjusting to the testing requirements. Evaluators and students inherently depend on cooperation from the staff, which requires that they be informed and willing to change some of their own routines to accommodate the essential aspects of the examination. The best context is one in which the staff is experienced and stable, and, following an orientation period, is cooperative and supportive of all aspects of the performance examination.

Other factors to consider in the context relate to the availability of essential supplies and equipment and the space in which care will be administered. Obviously, unless supplies and equipment are on hand or readily available, the examination can be frustrated. Because time is a key factor, it should not be wasted in writing requisitions or going to other units or departments to borrow needed supplies. The selection of units is in part dependent on this factor; however, in addition, once units are chosen, the evaluators and clinical associates can be held accountable for making sure that everything needed for care during the examination is on the unit prior to the beginning of the test. This protects the time for its intended purpose: examining the student's competence to administer nursing care in a selected area and under somewhat controlled conditions.

Furthermore, the space within which care will be administered has to be adequate for the student to function, as well as for the evaluator to observe continuously. Not all patient units provide the space and degree of privacy needed for the examination; therefore, when a choice exists, the committee should consider the influence of inadequate space on the examination process and outcomes. If the evaluator is forced to stand directly in view of the student and/or patient it will be more difficult to remain neutral and uninvolved. It also increases the student's anxiety.

Students assigned to patients in four-bed rooms crowded with suction, irrigations, dressing, or other equipment, will have greater difficulty meeting the critical elements than those students caring for patients in semiprivate and less cluttered rooms. Under the best of circumstances it is challenging to be organized and neat, to apply principles of asepsis, and to meet other critical elements in an environment overflowing with "things" on every flat surface. The finality and anxiety associated with an examination greatly compounds the stress and the chance for failure. Unless response to extremely stressful situations is the focus of the examination, such frustrations should be eliminated or minimized to the extent possible. Assuming the space is adequate, the evaluator can be responsible for ensuring that linen and basic equipment are available in the patient's unit before the test begins. Dealing with the problem of the proverbial absence of items such as washcloths, bath blankets, sheets, and blood-pressure apparatus is not usually a critical element and therefore should be taken care of by the evaluator to free the student to perform behaviors actually being tested.

THE SIMULATED EXAMINATION

In general, most of the criteria described above regarding the conditions and context of administering a performance examination apply to simulated as well as to actual situations. Naturally, more control can be exercised in a laboratory and fewer problems are likely to occur. Whether the total examination or a part of it is simulated, the criteria should be discussed and decisions made regarding each one that is relevant to the test.

The role and responsibility of evaluators is the same except for those considerations related to patients and the clinical staff. Neutral observation without teaching or assisting is just as applicable, and implementation of the concepts of objectivity, comparability, consistency, flexibility, etc., also is equally relevant in a simulated test. Too, the randomized selection of performance areas to be tested, drawn from a sample of the potential universe, is just as essential. The total number of areas to be tested, the predetermined criteria for passing and failing, and the number of times students are allowed to try to reach 100 percent accuracy all require explicit statements in the examination guide to ensure a fair and appropriate assessment. Criteria related to space, supplies, and equipment are equally important also, because they potentially influence the student's behaviors and the outcome of the test.

Depending on the nature of the simulated test, writing a nursing-care plan and evaluating the care at the conclusion of the implementation phase may or may not be required. There also are probably fewer "gray" areas requiring consultation prior to making a final decision about the students' competence. What the student wears also may be irrelevant in a laboratory setting.

In a simulated examination administered in a nursing laboratory setting, one evaluator may be able to observe simultaneously more than one student. While it is desirable consistently to observe one student at a time, when the number of students is large and the time available for the test is limited it may be possible to arrange the environment so that one evaluator can adequately observe two or more students. If such an arrangement is made, consideration should be given to the possibility of "cross contamination" from one student to another because of the close proximity. It may be possible to provide screens or some barrier between the simulated situations to preclude direct observation or communication among students who are simultaneously taking the examination without obstructing the view of the evaluator. Once again, it is important to point out that these concerns may be more or less relevant depending on the specific content, the level and comprehensiveness of the examination, the test's placement in the program, and its purpose in relation to other assessment procedures being used.

SUMMARY

In summary, the conditions associated with the examination process and the context in which it is administered are as important as the content being tested. The examination guide, developed by the faculty committee to be used both by students and evaluators, should contain statements for each of the areas addressed in this chapter. Students, evaluators, clinical associates, nursing staff, and the total faculty all need to know exactly *what* is being tested, as well as *where, when* and *how much* is being tested, as well as *who* is responsible for each aspect of the process. All of these details—along with the list of areas of care, their definitions, and critical elements—need to be clearly, systematically, explicitly outlined in the examination guide. This guide, then, serves as the basis for the orientation of students, evaluators, staff, and others to ensure that all points related to content and process are equally and comprehensively covered. The validity of the outcomes depends on the careful development and implementation of all of these points.

SUMMARY OF CRITERIA

A. Conditions that Focus on Students

1. All potential clinical competencies, procedures, and conditions pertaining to the clinical performance examination are clearly and comprehensively outlined and explained in the examination study guide, which is given to students well in advance of the testing period.

2. The nature of the relationships students are expected to form with patients, evaluators, agency staff, and others in the setting is explicitly described in the study guide and reviewed during the orientation period.
3. The type of clothing students are expected to wear and any articles they are expected to bring with them are identified in the study guide.

B. Conditions that Focus on the Examination Process

1. All conditions related to the examination process are included in the examination study guide.
2. The time allowed for each portion or segment as well as for the entire examination is specified, along with any qualifications or exceptions.
3. Characteristics of the kinds of patients to be selected for, or to be excluded from, the examination are specifically and clearly listed in the study guide.
4. The number and kinds of areas of care and the potential combinations for a given PCS are predetermined.
5. Guidelines for assigning students to patients for each PCS are predetermined and specifically outlined in the study guide.
6. The role and responsibilities of the clinical associate are specified, along with all other aspects of the examination.
7. The role and responsibilities of clinical evaluators are specified and clearly outlined in the study guide.
8. Mechanisms to control evaluator bias are preestablished and made known to both students and evaluators.
9. The basis for declaring a pass or fail result is outlined in the study guide.
10. The consequences of failure and any immediate actions to be taken are outlined.
11. A mechanism whereby students may appeal a clinical failure is identified and outlined in the study guide.
12. The forms required by the performance examination are developed, described, and illustrated.

C. Conditions Related to Context

1. The clinical units to be used routinely must have a sufficient number of available patients who require the nursing care needed for the examination.
2. The characteristics of the unit must be conducive to the administration of a clinical preformance examination.

CHAPTER 7

The Active Transition: A Matter of Reorientation

The transition toward objective performance testing is an evolutionary process that is both exciting and difficult. The prospect of having a nonsubjective, equitable, and reliable method of assessing the clinical competence of students is a powerful incentive to accomplish the substantial work that is required. Such a challenge can inspire the creative and concerted efforts of the faculty, but effective leadership is essential if those efforts are to be sustained to a successful conclusion. Excitement is experienced with the completion of every aspect—like the sheer delight in finding an elusive piece in a difficult jigsaw puzzle. But the pleasure is culminated only when all of the pieces have been "found" and the picture is complete—better yet, when the final product is exhibited with pride. The feeling of success is a prime motivator, and thus it becomes an important factor in planning for the transition period. Here again, leadership plays a key role in the developmental process to ensure that the "little successes" outnumber all of the failures and frustrations along the way, and that sufficient enthusiasm about the project is generated and sustained to counterbalance the difficulties encountered.

Going through such an evolutionary change process requires a planned orientation for all of those actually or potentially involved, including faculty, students, and agency staff. It requires a deliberate "reprogramming" of philosophy and attitudes toward teaching, learning, testing, and clinical practice. Because of the nature of the test and the length of time required for the transition period (several months to one or more years), plans have to be made from the outset to deal with the administrative, academic, psychological, and procedural problems that inevitably will occur. Among the highest priorities is the selection of a leader and the committee who will be responsible for development and implementation of the performance test. Throughout this chapter a sampling of the kinds of difficulties likely to be encountered will be explored, along with some suggestions for dealing with them. But regardless of the kind of problems, the influence of the committee chairman (and/or other leaders) is a major factor that should not be underestimated. This discussion of possible difficulties with faculty members, students, and agency personnel during the transition period is intended to help the committee—and especially the chairman—to anticipate potential problems in order to take steps to prevent or minimize them.

The reorientation effort is deliberately planned to confront the participants with the distinctions between the familiar traditions of the past and the new approach. It is designed to help them win in the struggle to outgrow past practices in favor of procedures not yet personally tested. The total reorientation must take into account both the initial conflicts as well as the sustained period of stress associated with learning to adjust to multiple changes in expected behaviors and procedures. All groups involved (faculty, students, and agency staff) will be called on to reverse the "doing-what-comes-naturally" attitude, as a true clinical performance examination is anything but natural. In fact, it requires the deliberate negation of certain "natural instincts"—such as the instructor's teaching, helping, coaching, showing, and telling students in the clinical setting, and allowing personal preferences and biases to influence judgments made about students' performances. For students, it means accepting the full responsibility for learning and actual demonstrating achievement without the opportunity to manipulate individual arrangements.

Implementing a performance examination as described in this volume also is in direct conflict with the "we've-always-done-it-this-way" attitude. Once again, faculty, students, and staff must be confronted with the obvious—and the not so obvious—consequences of these changes. The phrase "we've always done . . ." has to be recycled into a new attitude of openness and objectivity to accommodate entirely different expectations for all concerned.

BENCHMARKS ON THE CHANGE CONTINUUM

The transition away from bias is difficult and does not occur automatically, which is exactly why a period of adjustment must be planned and executed. Words such as evolution, transition, process, change, and growth characterize the period in which the performance examination idea is converted into a reality that is fully implemented in the program. Input and cooperation are essential from the entire faculty (as well as others) under the leadership of the committee that is responsible for developing and implementing the examination. Defining the content and procedures of the examination is only one part of the challenge; orchestrating the conversion of faculty and students to using the test as designed is an entirely different matter. Underestimating the critical importance of either part could prove disastrous to achieving the overall goal. It is certain that each faculty group will respond in its own characteristic and individual manner; however, some general reference points along the continuum of change can be predicted. Anticipating the behaviors associated with these benchmarks can be quite helpful to those responsible for overseeing the transition.

The process of change is difficult and is influenced by the extent to which long-established habits must be modified. Some of the problems likely to be encountered can be anticipated. It might be helpful to envision a continuum of change, representing an undesignated period of time during which the performance examination idea is introduced, developed, tested, and fully implemented. The progression along that line probably will be uneven and disjointed, and if the point of full acceptance and implementation is to be reached, conscientious leadership will be required. Some faculty groups are totally ready to initiate a performance examination and they may not go through some of the following stages. However, it is quite likely that when the idea is first introduced some faculty members (particularly in very large schools) will be resistant for one of several reasons. Some comments may include the following: it's too difficult a task; we're already overextended; there's no money in the budget for it; we don't have enough time to work on it or enough time to implement it even if a performance test were available; the faculty is ill-prepared to undertake such a project; our facilities are too limited for such examination; we can't delete any of the class content, therefore we have no time for it; there's too little time for teaching as it is; we've just gone through a major curriculum change—please not again; we don't have lab facilities; students are already too busy now so how can we ask them to practice more in the lab. This resistance is benchmark number one.

However, if a sufficient core of the faculty is committed to the idea and continuously apply positive persuasion, it is likely that others will show increasing interest. Most of the above arguments can be dealt with on a logical basis and most do not pose insurmountable

Fig. 7.1. The first two steps in the transition.

obstacles, e.g., some form of performance examination can be developed in essentially every kind of setting with all types of students. As each faculty member joins the core of "true believers," a greater pool of problem-solving power is available for confronting the issues and impediments. Figure 7.1 illustrates these first two benchmarks on the change continuum: (1) introduction of the idea with initial resistance, and (2) the temptation to try it by an enlarging group of the faculty.

Once a sufficient number of the faculty is convinced that a performance examination is a good idea and is attainable, it may be difficult to hold back their enthusiasm. In fact, they may have a tendency to want to develop and implement it quickly. It is a natural inclination to want to implement the examination in the next semester, or to have it completed along with other curriculum changes that already are well underway. Premature introduction of parts of the performance test (Figure 7.2) can only lead to problems. This is benchmark number 3.

While zeal and enthusiasm are essential, they cannot be allowed to override the necessity for understanding the multiple facets of such a major change and the need for logical and systematic development of content, process, and the planned transition period. Moving ahead too quickly, attempting to implement an examination prematurely, excluding certain basic concepts, or ignoring the need for pilot-testing, etc., almost certainly will result in a superficial and inadequate examination. It also results in frustration and unnecessary failure. In many cases, this could put a long-term moratorium on trying again.

If students are subjected to a comprehensive (or even to a limited) performance examination without a thorough and extended period of

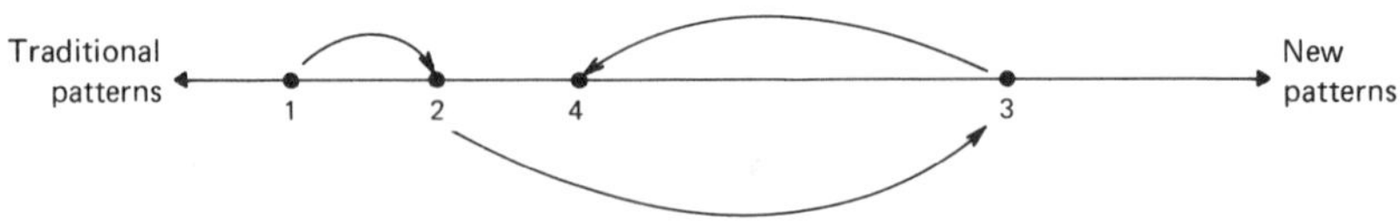

Fig. 7.2. Premature advancement and resulting setbacks.

planned transition, large numbers of them undoubtedly will fail, resulting in anger and frustration for all concerned. If the examination is introduced before all of the conditions of administration are explicitly specified, serious problems could occur because of ambiguity, inconsistency, and incomparability of testing episodes. If the staff members in the agency are inadequately prepared, patients could be neglected or the staff could become sufficiently upset to call a halt to examination procedures in their facility. Moving ahead before evaluators are adequately prepared could nullify all previous attempts at objectivity and comparability. These problems realistically can be expected if the examination is introduced prematurely by a faculty that is enthusiastic but ill-prepared. This is benchmark number 4.

Figure 7.2 illustrates the sporadic movement along the transition continuum (as described above). The setbacks resulting from the frustrations and failure of premature activities could cause the cancellation of the entire project. The natural instinct is to proclaim that "it doesn't work" and go back to former evaluation procedures, with everyone's being even more distressed than before.

ANTICIPATING AND PLANNING

This sequence need not occur, or certainly not to any extreme degree. Anticipation of such events and deliberately planning to prevent them is a function of the committee responsible for the project. The cooperation of the program administrator and the remaining faculty—who sometimes are inclined to push too hard without understanding the consequences—also are continually needed. However, the faculty that is truly committed to objective performance testing will not give up, but will learn from the growth process and will back up and start over again wherever they are along the continuum. Nonetheless, the committee and others involved will at that point have to contend with the discouragement associated with initial failure and the tendency to regress to previous assessment practices. Additional efforts will have to be made to rectify these problems along with instituting newly scheduled activities. In time, adaptations will be made in the schedule as well as aspects related to content, process, structure, and transition—indicated by benchmark number 5. This time, one hopes, sufficient planning and time will be allowed to maximize chances for success.

Ultimately, after completion of development and pilot-testing of the examinations, the final point on this change continuum is reached.

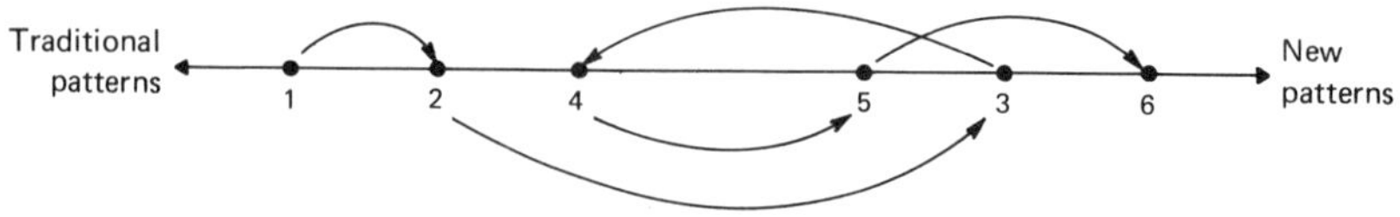

Fig. 7.3. Transition summary: the evolutionary process of change.

To continue this theoretical consideration of the change process, the majority of the faculty will then enthusiastically accept and are willing to implement the test; others may not be so enthusiastic, but will use it as mandated by the faculty. In time, as implementation problems are resolved and the entire examination is successful, all groups involved probably will come to embrace the philosophy and process, indicating that benchmark number 6 has been reached (Figure 7.3). Subsequently, of course, over a period of time the examination will be evaluated and revised accordingly.

As summarized in Figure 7.3, the entire transition period can be anticipated to include the following:

1. Initial resistance to the idea of objective performance examination: too many problems.
2. Temptation to try it: some development initiated (the turn-on).
3. Excessive zeal to implement too soon: content, process, and personnel not ready.
4. Discouragement and regression: frustration with problems and complexities.
5. Adaptation: development reinitiated with more deliberately planned long-term efforts (a time of learning).
6. Acceptance: enthusiastic support after successful development and pilot-testing to complete refinements.

The smoothness with which the faculty (and others) moves along the continuum depends upon the many variables that have been discussed earlier. Ideally, the changeover to objective performance testing moves gradually and progressively along the line—indicating steady, evolutionary growth. Key factors that influence this progress include the preparation, ability, and determination of faculty; the availability of resources; and the leadership exercised in planning and developing the entire project. Another factor is the degree to which the faculty committee anticipates potential problems and takes steps to prevent or minimize them all along the way.

It might be helpful with the above perspective in mind to review the major tasks associated with the planning, development, and implementation phases and to pinpoint some of the transitional problems associated with each one. This is not meant to be an exhaustive list, but rather suggestive of the kinds of concerns and issues that can be anticipated by many faculty groups during this period of change. Some will be more pertinent for one group, while others will relate more directly to another group (depending on the type of program and students, geographic setting, purpose of examination, etc.).

While it is possible for a faculty to proceed smoothly and systematically through the process of changing to a more objective and comprehensive system of clinical performance examinations, they also may encounter some problems. Basing conclusions on considerable experience in developing performance examinations, the following section explores some of the potential problems that can be anticipated and thereby avoided. Not all of them apply to every group, but wisdom dictates that they at least be considered.

FACULTY TRANSITION PROBLEMS DURING EACH PHASE

PHASE I

Phase I is the initial assessment and planning period. Typically this phase begins when the nurse administrator, a small group of the faculty, or even one person becomes convinced that objective performance examinations are not only possible but also desirable in the particular situation. The nurse administrator and/or total faculty are involved at this point with four primary tasks to be completed during this period.

1. Hold preliminary discussions to assess possibilities and make the decision to undertake such a project.
2. Make basic decisions regarding the nature, placement, and gross content of the examination.
3. Draft tentative guidelines to assist a committee in developing the test.
4. Appoint a subcommittee to develop the performance examination.

Preliminary discussions cover such considerations as budget, time, resources, existing priorities, and the degree of interest expressed by the overall faculty. Some discussions must obviously take place between the administrators of the nursing program and the parent institution. Without support from administrative authorities, difficulties will be compounded or become even insurmountable. The same result can be expected when a major discrepancy exists between the faculty and nurse administrator, or among subgroups of the faculty.

Some of the problems that might be expected during this phase emanate from a misunderstanding of the fundamental distinctions between clinical evaluation and clinical examination, and a conflict of philosophies among faculty members. Such problems are most likely to occur when the faculty—and particularly the examination committee—do not take the time to become thoroughly familiar with the literature and the basic concepts that must be applied, and/or they do not think through the changes that will be demanded by the implementation of objective performance examinations.

One of the most fundamental of these changes, of course, relates to the teaching–learning process and its relationship to objective assessment. Unless the faculty understand the differentiation from the outset the entire project could be undermined. Both students and faculty need to acknowledge afresh that learning and becoming clinically competent are the responsibilities of the student and that specific and focused practice time in the laboratory, as well as in the clinical setting are essential in preparing to meet the standard of performance established by the faculty. The separation of teaching and learning time from testing time is essential and influences to some extent the entire program. Changing teaching–learning attitudes and practice that already have settled into comfortable modes of expression can generate considerable resistance. The background, preparation, experience, and philosophy of individuals will determine the extent to which these kinds of problems will interfere with the project. In fact, it probably would be more helpful in the long run to encourage such conflicts to emerge so that participants can deal with them objectively rather than to allow them slowly to gather the momentum of discontent over time and erupt as serious problems later on.

Other kinds of problems that might occur reflect the type, placement and comprehensiveness of the performance examination being suggested. Different subsets of problems will emerge depending on whether the examination is to be administered in the clinical setting at the end of one year, or is one required at the conclusion of the entire nursing program. Problems also vary depending on who (and how many) suggests the idea, and how the plan is likely to influence other assessment procedures and the workload of available faculty. In instances in which unions exist and are active, these initial problems could be substantial and will require careful consideration. The introduction of a comprehensive performance examination could require changes in the number of work hours during the testing periods, as well as in the practice laboratory setting.

The problems of budget, time, workload, committee assignment, reallocation of some responsibilities, scheduling of priorities, etc., are obvious and usually can be discussed openly and resolved without too much difficulty. However, keen insight and concerted efforts are required by the leadership (individual faculty members, nurse administrator committee, and chairperson) to anticipate and prevent the kinds of philosophic problems suggested above. Because past practices and one's philosophy and opinions about teaching–learning and assessment are so ingrained in the personality and *modus operandi* of each faculty member, suggesting major changes in them is quite likely to engender disagreement and insecurity. Anticipating the likelihood of such problems and dealing with them early is to take a major step forward. (The nature and extent of such problems will, as stated earlier, vary depending on the characteristics of the faculty and the circumstances.)

Timing

Some faculties have arranged their curriculum into modules and therefore are faced with multiple discrete segments of nursing theory and practice to be presented and evaluated. It is quite natural to question the appropriate timing for the administration of performance tests. Some groups might feel strongly that a performance test should be required at the end of each module; in fact, some might even prefer that students master the content of the module and be tested on their performance in the laboratory before rendering that care to actual patients. This would entail scheduling theory and performance tests every one, two, or three weeks (depending on the length of the module), which would require considerable personnel time and effort, and of necessity reduce actual learning and practice time.

While administering performance tests this frequently may be desirable under some circumstances, the practice has serious disadvantages in addition to the time, resources, and expense already mentioned. Perhaps most importantly, it would reduce the overall time for learning by forcing all students to practice the related skills during the time allotted for the particular module. Many students learn a given skill better if it is practiced in relation to one or more associated others. Everything may not come together so systematically for some as for others, but given time, students can master all essential skills. For most students, clinical competence is achieved through cumulative and integrative efforts; therefore learners require an extended period of time and experience with the multiple aspects of clinical performance before they are able to master one or more particular parts. If they are tested prematurely a considerable degree of failure and mutual frustration can be expected for students and faculty. Thus the faculty should carefully think through the rationale and consequences of performance testing at the end of each module (or unit).

It may be much more sensible to conduct performance tests subsequent to the completion of a large cluster of modules. Simulated laboratory performance testing also would be preferable to repeated tests in the clinical setting simply because the latter is fraught with complexities and requires much more time, planning, scheduling, and budgeting. Applying these two suggestions, learning time would be increased, faculty time would be used more efficiently, and chances of success probably would be enhanced.

Simulations

If the faculty decides that simulated performance tests are desirable at the end of each module or course, perhaps some suggestions about process would be helpful. For example, it is possible in many situations—especially when large numbers of students are involved and few faculty are available for the laboratory practice sessions—to have students responsible for evaluating each other on a scheduled and generally supervised basis. During the practice sessions, those evaluating would be responsible for seeing that all aspects of the test are implemented as outlined. Students, therefore, would have actual practice time as well as vicarious learning from watching a classmate. This would give students valuable experience with both roles, which probably would be helpful to them at the present as well as in the future, especially in preparation for a final clinical examination.

All students would be held accountable for their behavior in these learning sessions and when necessary incentives could be developed to ensure that the practice and testing sessions in the laboratory were productive. When incompetence related to a previously "learned" aspect of nursing care is revealed, students could be required to return for mandatory retesting under the observation of a designated faculty or staff member. This approach might be quite functional in reducing the number of hours required for actual testing and one-to-one evaluation while still accomplishing the goals of promoting practice sessions and increased clinical competence of students. This approach or a modified version with more periodic faculty evaluation could be used throughout the program, until the time for the comprehensive clinical performance required of all students prior to completion of the educational program. At this time each student would be tested by an evaluator in the actual clinical setting, as specified by the examination study guide.

Anecdotal Notes

The problem of what to do about anecdotal notes is a very real one. Basically, such notes still can be used as a basis for providing feedback to students for their continued learning. In this way they serve as a teaching–learning tool and are not necessarily used in determining the students' clinical grades. A simulated performance test could be used at the conclusion of the course as the basis for the clinical portion of the grade in combination with other methods of evaluating achievement of the course objectives. It might also be useful to use anecdotal notes to comment on the appropriate critical elements also found in the performance test to be administered later in the program.

It is important, however, that faculty do not "throw out the baby with the bathwater" by totally abandoning the use of anecdotal notes. As stated, they can be a valuable tool in the students' learning program if they are understood and applied with that in mind. Students need the insight and perspective of a skillful and experienced role model. The notes, in actuality, should be used to guide the students' understanding of their own performance as observed by others. Some of this function can be satisfied by fellow students; other aspects can come only through the several possibilities suggested above. (Different faculties undoubtedly will determine the approach best suited to their particular circumstances.)

This first phase in the faculty transition corresponds to the first two steps on the change continuum described earlier. There might be resistance to the idea by some and acceptance by others. The decision to implement objective performance testing must be balanced by persuading all of those directly involved not only that it is possible but that it also requires a number of other changes, particularly in the attitudes and behavior of the faculty and students.

PHASE II

After preliminary assessment, planning and decisions have been made and a representative committee is appointed; phase II of the examination development begins. This is the period of initial development during which more definitive aspects of the examination are outlined. Fundamental decisions are still being made, thus considerable dialogue is necessary between the committee and the total faculty. The overall primary objective of this phase is developing a detailed outline of the content and conditions of the examination. More specifically, the following subobjectives have to be accomplished.

1. Determine the time frame and meeting schedule that fits the needs of the project and the faculty's other responsibilities.
2. Identify and define preliminary list of areas of care (content to be tested).
3. Relate examination content to program/course objectives, realistically approaching placement, comprehensiveness, and level of expectations.
4. Write first draft of critical elements for areas of care, or draft an adaptation from another existing performance examination (such as those developed by the New York Regents External Degree or other programs).
5. Identify conditions under which the test will be administered (i.e., where, when, who, criteria for passing/failing, etc.).
6. Facilitate exchange of ideas and exam development by involving faculty and students.
7. Conduct preliminary minipilot-tests as each aspect is developed.
8. Obtain consultation from testing experts and/or those experienced in performance testing.

During this phase responsibilities shift from the nurse administrator and total faculty to the examination subcommittee. However, one essential strategy in the transition period is to schedule regular sessions with the total faculty group in order to discuss progress and to seek clarification and cooperation from them as each aspect is developed. In programs that have a small faculty (fewer than eight to ten members) it is quite possible that the entire group would work on developing the performance examination. Some aspects of it, however, might be assigned to a subgroup for initial development. Depending on the nature of the examination, this phase could take from a few weeks to a year. Consequently, the faculty as a whole needs to be kept informed, to promote both their interest and their continued input over a prolonged period of time.

If the committee tends to work in isolation and does not repeatedly share the ups and downs of progress, or does not engage others in the preliminary trials of various aspects of the test-in-development, the reorientation efforts later on will be compounded and the potential assistance from colleagues will be lost as well. During these discussion sessions (with the total faculty or subgroups of the faculty), another reprogramming strategy can be implemented by getting the faculty to verbalize their reactions, fears, concerns, and other feelings honestly to prevent them from building up to a point where serious setbacks might occur. Involving as many faculty members as possible all along the way helps to increase their understanding and to defuse unnecessary anxieties; it also proportionately increases the creative input for solving the inevitable problems associated with the project.

Support System

During this phase of the transition period, committee members probably will vacillate between enthusiasm about progress being made and feelings of anxiety and uncertainty about what is expected of them. Unless the nurse administrator (chairman, director, dean) and remaining faculty members develop a support system to assist where necessary, the undercurrent of stress could build up (consciously or unconsciously) and express itself in disruptive ways. Committee members might begin to find other priorities and to make excuses for not attending the scheduled meetings or for not doing their assigned homework. They also might become discouraged and want to give up the project or greatly minimize it, especially when those not directly involved criticize or do not follow through with needed psychological and procedural support (e.g., assuming increased responsibility for faculty duties to relieve the committee for their added workload, etc.). As pointed out in an earlier chapter, the composition of the committee could be the source of major problems unless this possibility is anticipated and steps are taken to prevent it. Clinical emphasis, academic preparation, experience, understanding of the project, and personality factors are major variables to consider. Once again, leadership in the committee is extremely important in meeting the scheduled objectives in resolving problems related to content and procedures and in assuring the implementation of the fundamental concepts.

During this phase (and the next one) the committee could progress steadily and productively or respond in any one of three problematic patterns: (1) get bogged down with excessive minutia; (2) give up as too difficult; or (3) move ahead prematurely. Becoming lost in details and caught up in developing "the perfect test" is a very real possibility—especially when a comprehensive performance examination is being developed. It is very easy for a group of nurse educators, sitting around a conference table, to become unrealistic, excessively idealistic, and inordinately preoccupied with details. It is essential for the group leader to help the committee to keep the key concepts, purpose, and goals clearly in focus. The natural tendency will be for the group to regress to writing a procedure manual, to want to test everything, to include theory as well as performance, and to spend excessive amounts of time debating particular behaviors, a description, or even a single word. Precision of wording is important but it is not easy to achieve consensus on which words to use. If these kinds of problems are allowed to dominate the meetings, the entire project could get bogged down, or the committee could develop such negative attitudes that progress is retarded or even stopped altogether. The group leader has the difficult but challenging role of negotiating disputes, stalemates, and discrepancies.

Maintaining Patience

Another response equally as likely, and as problematic, is that the committee could give up the whole idea once they become aware of the difficulties to be resolved, the time required, and the long-term requirements of the project. After making some initial progress, the group may tend to forget the evolutionary nature of developing and implementing a performance examination. The first (and subsequent) drafts of critical elements and procedures take time; they usually are far from perfect, and are full of inconsistencies.

Furthermore, when these first attempts are shared with colleagues they are often met with the kind of criticism that is well-intentioned but should be reserved for the final product. Unwarranted criticism and misunderstanding, or taking the draft out of context, can be disconcerting to those who have worked diligently on it. Again, the quality of leadership is important in keeping these situations and responses in perspective. (Using or modifying already-developed instruments obviously has major advantages.)

Another response by the committee could be moving ahead too quickly, prematurely attempting to implement aspects of the examination before content and/or procedures and fully developed and tested out. (This corresponds to steps 3 and 4 on the transition continuum as previously described.)

Unfortunately one of the potential results could be the return of the negative conviction that "it just doesn't work." True. If the examination is improperly developed, ambiguously worded, and prematurely introduced without pilot-testing, it probably will not work—and it should not work. If the resulting problems are serious, or the initial commitment was weak to begin with, this could cause the termination of the project. However, this danger could be prevented by paying more careful attention to the steps in the developmental process, integration of the basic concepts, and a deliberate and methodical attention to the kinds of details suggested here. All too often, ample attention to these seemingly unimportant matters influences the success of the entire project.

PHASE III

Phase III is the period of evolutionary development, in which successive drafts of all documents are written, tested-out, and revised. As with all other phases it is essential that leadership be exercised to keep the group on target in both content and schedule and to be alert to certain predictable problems. As this stage is a continuation of phase II, all of those concerns are still applicable—some even more so during this time of rewriting and preliminary trials. The following objectives relate to some of the major objectives for this specific period.

1. Write successively improved drafts of entire instrument, including content and procedures, until an acceptable total version is ready for preliminary pilot-testing.
2. Write successively improved drafts of the examination study guide, evaluators' manual, and other essential forms.
3. Obtain frequent and periodic input from faculty members not on the examination committee, to obtain their assistance in revisions and to lay groundwork for later implementation.
4. Conduct minipilot-tests of each aspect of the examination as it is completed, upon which results revisions are based.
5. Initiate orientation of students and agency staff as a foundation for the full-implementation phase.

This phase corresponds to the segment on the continuum between numbers 4 and 5 and represents a period of steady and progressive development and adjustments. By the time the committee is well into phase III, the likelihood of giving up becomes more remote. Too much already will have been invested. One of the most obvious kinds of problems, however, is the tendency either to get lost in the plethora of detail or to begin to accept language that is imprecise and ambiguous. Constant vigilance has to be maintained against the intrusion of value-laden words or subjective behaviors that are not observable or that are inappropriate for the particular examination being developed.

It is not uncommon that the conference-room atmosphere fosters some expectations that are unrealistic—e.g., use of erudite words that sound good but may have little actual relevance for an objective performance examination. When the committee becomes tired of rewriting the same material or simply wants to be finished with the job, they are less apt to remember the criteria for writing critical elements or to be concerned with all of the nuances associated with the basic concepts. The role of the group leader, again, is crucial. As with any long-term project (e.g., writing a book or conducting a lengthy research project), some individuals become discouraged with the time required; others are so immersed in the subparts they lose sight of the total entity and its central purpose; still others want to conclude the work and are content to implement the project as soon as most parts look O.K.

Some of these concerns were discussed under phase II; others are reasonably clear and need little elaboration. The key point to be made is that these and similar problems are typical and can be anticipated and confronted before they blossom into major difficulties. The committee needs to be aware of these potential reactions and their significance; the leader has the job of moving the project ahead toward a successful conclusion while at the same time being sensitive to the behavioral responses of the group (and individuals). Frequent interactions with students, other faculty members, and practitioners in the service setting also are helpful in keeping all of the multiple aspects in perspective. These people are a valuable sounding board, particularly during phase III when the conference-room ideas have to be modified to fit within the context of the real world of the clinical context.

PHASE IV

After a final total version of the examination is developed—including all aspects related to content, structure, and procedures—phase IV begins. At this point most of the initial creative and developmental work is finished, leaving the overall objectives of testing, orientation, and precise final adjustments to be made. Specifically the following objectives need to be systematically achieved during this final phase.

1. Conduct the final pilot tests to identify problems with any aspect of the content, the process, location, scheduling, forms, etc.
2. Refine the examination based on the prepilot-test.
3. Complete the examination study guide, evaluator manual, and other forms required (for assignments, nursing-care plans, recording of critical elements, etc.).
4. Orient all faculty, students, and staff to all aspects of the examination in its final form, building on previously preliminary discussions.
5. Orient faculty who will serve as evaluators and clinical associates to their unique roles.
6. Conduct final pilot-test and validation study, implementing every aspect of the examination exactly as developed (to the extent possible); make minor revisions as necessary.
7. Establish agreement with clinical agencies for special considerations required for testing periods (this may or may not require a formal contract, but conditions should be clearly outlined and understood by all parties involved).
8. Administer to first group of students for actual grading purposes.
9. Reassess and adjust any aspect of content, process, or structure based on real testing experience, as well as feedback from students, evaluators, staff, etc.; modify study guide and/or other documents as necessary.
10. Take a well-deserved break (the first final version is finished), at least for awhile; other modifications may be required after several actual administrations.

This phase corresponds to the fifth and sixth interspace on the change continuum and relates to completion, full acceptance, and implementation. Pilot-testing and final evaluation of the project involve special procedures and considerations and thus will be discussed at length in a subsequent chapter. Basically, phase IV focuses on completing necessary refinements, orienting everyone involved, and actually administering the test. However, several problems are certain to emerge during this period, if they haven't done so already. Staying alert for these potential problems and recognizing the symptoms will provide a head start for resolving them.

The innate struggle to achieve perfection of course, did not disappear during the development of the performance examination; it now persists with a new focus. Consequently the examination committee members may be reluctant actually to declare that the test is "finished." Consciously or unconsciously, they may perpetually keep looking for various facets, wording, nuances, areas, etc., that should be revised. Once the idea of writing evolutionary drafts of the material really takes hold, some members may find it difficult to call a halt to the process of refinement. This can be likened to the "developmental do-loop" discussed early in the book, i.e., the writing—trying—refining—writing—trying—refining, etc., complex. This searching for perfection can be carried to extremes and can delay the actual implementation of the examination. Much will be learned from the first actual administration. A balance has to be achieved between moving ahead before the test and persons involved are ready, and resisting implementation because unanticipated problems might emerge.

In actuality, this process may be symptomatic of the "avoidance phenomenon," reflecting to some degree the committee's resistance to putting their work on the line. Rather than concern with aspects of the test, such behavior could be an indication of anxiety regarding whether or not the test really works, and whether or not it will be well received by colleagues. The fear of failure may be conscious or unconscious, and may or may not be well-founded; nonetheless, it is real and must be recognized and resolved in as logical a manner as possible. The kind of support system and feedback from the faculty and administration during the developmental period have a significant influence on the emergence and extent of anxiety at the time of completion and implementation. Positive reinforcement and cooperative assistance throughout the months of committee work and prepilot-testing more than likely will help to minimize anxiety during this last phase.

Finishing

The clinical performance examination developed by the Regents External Degree exemplifies a maximum comprehensive approach to objective clinical testing. The faculty subcommittee was extremely careful to ensure that the examination was comprehensive and that all aspects were meticulously worded and based on data obtained from several pilot-tests. The committee worked for nearly four years on the CPNE and was not satisfied that the test was actually ready until the eighteenth draft and several pilot-tests were completed. Even then some members kept finding items that "needed revision"; but finally a moratorium on modifications was declared until after actual administration to the first group of 50 candidates was completed. To be sure, the stakes were high and the potential problems awesome; thus the level of anxiety also was appropriately high. However, the time finally came when avoidance had to be confronted and the examination administered.

The imperative for success was great enough to require repeated adjustments and pilot-testings. However, some modifications were made after two to three months and, again, three years later.

Other faculty groups, similarly, must distinguish between the time the test is actually ready and when they are simply avoiding the reality of administering it. How much pretesting and refinement is enough is a difficult question without a standard answer.

Another potential problem is the "clinging phenomenon." The symptomatic behavior here is difficulty in relinquishing some aspects of the test even though pilot-testing and experience prove it to be unnecessary, nonfunctional, or ill-conceived. This is another reminder that just because an idea, approach, or word had its birth in the conference room of good intentions is no guarantee that it will (or should) survive in the final version. Faculty members are constantly amazed at their colleagues who refuse to give up their favorite words or an aspect of content to which they are particularly attached. Unfortunately, this is not a unique phenomenon; it is a common characteristic of most involved (and even uninvolved) faculty members.

Clinging to favorite words or approaches occurs throughout the developmental phase; it also arises subsequent to pilot-testing when the need to revise the scope, complexity, or specific aspects of the examination become obvious. Originally the committee may have been thoroughly convinced that students should be expected to engage in 10 areas of care in each PCS. However, pilot-testing might reveal that: (1) it is difficult to find enough patients who require ten areas of care during the days or hours of the testing period; (2) if such patients are found, they are too ill to be subjected to students during an examination; (3) it takes much longer than three hours to administer such care; and (4) the level of expertise is far beyond the beginning practitioner's ability. Logically, the committee should revise the requirements to a more realistic and functional number of areas of care; but they may feel instead that any change that reduces demands on students is downgrading or "watering down" the test. They resist, argue, debate, and rationalize rather than recognize that their original perspective was more colored by conference-room theorizing and wishful thinking than by functional realism.

It is more difficult for some than for others to give up their "beloved" plan or idea, but the kinds of modifications suggested above are essential. Pilot-testing is imperative to identify and work out such problems, but the committee (and/or total faculty) has to be willing to use the resulting data without feeling unnecessarily anxious or frustrated when changes are clearly indicated. Clinging to original and/or refined aspects of the test simply because someone thought of them, worded them, and got them accepted by the committee is non-productive behavior and potentially could threaten the positive outcome of the project. One must constantly watch for clinging behavior, obtain necessary factual data, and use it persuasively for the good of the test and its purpose.

Reactions to Criticism

A third type of behavioral response that occurs during phase IV (as well as throughout the project) might be called the "overprotection phenomenon." It is characterized by degree of negative reaction and sensitivity to the criticisms made about the examination and, consequently, about the caliber of the work being done by the committee. Those who have created, nurtured, tested, and refined the examination (in all of its complex dimensions) may feel anger or offense when their colleagues make negative remarks, suggest substantial or fundamental changes, or make comments that reveal a startling lack of comprehension of obvious (or subtle) points. This may be equally true when the criticism is constructive and well-intentioned or when the comments actually are meant to be denigrating or hostile. The feelings of the recipient may be the same: some degree of psychological trauma.

Feeling sensitive to the remarks of others is natural, given the circumstances of this type of project. The very fact that the examination has been developed might arouse feelings of guilt by those who thought they should have done it years ago.

Furthermore, once the entire test is finished and worded as objectively and clearly as possible it looks quite simple and logical. It then becomes natural to think: "Why didn't we do this before?" or "What's so difficult about that?" (Experience and hindsight are invaluable to understanding and to the wheels of progress.) These kinds of feelings generate comments that might seem to undermine the committee's achievements and minimize the weeks and months of their steadfast efforts.

Sharing each aspect of the test as it is developed—using uninvolved faculty members and others as a sounding board and encouraging their active participation and feedback—are positive ways to prevent excessive criticism and misunderstanding. The committee that tends to work in isolation and that reserves sharing the test with others until it is finished and "presentable" may be committing a tactical error. They probably will be subject to more criticism, misunderstanding, and negative reactions than if the regular sharing of problems, struggle, and progress were seen as an essential part of the reprogramming of the faculty.

Another problem likely to occur during this phase could be called the "detail-overload phenomenon." This typically emerges when the examination is being presented to a group of people who have heard little or nothing about it—as in orientation sessions with students, agency staff, or some faculty or administrative groups. The committee members responsible for describing the test—i.e., its specific content, approaches, process, structure, and conditions—may have a tendency to focus on multiple and diverse details without first of all summarizing the whole. The unending details could totally overshadow or obfuscate the major fundamental aspects of the test—the skeleton on which the details must hang. This is quite natural as those totally involved in the project over a period of time have grown in their understanding of it, have accepted it, and have moved on to a preoccupation with the specifics that make the test function to achieve its purpose.

It is difficult to step back and look at the whole, as newcomers inevitably must, and yet the ability to do so is fundamental to gaining acceptance of the examination and its usefulness in the particular situation. Those who take time to prepare and to present the examination succinctly but comprehensively probably will be more positively received. Questions and discussions about specifics will follow naturally or can be introduced appropriately. A positive orientation for students, agency staff, faculty, and administration is crucial to successful implementation; consequently, those responsible for this aspect of reorientating these groups are well advised to be aware of and to take steps to prevent the detail-overload complex.

OVERVIEW

The foregoing discussion suggests some of the kinds of problems faculty members can anticipate; they are likely to occur during one or more of the four major phases of developing and implementing the performance examination. A comprehensive and clinically oriented examination has been envisioned as a backdrop, but regardless of the kind of examination (its scope, placement, and specific nature), many of these problems probably will emerge to one degree or another. The more complex and extensive the test, the more likely the possibility of problems. The difficulties described above are merely suggestive; the particular configuration of problems will depend upon multiple complex factors that characterize the faculty and the circumstances. However, by being alert to these concerns, those individuals developing performance tests can take steps to prevent problems from occurring, or to minimize their potentially negative consequences.

THE TRANSITION FOR STUDENTS

Students need very special consideration during the transition period in which objective performance examinations are being developed and implemented. The first one or two groups of students to be evaluated this way are at a distinct disadvantage until the all-important grapevine system of communication is fully updated and once again functional. Currently, students pass on information about their experiences to those who chronologically follow them, thus perpetuating the traditions of survival in the present subjective system. The preferences of individual clinical instructors as well as their biases and pet-peeves have been passed down from one generation of students to another, along with instruction on how not to get caught, and if you do, how to get out of a difficult situation. Successful ways of manipulating instructors, keeping out of sight, convincing them that everything is going as planned, and priming patients to come to the rescue when needed, are some of the skills passed along. Some students also have used threats of legal action to gain a more positive standing; the absence of an objective system has made this a rather successful ploy in some circumstances.

In the absence of an objective and consistently administered performance examination these behaviors are commonly encountered and they form an important aspect of the students' underground system of communication. However, when objective tests of simulated or comprehensive clinical examinations are used, this customary and historical system of information sharing temporarily collapses. The rules are all new; the faculty's behavior is different; the expectations for performance are different; the faculty's response to pressure is not the same;

the chances of reversing a failure are much less likely; the excuse of not knowing what was expected is no longer applicable; the possibility of avoiding the instructor's scrutiny is nil; and the chances of successfully threatening legal action is markedly reduced.

However, it takes time for the reality of this new system to sink in and take hold. Students might be overheard saying things such as: "Who really believes all that dialogue about objective performance testing and being held accountable for actions? Haven't we heard all that before? This is probably another phase the faculty is going through and soon the symptoms will pass and they'll be back at their old routines again. Seeing is believing." They simply have not had past experience, actual or shared, to prepare them for current expectations, and, typically, until convinced otherwise they will follow a known pattern. However, this could be disastrous when the first real performance examination is administered and students are held fully accountable for the results. Only when it actually happens and large numbers fail, does the new reality begin to come alive for many students. Unless the faculty plans a thorough and comprehensive reorientation effort focused on the particular needs of students, the first testing experiences could be devastating and cast a dark shadow of suspicion on the applicability of the test and on the work of the committee to enhance objective evaluation.

SYSTEMATIC REORIENTATION

Therefore, regardless of the type of students the scope of the examination, and its placement in the education program, a comprehensive and systematic orientation for students needs to be planned and implemented well in advance of the actual administration of the performance examination. A gradual and progressive approach probably will be more effective than a single-session group conference. This is definitely a case when "once is not enough"; students need to hear repeatedly the detailed explanation of changes in expectations of them, and the basis upon which judgments will be made about their clinical competence. The orientation might be implemented over two or more semesters, and in some cases, aspects of the new approach should be incorporated throughout the entire program (whether that involves a few weeks, months, or two to four years).

The length and nature of the scheduled transition for students is dependent upon several factors, including the developmental process being used by the faculty and the number and the type(s) of performance examination(s) to be used for the entire program. For example, if the faculty wants to start the objective testing gradually by developing segments and trying them out on incoming students, a little at a time, the orientation begins there. In fact, that is one way of planning for the reprogramming: begin with a new group of students who have little experience with the "old system" and who can accommodate to the changes gradually, as the faculty develops and implements them. The first test probably will be administered in the nursing laboratory and will require documentation of simple skills, but at the same time will introduce the concepts of objective critical elements, one-to-one direct observation, and the expectation of 100 percent accuracy in performance.

In some other situations the faculty might decide it is preferable to begin with a comprehensive, end-of-program performance examination, in which case a very different type of orientation is necessary. This requires that the entire examination be completely developed, pilot-tested, and refined before it is administered; therefore, the first time students are directly exposed to the examination is when it is being pretested or administered to them for grading purposes. It seems fairly obvious that this approach will engender more anxiety among students (and faculty) and the response of some students may be that of disbelief and resulting poor preparation. If this approach is used, a series of meetings with students should be planned to ensure their understanding and internal integration of all aspects of the examination. Whenever possible, required laboratory sessions also should be scheduled to familiarize students thoroughly with both content and process. For the first several administrations, it might be advisable to make practice sessions in the laboratory mandatory, until the grapevine effectually conveys the message that, indeed, everything included in the study guide and reiterated orally by the faculty really is true.

Students, like faculty, have to be taught to change their perception of what clinical evaluation means. They have to learn the difference between the time for learning and the time for testing. They have to learn that an objective performance examination is just that, and a very different entity from evaluation for the purpose of guidance and improvement. They have to learn that critical elements must be performed with 100 percent accuracy, and that failure of just one of them might have serious consequences. They also have to learn to administer care (actual or simulated) under the ever-present watchful eyes of an evaluator who observes with a preestablished testing tool in hand, so that errors in recall and in interpretation rarely occur.

Adjustments

Perhaps most important of all, students (and faculty) will have to learn that they are fully accountable for their actions or inactions, once they have been thoroughly oriented to the expectations held for them. This is perhaps the most difficult adjustment, which therefore requires special attention for the first several groups of students. Once the examination guide is developed, approved for implementation, and administered, students can no longer dismiss responsibility for their actions. However, because of past practices among the faculty (e.g., subjectivity, inconsistency, uncomparability, helping and teaching, etc.), students need special assistance in making the transition to this more objective type of clinical assessment. In many cases their past disbelief of faculty plans and programs has been well founded, and they need help in realizing the consequences of not taking this test seriously. This is the basis for the earlier suggestion that practice in the laboratory should be made mandatory for the first several groups, as a way of impressing students with the change. Thereafter, if students choose not to practice, not to learn the critical elements, and not to achieve the expected standard as described, they and they alone are held responsible. If they fail to achieve, for whatever reason, they are held accountable and have little or no recourse for modifications, since one of the new conditions is that the rules cannot be modified for individual students; rather, students must learn and adapt to the examination requirements. In some programs a few students may have to experience unnecessary failure before the message gets across that acceptable clinical competence is defined by the content and procedures of the performance examination, and that the test will be objectively and consistently administered. Preferably, the faculty will help students make the transition and avoid the disappointment and frustration of failure out of carelessness. The problem is serious enough to warrant a deliberately planned systematic reorientation of students as soon as the examination development is well under way.

One major thrust of the transition period is to help students realize why this approach is preferable and to point out the potential benefits to them in nursing practice as students and ultimately as graduates. They need to understand that this is a valuable learning device, for it establishes the baseline for expectations in their practice. They no longer have to guess what is required, or what is deemed appropriate and acceptable nursing behavior; a comprehensive performance examination serves as a guide to learning, even though expectations in the learning phase are enlarged and more idealistic. The purpose of the examination is to determine the extent to which students have learned to practice nursing as defined by the faculty. If properly constructed the examination is not a game, and definitely is not a "Mickey Mouse" experience to be treated lightly—by students or faculty. It becomes a primary vehicle for preparing students for actual practice in their chosen profession, by establishing clear-cut standards of expected behavior that must be achieved before leaving the educational program.

Central to this scheme is the necessity for students to know in advance, while the learning process is going on, exactly what is expected of them. Knowing the criteria for acceptable performance sets the stage for purposeful learning, which in turn is the keystone for influencing present and future practice. In addition to the planned reprogramming of the students, the faculty also should be aware of the informal, and sometimes unconscious, orientation they provide. Just as surely as students learn through the discussions and systematic review of the new expectations, they are influenced by the individual and collective responses of the faculty themselves. Internal disagreements and lack of compliance with any aspect of the adopted examination protocol as potentially serious consequences for students and their performance. Sometimes disagreement or noncompliance results from simple lack of interest or lack of knowledge about what's been going on, or the importance of their role in the successful implementation of the objective test. This is an important consideration because students are so directly influenced even though they are not aware of the conflict or confusion. It is another reason for total faculty involvement in the transition period.

FACULTY VIOLATIONS

There are several major categories into which the consequences of faculty violations fall; they are briefly described below. While it is possible that none of the following problems will occur, anticipating their likelihood could help to avoid their occurrence. Preventive considerations and a plan for prompt corrective action probably form the best defense.

1. When some faculty members reflect a superficial view of the newly approved examination procedures and this is transmitted directly or indirectly, students have very little basis for regarding the test seriously. They may tend to be confused because of the discrepancy between the formal message and the informal mes-

sage, and because they have little or no reliable grapevine data, the other mixed communications could be difficult to sort out. Again, this is particularly crucial for the first few groups of students who take the examinations. Students don't know which parts to take seriously and the result is a return to the guessing game of "What's expected today?" in clinical performance. It also means an eroding tendency back toward subjectivity and inconsistency, which is counterproductive for students and faculty.

2. Similarly, when students overhear disparaging remarks or observe denigrating behavior among instructors, their inclination is to copy it. This leads to unnecessarily negative attitudes about the examination even though students have no choice about taking it. Such circumstances can only add more pressure on students' already high level of stress, which could have damaging consequences on their performance (and, indeed, on their success in the program). Faculty members need to be reminded that negativism is not in the best interest of students or the program.

   Once the examination has been fully developed and approved, faculty members have an obligation to comply for the sake of students (if for no other reason).
3. Another consequence of faculty infractions and/or insufficient student orientation is that students feel like subjects in an experiment, except that their careers are potentially at stake. They may feel that unfair advantage is being gained at their expense.
4. A fourth potential problem is the emergence of hostility associated with failure, especially when students feel they were poorly prepared for the reality they experienced. This is a possible source of legal suits and certainly grounds for long-standing feelings of anger at the faculty, the program, and even at the profession itself. Frustrations are an inevitable result of a lack of understanding of expections.

These kinds of problems actually have been experienced by students in more than one nursing program that made the transition from subjective evaluation to objective clinical examination. Students were oriented by the faculty, according to the perception of the faculty; the students had another view, which became clear only after the first administration of the examination. Several students failed—some because they did not prepare sufficiently, some because they did not understand the conditions (even though they had participated in orientation conferences), and some because of faculty deviations from established procedures. The students felt caught in the first wave of uncertainty as the faculty implemented a well-conceived and comprehensively developed examination. Fortunately the schools were able to find ways to help students, as the apparent problem was inadequate reorientation even though considerable effort was exerted to avoid the problems. It simply is difficult for students to accept changes of such magnitude unless these and other potential problems are anticipated and a plan is designed to prevent or minimize them. It probably is impossible to avoid all problems but a carefully planned transition for students is among the major considerations in reducing serious difficulties.

TIMING AND EXTENT OF ORIENTATION

As previously suggested, the timing and extent of the orientation depends on the nature of the performance testing procedures adopted. In a four-semester basic program (associate or bachelor's degree) in which both simulated and comprehensive examinations are planned, the following basic outline is suggestive of the transition agenda for students. The principle is gradually and progressively to introduce objective performance testing throughout the program, holding students accountable for increasing level and scope of practice.

> First Semester:
> Introduce some aspects of simulated objective performance testing at the end of the term, using critical elements and prescribed conditions, and incorporating as many of the key concepts as possible, mandate practice sessions with fellow students as "objective observers" and hold students accountable for their actions. Emphasize the difference between learning time and testing time; hold conference sessions to review written materials related to the examination. Involve students in the development process.
>
> Second Semester:
> Add other areas of care to simulated laboratory examination and reinforce accountability for all critical elements and specified conditions. Possibly add some limited aspect of the examination in the clinical setting. All the while the faculty are evolving better testing procedures and materials, preparing evaluators and orienting agency staff. Distinctions are made between simulated and clinical testing. Continue to involve students in the developmental process.
>
> Third–Fourth Semester:
> Depending on the curriculum arrangement and the preference of the faculty, a comprehensive clinical performance examination can be implemented. This might be the only such examination for associate students but one in a series for bachelor students. For instance, in addition to the hospital oriented examination, the BSN students also might be tested objectively on other dimensions of practice such as leadership, client teaching, clinical decision making, collaboration, health assessment, etc. A complete study guide should be given to

students at least one semester before the examination is to be administered to ensure that they have 3–4 months to prepare. In many cases it may be desirable, after all materials are developed, to make them available even earlier. Be sure several conference discussions are held—and perhaps even a written test given—to assure that students understand *all* aspects of the examination sufficiently in advance to correct their deficiencies if necessary. Practice sessions in both laboratory and clinical setting should be encouraged and assistance made available. Students still could work in pairs, with one demonstrating and the other playing the role of objective observer. This is an important part of student learning, and good preparation for actual practice roles, especially for the BSN student.

Initiating these and similar procedures helps students to learn that direct observation is not just for the inadequate or weak student but for everyone. If done properly, it also should teach them that neutral observations can be made and that they play an important part in the role of assessment. whether for students, other coworkers, or patients. It should help take the guilt out of finding errors in their own practice or in that of others.

THE TRANSITION FOR AGENCY STAFF

When a performance examination is to be administered in a clinical setting, a transition orientation also must be arranged for staff members of the agency. It is essential that it include all individuals who are likely to be providing nursing care during times when the examinations are being given, in addition to the supervisors, in-service education staff, the director of nursing services, and hospital administrator (to a certain extent). For purposes of discussion here, it is assumed that the clinical examination (limited or comprehensive) will be administered in one or more agencies already being used for clinical instruction. It is further assumed that some type of formal (contractual) arrangement already exists and that it can be modified, if necessary, to accommodate the changes associated with the examination.

Once the decision is made and the initial phase of development has been completed, it probably would be helpful to begin tentative discussions with authorities in the clinical agencies that potentially may be used. The first discussion might be with the unit staff or with the director of nursing services; in either case the intent is to share information about the purpose and nature of the clinical examination and the plans for its development and implementation by the program. Gaining early cooperation from the clinical staff sets the stage for subsequent detailed orientations. The director and other members of the staff may contribute some good ideas that could be quite helpful even in the early period of development.

After the completion of the first draft of content (but prior to the first prepilot-test), orientation sessions should be arranged with those staff members most likely to be directly affected, i.e., supervisors, in-service personnel, and head nurses and team leaders on units likely to be used. These sessions have a twofold purpose: (1) to inform the staff about the introduction and use of an objective performance examination and (2) to gain feedback from them which might be useful in completing the project. The importance of these staff-orientation sessions cannot be overemphasized; they establish a frame of reference for subsequent detailed sessions required for pilot-testing and ultimately for actual administration of the examination.

It is important that the early sessions not get bogged down in too many specifics, as many of the details undoubtedly will change during the redrafting and refinement periods. Most helpful at this stage is a discussion that includes the following kinds of topics: (1) the basic reasons for developing and using an objective performance examination; (2) distinctions between clinical evaluation and clinical examination; (3) distinctions between learning time and testing time; (4) changes in roles (for those in service and in education) during an objective examination, in contrast with roles during learning experiences; (5) potential changes in time and schedules during the examination periods; (6) gross description of the examination as it is being developed; and (7) contributions the staff can make to the project—now and later.

The staff probably will be most concerned about the influence the examination is likely to have on patient care, nursing-staff time and schedules, and the ways in which the test will modify their roles. Some of these questions may have to be answered later but in time the staff will need to know all details related to patients and scheduling. They can be told, of course, that patients will continue to receive well-supervised nursing care and that the best interests of patients will be protected. This will not change; in fact, it will be more assured during the one-to-one examination than at any other time.

ROLE MODIFICATIONS

Staff do need clearly to understand that this examination is just that—an examination, not another clinical experience, and as such their role will be modified accordingly during those periods. This means that they must understand the requirements of the examinations, the expectations for students, and the modified roles for all parties concerned. Instructors become objective evaluators; staff function within the protocols for objectivity and do not overtly help or hinder students; patients are not told of the "examination," but their agreement to have students provide their care is obtained as usual; physicians and others are informed as usual and are urged to cooperate with the efforts being provided to assess the students' clinical competence objectively. Failure of staff to cooperate in these and other prescribed ways could create some serious problems and cause frustration and scheduling problems for all concerned. Prior to actual implementation the staff should receive a detailed written study guide and participate in discussions regarding their specific responsibilities during the examination.

Some of the typical staff responses that cause problems can be grouped into four categories: (1) helping too much; (2) helping too little; (3) being too busy; and (4) being resentful of changes. Most head nurses, team leaders, and staff nurses are usually quite helpful to students, and except when too busy, they probably enjoy participating in the clinical instruction. However, during the examination this behavior has to be modified to satisfy the purpose for that occasion. Staff, therefore, need to understand that when they do certain things "to help" the student, that corresponds to their direct answering of questions for the students on a written test. Sometimes nurses get caught up in their own routines and "forget" about the students' assignments. However, when the staff nurse gives medications to be students' patients, those students are deprived of their scheduled examination and must start over again. When someone regulates the patients' IV, give their baths, and completes other procedures, this means the student cannot be tested on these competencies and the examination must be terminated and rescheduled. Once the staff understands the difference between clinical experience and examination and are fully informed of their role, they undoubtedly will cooperate. They do, however, need some repeated and gentle reminding of their new role prior to pilot-testing and the actual administrations.

On the other end of the problem spectrum, staff sometimes detach themselves too much and the patients' care could suffer as a result. This also results from a basic lack of understanding about the nature and requirements of the examination. For example, on their clinical learning days, students ordinarily are assigned to care for patients for an entire morning; however, during the examination they may be with the patient only two hours, and that period may not begin until 10:30. The staff can easily make the assumption that because students are on the unit that day they are with the assigned patients for the entire period. It is possible, therefore, that some patients might be neglected for two to three hours. Consequently, it is essential that this distinction in scheduling be clearly understood and that the specific hours for assignment of specific patients be orally reviewed with the staff as well as posted on the bulletin board.

Other problems that sometimes interfere with the conduct of the examination occur when the staff are excessively busy and are hard to find—to get or give report, to clarify particular aspects of the patients' care or nursing routines, or to obtain other forms of customary assistance during the examination. This slows the process and interferes with the already tight time schedule, especially when two or three students are being tested consecutively within a specified time period. Again, when the staff understands the importance of the timing as it relates to the students' examination they usually cooperate unless the situation is beyond their control.

Sometimes staff nurses (head nurses, team leaders) also express resentment of the interruptions from students and/or evaluators. They also may be resentful when students do not complete all care for the assigned patients—especially when the student fails and leaves the situation before completion. This is another difference between clinical experience and examination; the rationale for returning patients to the staff after failure has to be carefully explained, along with the reasons that the evaluator cannot be responsible for completing care. If students fail one or more critical elements in the care of the patient, they have failed in that situation and there is no reason to allow them to continue; they have already been judged as not competent in that situation.

Feelings of resentment about changes from the usual, comfortable circumstances are perfectly understandable; however, one of the purposes of the orientation for all members of the staff is to minimize this and other psychological and procedural problems. Clearly, all of the implied changes cannot be fully integrated in just one hearing, therefore several sessions may be scheduled over a given period. These are especially helpful just before major prepilot-testing episodes and again before the scheduling of actual examinations. Maintaining communications with key members of the staff and getting feedback from them is a positive way of promoting their understanding and obtaining ideas from them. Frequently these contributions help to minimize the educator-idealism and increase the functionability of the examination within the real setting. In-service personnel are particularly helpful and in some cases it may be beneficial to have a particularly able representative on the examination committee as a participant or consultant.

Those planning for the transition and reorientation of agency staff should keep in mind that, as with faculty and students, the more the agency staff are informed and included in the development period the less likely that problems occur later in the administration phase. In most cases the problems that do occur emanate from inadequate understanding, not from an overt wish to obstruct or cause difficulties. To the extent that agency staff are regarded as colleagues in the nursing profession, with mutual interests in patient care and preparation of nurses, they will cooperate in the examination effort. With this in mind, it also would be helpful for the faculty to point out that the long-range outcome of requiring a clinical performance examination is improved quality of nursing care and services to patients.

It also may interest the staff to realize that the same concepts of examination for students are just as applicable in nursing service. Performance examination could be developed for screening of potential new employees, or for making judgments regarding promotions. They also could be used at the conclusion of refresher courses for nurses, or for hospital-based courses for specialty areas. These and other uses in the service setting will be discussed in a later chapter.

SUMMARY

During the transition period many problems will emerge. Most of them can be anticipated and thus their consequences can be minimized. Most of the changes inherent in implementing a comprehensive performance test cause problems for the faculty, although students and agency staff also have to make adjustments. All three groups need an extensive period of transition and reorientation to acclimate to the changes and their own new roles and responsibilities. Planning and conducting these orientation sessions probably is best accomplished by the committee that develops the examination. The discussions are probably most effective if they begin early and continue throughout the development and implementation phases. This allows for gradual adjustments in attitudes as well as providing helpful feedback in refining the examination.

While the examples used focus on a clinical, in-hospital (technical) examination, the problems addressed relate equally to other types of performance tests. Simulated tests in the laboratory setting, and circumscribed or highly specialized tests in which actual or mock clients are used also require similar considerations, although they are much less complicated.

CHAPTER 8

Scheduling: Problems and Suggestions

Yet another concern that is frequently voiced about performance testing is the amount of time it required to administer—especially to large groups of students. This is needed for development and for administration to be sure, but anxiety about time expenditures may be exaggerated out of proportion unless actual requirements are carefully analyzed. Preceding sections of this book have been devoted to time and other considerations for the developmental phases. At this point, some attention will be paid to scheduling problems that are associated with actual, ongoing administrations of performance examination. Consideration will be given to the need for evaluators, facilities, and a preplanned time schedule. Introducing a performance examination obviously changes a number of things, including utilization of the designated number of weeks per term, hours per day, or even days in the week. Clearly, certain aspects of clinical and/or class time and teacher time may be modified, but this can be accomplished to the improvement of the program and the outcome competencies of the students.

Not every program will be able to implement the most comprehensive performance examination described in this volume, but it is possible for every program to apply to some extent the concepts described and some version of a limited-scope or simulated performance test. The decision, in part, will be based on the philosophic commitment of the faculty to realization of a performance examination and their willingness to reorganize their thinking as well as their currently accepted schedules. As discussed early in the book, the introduction of a comprehensive clinical performance examination involves more than merely adding another test to the existing schedule. It means a change for both teaching–learning and for assessment; it means a reorganization of time schedules and a rethinking of the priorities for the time available.

If the faculty (however small or large) wants to implement more objective performance testing it can be done. The type and extent of assessment and the amount of testing time proportionate to learning time can be worked out. This chapter is designed to review some possible approaches to this difficult problem. For the purposes of illustration, the focus will be directed on in-hospital clinical performance testing to assess the students' competence to administer technical aspects of nursing care. A basic clinical examination (or an outgrowth of it) is applicable for associate or baccalaureate nursing programs, for screening into either of those or into master's programs; for use in career-mobility programs, for use in specialty certificate programs or extensive staff development or refresher course, and the like. The purpose here is to illustrate a variety of approaches to the problems of scheduling, including the amount of time and number of evaluators necessary to get the job done. Most of these ideas have emerged from the approach used by the Regents External Degree Nursing Programs in its three performance examinations and other programs engaged in developing similar tests. Different schedules and formats are necessary for some simulated examinations, but the ideas presented here can easily be adapted to meet a variety of needs.

BASIC ELEMENTS

The basic elements essential for the examination as envisioned in following discussion include:

1. The concept of a comprehensive patient-care situation (PCS) involving care to one patient at a time that focuses on planning, implementation, and evaluation of care.
2. One evaluator to observe one student during the entire PCS.
3. Approximately two to three hours allotted to each PCS, including all aspects of the nursing process.
4. A "cushion" time of approximately half an hour between PCSs to allow for a break and movement from unit to unit when this is required by the examination structure.
5. Different evaluators' being stationed on different units in order to increase objectivity and sampling.
6. One clinical associate or coordinator who is not directly involved in direct student evaluation to serve as the student-evaluator-patient-staff advocate during the examination.

Clearly, the amount of time for each PCS depends on the complexity of the content to be tested; the number of evaluators depends on the number of students and the length and complexity of the test; the number of units to be used depends on the needs and on the number of units available for the designated purposes. The time of day to be used also may vary, depending on the actual content to be tested and the time made available by the clinical agency. With use of the following suggestions it should be possible for any particular faculty to determine which approach is best and to adapt and elaborate it for their purposes.

SPECIFIC PLANS

Table 8.1 illustrates a basic format that uses an entire day for testing, from 7:30 a.m. to 4:00 p.m.; three different evaluators, each assigned to a different patient unit; a 2½-hour testing period for each patient-care situation (PCS), and a half-hour interval between each PCS. Using this approach the three evaluators can examine a total of nine students for one PCS each, as illustrated. They also could test three students for three PCSs each, or three students for two PCSs, with time to spare. As the number of students and the number of required PCSs are increased, obviously the number of evaluators and the number of days necessary for clinical examination have to be increased proportionately. Students simply sign up for the time period available, or preferred, without knowing the evaluator or specific location until the day before the test. When more than one PCS is to be examined, students probably will sign for one slot—which automatically will put them into a predetermined, randomized rotation pattern (as described in chapter 6).

If more evaluators are available and/or only the morning hours are available or preferable (given the specific objectives of the performance examination), the format illustrated in Table 8.2 can be used and duplicated *x* number of times to evaluate the number of students for the desired number of PCSs. Obviously, using more evaluators is

TABLE 8.1
Basic format for three evaluators and three PCSs per day.

Time Periods	Evaluators/Units		
	1	2	3
7:30–10:00	Jones	Smith	Wong
10:30– 1:00	White	Emory	King
1:30–4:00	Rosettie	Schwartz	O'Day

TABLE 8.2
Format for six evaluators, using only morning hours.

Time Periods	Evaluators/Units					
	1	2	3	4	5	6
7:30–10:00						
10:30– 1:00						

helpful in meeting the time constraints that may be imposed by the schedules of both students and faculty. Six evaluators working simultaneously under the coordination of one clinical associate, using three to six patient-care units, seems to be an ideal arrangement. In large institutions and with large numbers of students, duplicate teams could be used to complete multiples of the basic format. By using six evaluators, for example, 12 students could be observed for one PCS each, or six students for two PCSs each.

By using the same format for a three-day period, any of the following combinations potentially could be accomplished. The most desirable one depends upon the nature of the examination and the context in which it will be administered.

1. Six students evaluated on six PCSs each.
2. Twelve students evaluated on three PCSs each.
3. Eighteen students evaluated on two PCSs each.
4. Thirty-six students evaluated on one PCS each.
5. Other combinations—using 36 PCSs over a three-day period, with fewer or more evaluators working simultaneously.

Table 8.3 illustrates the schedule for six evaluators using three time periods per day. With this format, 18 PCSs could be tested in one day, with the following potential combinations:

1. Six students evaluated on 3 PCSs each.
2. Nine students evaluated on 2 PCSs each.
3. Eighteen students evaluated on 1 PCS each.
4. Other combinations using 18 PCSs.

By duplicating this schedule for four days, six evaluators could observe a total of 72 PCSs and provide any one of the following potential combinations:

1. 72 students evaluated on 1 PCS each.
2. 36 students evaluated on 2 PCSs each.

TABLE 8.3
Format for six evaluators and three time periods per day.

Time Periods	Evaluators/Units					
	1	2	3	4	5	6
Day 1						
7:30–10:00						
10:30– 1:00						
1:30– 4:00						

3. 24 students evaluated on 3 PCSs each.
4. Other combinations—using 72 PCSs during a four-day period.

By adding one more day of examination time periods, but using the same format, the following could be accomplished in one week (5 days × 18 PCSs per day = 90 PCSs):

1. 90 students evaluated on 1 PCS each.
2. 45 students evaluated on 2 PCSs each.
3. 30 students evaluated on 3 PCSs each.
4. Other combinations—using 90 PCSs during a five-day period with x number of evaluators working simultaneously.

These are some of the possible approaches to scheduling. Other hours of the day could be used and less time could be allotted to each PCS, depending on the content being tested. The number of evaluators available at a given time also influences the schedule. All of these factors require careful consideration during the early developmental phase to assure that the examination is functional once it is ready for implementation. Whether one, two, or more PCSs are used, single or multiple testing periods can be scheduled. The reality of the particular program essentially will dictate the amount of time allowed for clinical testing.

SCHEDULING THE TIME

In conventional on-campus educational programs—especially those with large numbers of students—it may be necessary, and even desirable, to use more than one block of time to administer performance examinations. It is possible to use both the regular midterm period as well as a week at the end of the term to administer the performance examination (along with the essential written tests). In some cases the midterm and final weeks are devoted exclusively to testing; if the usual classroom schedule is suspended, students and faculty may have a little more time. There is no basic reason why the clinical performance examination could not or should not be scheduled along with all other tests during these periods. However, in some cases, when faculty members are randomly assigned to proctor final examinations throughout the college, other scheduling arrangements must be made.

For example, one week at midsemester and the last one to two weeks of regular clinical weeks could be devoted to testing on a scheduled basis rather than to learning time. The use of two periods is probably most desirable for comprehensive end-of-program examinations, although the concept and schedule are applicable even for limited end-of-course and/or simulated examinations. As already outlined the purpose of the test, the number of faculty available, the type and number of students, the agency resources, the placement of the test in the total program, etc., are factors that converge to influence the decision about which kind of test to give, how many patient or simulated situations to test, and whether or not to use one or more testing periods. Similarly, whether the test is given at the end of the second semester, third semester, or total program depends on the same factors.

For end-of-program comprehensive performance testing, the following options are possible.

1. Use the midterm examination week of the final semester (or next to final semester) to administer one PCS to all students. This could be envisioned as a trial, to be administered precisely as designed, but without penalty: a "practice session" in which the same content would be tested, applying all rules and conditions. Students could see how well they perform and which skills need to be practiced further in order to meet the expected standard. Regardless of the outcome it would help to orient both the students and faculty for the "real" final test at the end of the semester. The final examination week or the last week of regular class time (clinical assignments) then would be used to make a conclusive decision about the student's clinical competence in reference to the predetermined standard. One or more could be used, depending on the number of students and evaluators and the availability of facilities, resources, and time.
2. The midterm examination week could be used as phase I to administer the first of three PCSs, for example—results of which would count toward the final decision. At the end of the term,

either before or during the final examination week, the second PCS would be administered, and the results combined with the midterm PCS. This approach would increase the number of PCSs and the time available for testing, thereby increasing the possibility for comprehensive testing.

If both PCSs are passed according to preestablished protocol, the student would be judged as successful (given the criterion that two of three PCSs must be passed). If the student failed either PCS 1 or PCS 2, a third PCS would be required by individual appointment within a specified period of time. The schedule for PCS 3 (the repeat session) would depend upon how many students needed to be retested, but undoubtedly it would be a small number. Technically, all PCSs probably could be administered during the final two weeks of the term. If necessary the testing period could be started earlier or extended, depending on the situation.

3. In some situations it may be quite possible and desirable to allow students to sign up for the comprehensive performance examination far in advance of the mandatory test period. For example, they could be tested at any time during the last two to three months of the program, through examination appointment periods that are mutually convenient. This mechanism would spread the testing period, decrease the pressure for both students and faculty, and offer a flexible option to the more able students while allowing maximum learning time for the less able students.
4. Other arrangements also could be worked out, depending on when in the program the performance test is to be administered, how many PCSs are judged to be necessary, the number of faculty actually available during the examination period, and other such considerations. Actual PCSs also could be combined with simulated laboratory situations in sessions to be administered at the same time or during the midterm period.

As with all of the other aspects of developing and implementing the performance examination, these decisions about scheduling have to be made after considering all of the relevant variables. The best schedule will be worked out after the faculty committee outlines all of the possible options generated from consideration of the multiple complex variables in the situation. The usual responsibilities of the faculty may have to be altered to accommodate the implementation of a comprehensive performance examination. For example, those assigned to administer the performance test may have to be relieved of other responsibilities by those not directly involved. In many cases, every faculty member in the program may be needed to administer the examination during a concentrated period of time.

EXAMPLES OF SCHEDULES

Because the time required and scheduling problems present substantial concerns to so many faculties, some detailed examples may be helpful. Take for example, a typical local community college program. The nursing faculty chooses to improve the quality and objectivity of clinical evaluation by implementing a comprehensive performance examination at the conclusion of the two-year program. As they begin to work out details of the examination, they are unsure about how many PCSs should be required, given the number of students (100), the number of instructors (20), and the hospital facilities available to them (5). If the faculty decides that one PCS is all that can be managed, one of several scheduling patterns could be used. In addition to the above variables, at least two others are relevant: the time required for each PCS and the number of days available for performance testing.

In the following examples a period of two-and-a-half to three hours is allowed for each PCS because of the proposed comprehensive nature of the examination. However, the faculty committee could design an examination that requires fewer areas of care and less complex situations and therefore one that requires less time for each PCS (say, one-and-a-half instead of three hours). This would alter the time schedule significantly. Great care, however, should be exercised to allow enough time for the students to demonstrate the competencies demanded by the test. Pilot-testing will ultimately determine how much time is necessary for the particular test.

Table 8.4 illustrates that all 100 PCSs potentially could be evaluated in one day. This would require, however, that each evaluator test 5 students sequentially, and that 20 students be tested simultaneously, using 4 units in each of the 5 available hospitals. While this is possible, it would require Herculean strength and is not very reasonable. A detailed analysis of the table shows, for example, that Hospital I has units A, B, C, and D available for testing. Furthermore, 5 students can be tested on each of the 4 units designated for the examination but this requires a 12 hour day. A different evaluator is randomly assigned to each unit and students sign up for one time slot and are randomly assigned to a unit in one of the five agencies. To control

TABLE 8.4
Schedule for testing 100 students per day, using 20 evaluators, 4 units each in 5 different agencies, and 1 PCS per student.

Hospitals	I*	II	III	IV	V
Units/Evaluators	A B C D	A B C D	A B C D	A B C D	A B C D
PCS 1. 7:30					
PCS 2. 10:30					
PCS 3. 1:30					
PCS 4. 4:30					
PCS 5. 7:30					
Total students (100)	5 5 5 5 (20)	(20)	(20)	(20)	(20)

*Students are randomly assigned to each time slot.

potential bias each student is paired at random with an evaluator and tested one at a time during a three-hour test period. Therefore, 20 students are tested in each of the agencies; multiplying this times the five agencies, 100 students could be tested. However, the day extends from 7:30 a.m. to 10:30 p.m., which would result in 20 totally exhausted evaluators at the end of the day—hardly a desirable or sensible arrangement! Furthermore, one could legitimately question the evaluators' ability objectively to administer the examination after the third PCS.

This extreme example is used merely to illustrate the constraints imposed by trying to do too much in a single day. The schedule should be modified either by changing the time required for each PCS or by extending the testing period over one or more days.

In Table 8.5 the 100 PCSs are evaluated in two days instead of one. Each evaluator tests three students the first day and two students the second day, and the examination day extends from 7:30 a.m. to 4:30 p.m. for day 1, and 7:30 a.m. to 1:30 p.m. for day 2. This is a much more realistic schedule.

The illustration shows that in Hospital I a total of 20 students could be examined over a two-day period, 12 on the first day and another 8 on the second day. Each evaluator would be responsible for testing a total of five students. By multiplying this arrangement times the 5 agencies and 20 evaluators available, each of the 100 students could be tested on one PCS during the two-day period. The random matching of students, evaluators, and agencies is the same as described earlier.

TABLE 8.5
Schedule for testing 100 students on one PCS each, over a 2-day period, using 20 evaluators, 4 units in each of 5 different agencies.

Hospitals	I*	II	III	IV	V	Total
Units/Evaluators	A B C D	A B C D	A B C D	A B C D	A B C D	
Day 1						
PCS 1. 7:30						
PCS 2. 10:30						
PCS 3. 1:30						
Total	(12)					
Day 2						
PCS 1. 7:30						
PCS 2. 10:30						
Total	(8)					
Total Students (100)	5 5 5 5 (20)	(20)	(20)	(20)	(20)	

*Students are randomly assigned to each time slot.

Other variations also could be worked out. For example, 20 students could be tested on each of 5 days by using only the early morning PCS in the 20 units as in the above-cited examples. This means that each of the 20 evaluators would test only one student per day on each of the 5 days. This schedule would be desirable if the available amount of time for testing was limited on any given day.

In situations in which fewer hospitals are available, more than one evaluator could be assigned to each unit, with two or more students being tested simultaneously on each unit. This arrangement assumes that a sufficient number of patients who meet the criteria are available. The schedules in Tables 8.4 and 8.5 are based on one evaluator's being assigned to each unit. When fewer evaluators are available, the schedule would have to be extended to more than two days with each evaluator testing several students.

More students could be tested and/or the time reduced if PCSs were less demanding and required less time. For example, if one PCS required one-and-a-half hours instead of three hours, twice as many PCSs could be administered in the same period of time. However, this also means that the examination would be less comprehensive, and the students could be tested on fewer areas of care. The amount of time required for each PCS depends upon the number and complexity of areas of care being tested. In all fairness to students, and to patients, sufficient time must be allowed as determined by pilot-testing of the final instrument.

Testing students on one PCS clearly is possible in most programs, even with large numbers of students. The problem is how to multiply the schedule to accommodate the need for testing two or more PCSs, which seems more desirable for a comprehensive performance examination. One suggestion is to use a schedule comparable to that shown in Table 8.5, but applying it during the midterm week to test one PCS and then repeating the same schedule at the end of the term or during the final examination week. Those students who failed either PCS 1 at midterm or PCS 2 at the end of the term would be required to take a third PCS to be arranged by appointment with the faculty (using objectively predetermined and written rules of administration). The requirement of passing two of three PCSs with 100 percent accuracy means that the third PCS would have to be successfully completed in order for the student to pass the total clinical examination.

A split schedule such as the one just mentioned is appealing because it offers the advantage of spreading the time required throughout the midterm and final examination weeks. It also gives students the opportunity to discover areas of care for which they need additional practice before it is too late for them to do anything about the situation. Between the midterm and final periods students can spend whatever time is necessary to master the essential skills. They alone, then, bear the responsibility for the outcome of the total examination. A schedule such as this one probably is fairer from the students' point of view, is more manageable from the faculty's point of view, and ensures more accountability from the consumers' point of view.

However, when the faculty decides that all PCSs should be administered during a consecutive and consolidated examination period, a different arrangement is clearly necessary. Assuming the same requirements (that two of three PCSs must be completed with 100 percent accuracy, and that different evaluators, patients, and nursing-care units must be used), the following schedule illustrates an adaptation of the previous models.

Let us consider the rotation pattern for 20 students in a clinical performance examination that required three consecutive PCSs for each student. As shown in Table 8.6, it allows three hours for each PCS and uses 20 evaluators and four units in each of five different hospitals. The schedule requires that each student be tested by three

TABLE 8.6
Rotation Patterns for testing 20 students on three consecutive PCSs.

Hospitals	I	II	III	IV	V	Total
Units/Evaluators	A B C D	A B C D	A B C D	A B C D	A B C D	
PCS 1. 7:30	1 2 3 4	5 6 7 8	9 10 11 12	13 14 15 16	17 18 19 20	(20)
PCS 2. 10:30	2 1 4 3	6 5 8 7	10 9 12 11	14 13 16 15	18 17 20 19	(20)
PCS 3. 1:30	3 4 1 2	7 8 5 6	11 12 9 10	15 16 13 14	19 20 17 18	(20)
Total PCSs	(12)	(12)	(12)	(12)	(12)	(60)
Total Students	(4)	(4)	(4)	(4)	(4)	(20)

different evaluators, on three different units and with three different patients, all on a given day, with appointments arranged on a random basis. A total of 60 PCSs can be tested in a single day (three for each of the 20 students). The pertinent data follow.

- 100 students are expected to complete the second year.
- 20 instructors are employed in the total nursing program; while they usually are divided between the first and second years, all of them could be used as evaluators for the final comprehensive performance examination.
- 5 hospitals in the area are used for clinical experience and are available for testing.
- 4 units in each hospital are available for the clinical use of students.
- 3 PCSs per student is the maximum number of testing episodes required to assess clinical performance. The faculty also decided that the students should be tested by different evaluators and different patients on different units for the three PCSs.
- 2 of the 3 PCSs must be passed with 100 percent accuracy as concerns stated critical elements and guidelines.

The following steps summarize how the schedule could be worked out, incorporating the above data.

1. 100 students $\times$ 3 PCSs each = 300 total PCSs needed.
2. 300 PCSs $\div$ 20 evaluators = 15 PCSs/evaluator (maximum).
3. 15 PCSs/evaluator $\div$ 3 PCSs/day = 5 days required (maximum).
4. 20 evaluators $\times$ 3 PCSs/day = 60 patients/day (maximum, as some patients could be used more than once per day, and not all students will require 3 PCSs).
5. 60 patients/day $\div$ 5 facilities = 12 patients/facility/day (maximum).
6. 12 PCSs/day/facility $\div$ 3 PCSs/day = 4 units/facility/day.

Over a five-day period, 20 instructors-turned-evaluators could test 100 students on three PCSs each, sequentially and simultaneously. A combined maximum of 60 patients would be needed per day. With use of five hospital facilities, 12 PCSs per day per facility would be needed and if four patient units were available in each facility, only three patients per day would be necessary. From all of the patients available on a given unit, evaluators would select one patient for each of the consecutive time periods designated for testing, for a total of three patients per day on each unit. At the end of the day, the four evaluators in each particular agency would have tested three students each, for a total of 12 students; in the five agencies the 20 evaluators would have tested a total of 60 students between 7:30 a.m. and 4:00 p.m.

SUMMARY

Time and scheduling present major problems for most faculties. The use of the allotted time for a given term or program has to be reconsidered when objective performance examinations are to be implemented in addition to learning and practice time. The amount of time and kind of schedule needed are determined by the complexity of the examination and the context within which it is to be administered, along with other variables discussed. The most essential requirement is the faculty's commitment to implement an objective test to determine the students' competence; everything else will follow.

In some instances a single patient-care situation may be sufficient to meet the objectives; in other cases two or three PCSs may be required. Sometimes a simulated laboratory examination may be enough. Whether the purpose is to screen LPNs into an associate-degree nursing program, to place an RN into a bachelor's program, or to certify the competence of a basic student near the conclusion of the generic program, some form of performance examination can be developed to meet the content and scheduling requirements. The examples presented in this chapter illustrate some of the possible approaches; it is hoped that they will suggest a course of action appropriate for a wide range of programs that need some form of objective performance testing.

CHAPTER 9

The Conversion of Teachers to Objective Evaluators

A cartoon appeared in *Time* magazine some time ago in which two judges were walking away from a courtroom setting (see next page). One judge is looking distressed and the other one says: "Don't worry about it. One day you're feeling down and you dish out twenty years to some poor devil. The next day you feel great and everybody gets a suspended sentence. It all evens out in the end." This just as easily could have been two nurse–teachers leaving the clinical setting after completing final clinical evaluations for nursing students: "Don't worry about it. You did your best; after all, when every student passes that only makes it look like the course is too easy. Some make it and some don't. It all evens out in the end."

Such rationalization—whether overt or covert—is not uncommon. There is a feeling that "things will even out" by some unknown magical influence and that this somehow relieves the teacher of the responsibility for making decisions on an objective and logical basis. This seems to be especially true when previous judgments have been made on ambiguous information or inconsistent use of procedures. If the traditional practices being followed allow for subjective interpretation, the decisions will reflect the personal bias and feelings of those making the decisions.

During a meeting with nursing instructors in which clinical performance evaluation was being discussed, one teacher related her approach. She reported: "I observe the students and get a feeling in my mind about how able they are to provide nursing care." Based on this feeling she devoted more or less time and attention to the students and subsequently made decisions about their clinical competence. Un-

DRAWING BY VON RIEGEN: ©1964 THE NEW YORKER MAGAZINE, INC.

"Don't worry about it. One day you're feeling down and you dish out twenty years to some poor devil. The next day you feel great and everybody gets a suspended sentence. It all evens out in the end."

doubtedly, much more goes into the process of grading students in the clinical area, but the thought she shared was most revealing about the fundamental nature of one approach to clinical assessment.

Her approach is shared by a multitude of nursing instructors who, knowingly or unknowingly, evaluate students on the basis of "the feelings they get in their minds." Such feelings are influenced by a number of external and internal factors, such as how the instructor feels that day (as with the judge in the cartoon). There is a fairly strong opinion among nurse educators that their initial "feelings" about students are accurate and are a valid foundation for determining clinical grades. This assumption springs, in part, from the traditions passed

---

Cartoon drawing by Von Riegin: © 1964 The New Yorker Magazine, Inc. Reprinted in *Time*, December 12, 1977. By permission.

from one generation of teachers to another and in part from the lack of objective methods of clinical assessment. When this approach is analyzed rationally, its weaknesses are too obvious even to mention. While subjective data are useful in some aspects of evaluation, it generally forms a very shaky foundation. Some nurse educators—in basic academic programs, specialty programs, or in-service programs—somehow believe that their ability intuitively to perceive the competence of students is sufficient for the task. It is not uncommon to hear an instructor exclaim: "I just know when the student is capable of giving good nursing care." Similarly, some teachers are reluctant to use a predetermined and exclusive testing instrument in the clinical setting because presumably it restricts the influence of their personal opinions and professional judgment. Some resist the idea on the claim that it will restrict their "academic freedom." Many clinical teachers experience conflict between their desire for more objective testing procedures and their need to assess students on the basis of their subjective impressions and experience.

Nursing is not alone in this problem. The need for teachers objectively to document competence is evident in practically every applied discipline. Commercial pilots provide an example. According to federal aviation regulations, airline pilots must submit to performance testing one to two times a year and every time they are assigned to fly a different type aircraft. They also take written examinations and are then tested in a cockpit simulator; they are required to respond to a variety of situations that are likely to occur during actual flight.

The evaluators for these simulated examinations usually are senior pilots. While some structured situations (and their correct responses) are prescribed during the test, the final decision about the competence of the pilot being tested is based on the individual judgment of the senior pilot. He is supposed to "know" the appropriate responses for the simulated situations and whether the testee properly performed the circumstances prescribed.

Those responsible for administering these performance tests for pilots indicate that there are few if any actual "critical elements" or predetermined, specific behaviors to be tested consistently with every pilot. They suggest that this would be too difficult to achieve. Furthermore, they report that the senior pilot is the best judge of correct responses to the test, therefore judgments are left to his discretion. This system has definite advantages but it does not take into account the subjective perceptions and influences of the evaluator, regardless of his experience. However, the purpose, frequency, and candidates for testing all have to be taken into account.

THE CONVERSION PROCESS

This chapter focuses on the problems associated with the conversion of teachers to evaluators. As discussed in previous chapters, achieving objectivity is dependent upon the precision of the instrument as well as the objectivity of the evaluators in applying it; in this chapter the evaluator is in the spotlight. Problems to be discussed relate to the strategies for conversion, psychological aspects of changing to objective assessment, the most common recurring problems experienced by evaluators, the process of administering the test, as well as the roles and responsibilities of evaluators and clinical associates. The central objective for the faculty is attaining a perspective of "positive neutrality" during the performance testing period in place of the more traditional and subjective approach.

Fundamentally, the problem emanates from the strong magnetic pull of the past—with its traditional practices of subjective evaluation. The transition requires that these practices be acknowledged, deliberately confronted, and exchanged for a more neutral and effective mind-set essential for objective testing. Both during development and implementation of performance testing, teachers will experience the tendency to "regress toward the mean" and find themselves unconsciously slipping back into familiar instructor habits that are essential for the teaching–learning phase, but inappropriate for objective assessment.

STRATEGIES FOR CONVERSION

The fact is that not all teachers want to become (or are capable of becoming) "good evaluators." Those who may be excellent in instructing and coaching students during the learning process may have substantial difficulty in being detached and neutral during the testing of those very same students. Their psychological investment may be too great and their teaching habits too entrenched to accommodate an easy transition. The change can be made, but for these teachers the task requires considerable and sustained efforts and assistance. For those who have continued difficulty, it probably is desirable to find other responsibilities for them rather than to try to force change on unyielding habits.

In some situations only a portion of the faculty will be required as evaluators; in other programs everyone will be needed—and then some. In still other situations it may be possible to employ (or "borrow") a cadre of qualified evaluators who are not required also to fulfill the teaching function for the students being tested. When possible to effect, this approach has distinct advantages; but it probably is not too likely for most programs, in education or in-service settings. Given these realities, a plan should be drafted in which maximum attention is focused on using the existing faculty members and assisting them to develop those behaviors essential to conducting the performance examination as intended. As already suggested in this text, the need for and the complexity of this transition cannot be underestimated. Achieving the goal of objective student assessment depends as much on the evaluators as on the instrument itself. Consequently, four strategies will be suggested and explored to assist in this important task:

1. Change the title of teachers during the testing period to one that conveys a more neutral imagery.
2. Conduct faculty seminars in which the individuals and the group analyze their specific strengths and weaknesses related to the behaviors required for objective performance testing.
3. Initiate a planned transition period during which faculty deliberately focus on how to reprogram certain behaviors to comply with the responsibilities and demands of the evaluator role.
4. Establish criteria for evaluating the behaviors of the evaluators during the administration of clinical examinations.

WHAT'S IN A NAME

The title given to someone performing a particular job may or may not have a direct relationship on that person's behavior; however, there is little doubt that behavior can be influenced indirectly by the title. That influence springs from such factors as the title itself, traditional behaviors associated with it, the status associated with it, the expectations held for the person holding the title, and the rewards likely to accrue from successful performance of the job.

The titles "teacher" and "instructor" convey certain images that are firmly entrenched in the minds of most people. They project instant replays of experiences collected over many years and suggest behaviors such as helping, telling, showing, coaching, correcting, rewarding, sanctioning, etc. The name itself is a powerful stimulus for the kind of behaviors expected of the one who holds it. But these teaching behaviors are inappropriate during objective testing. Consequently, another image and set of behaviors are required. A different title and "job description," therefore, may help to stimulate the use of the kinds of behaviors necessary during the examination period.

Titles such as "evaluator," "tester," "proctor," and "examiner" convey more neutral behaviors, usually free of the images typically associated with teaching activities. By adopting one of these titles, and orienting faculty members to its specific connotations, the possibility of more objective clinical examinations is enhanced—not in and of itself, but as part of a planned and comprehensive transition toward objective performance testing. Thus changing the title to fit the role is one of the strategies that may help to accomplish the conversion of teachers to neutral evaluators. Discussing these distinctions during faculty orientation seminars and exploring the psychological investments associated with each title is very helpful in setting the stage for behavior change. This kind of overt clarification is one of the initial activities during the transition period.

BEHAVIOR ANALYSIS SEMINARS

Conducting faculty discussions to explore the relationships between teacher behavior and student assessment can be very useful. Open discussions to identify those behaviors that help and those that hinder objective evaluation establish the commonality of the problem and highlight directions for change. When all faculty actively participate in these sessions, each individual is more likely to understand the importance of her or his own behavior and its impact on accomplishing the goal. Every effort should be made to avoid negative criticism that tends to threaten the individual and to undermine good intentions. Identifying ineffective behaviors without unnecessary intimidation of those involved may not be easy, but it must be done to make way for the adoption of approaches that are more useful during the examination period.

Merely listing positive and negative assessment behaviors is probably too superficial to be of much value, even though it is a good beginning. The active exploration of differing philosophical orientations and psychological attachments to certain behaviors is more meaningful and makes change more possible. Rather than being just a planned exercise to be accomplished, these discussions are essential in making the transition from a traditional subjective evaluation mind-set to a markedly different and more objective frame of reference. Maximum value can be derived when faculty members engage in the candid analysis of the behaviors that characterize their evaluation approaches, their satisfactions and dissatisfactions with these behaviors, and the significance of changing or retaining them. This process of self-analysis and change is enhanced when some kind of psychological support system also is implemented; the kind of support will depend on the faculty and available resources.

Faculty Retreat

Conducting a faculty retreat for three or four days in a location removed from the work setting (and preferably with an outside consultant) has proved to be a useful strategy for initiating change of the kind being discussed here. A well-planned conference that is conducted with enthusiasm generally is effective in setting the stage for change. The objective is to saturate participants with new information while continually demonstrating its relevance to their concerns (in this case, objective performance examinations). All members are encouraged to participate actively to explore their specific concerns, problems, questions, and goals. The interaction among the group and the skillful direction of the leader all focus on the transition to more effective evaluation procedures. Presenting and discussing theoretical material is important, but providing opportunities for experiential learning is also necessary. Role playing, the use of simulated situations, small-group interaction sessions, and specific assignments are all useful techniques in helping the faculty to alter habitual and comfortable approaches to a different but more effective mental frame of reference. Maximum and sustained involvement, without the day-to-day interruptions is a key factor; hence holding the meetings away from the usual work setting is desirable. References on group process, change theory, and leadership should be consulted for more detailed information.

REPROGRAMMING BEHAVIORS

In addition to faculty discussions focused on identifying effective and ineffective evaluator behaviors, consideration should be given to activities to assist in the reorientation. Talking about the behavior is insufficient; practice is required. Therefore, at some point the faculty members make the decision to try to enact some of the behaviors listed in the "more effective" category. This can be done to some extent during clinical laboratory periods and particularly during simulated testing. If objective procedures are being introduced gradually over a period of several semesters, instructors have the opportunity to conduct several minitests and to implement different (more objective) approaches.

As suggested earlier in this book, it probably would be helpful to initiate the change to clinical examinations by starting with one course, or even one segment within a course, preferably early in the program. This approach provides a more manageable challenge for the faculty both in organizing content and in changing their assessment behaviors. Furthermore, starting with a small number of students prevents the kind of psychological overload that forces a return of automatic behaviors that are viewed as undesirable.

In those programs in which the performance examination is being used to screen applicants or to provide a basis for advanced placement, the same principles hold true. By initiating the project with a small number of students, faculty members have a chance deliberately to concentrate on the desired behaviors. If possible, several miniexaminations should be given for practice, and to refine the content, the procedures, and the behavioral approaches of evaluators.

Faculty members must focus on their behaviors during these times and deliberately curtail the teaching–helping–advising impulses and force themselves to observe in reference to the stated critical elements. Following such practice sessions or initial efforts, discussion with other faculty members is very useful. Sharing of attempts, successes, and failures leads to further understanding and growth. These kinds of preliminary sessions are also helpful to students. Both students and teachers need repeated practice with these new roles and expectations before a sense of comfort is achieved.

However, evaluation of self-behavior is difficult. The clinical situation demands that attention be directed at the needs of students, patients, staff, and others. It is easy to be distracted by immediate circumstances and to allow old habits to take over. For these and other reasons, having a person assigned periodically and unobtrusively to observe the evaluators' behavior is very useful, especially during the orientation and transition period. This faculty member (called the clinical associate in previous chapters) has the responsibility of overseeing the administration of the test and simultaneously observing the evaluators to ensure that their behavior is consistent with the procedures and protocol approved for the test. The associate can be quite helpful to the evaluators by pointing out the occurrence of "teaching" or other ineffective behaviors during the testing period. Quite often the teacher-turned-evaluator is unaware of these automatic behaviors. Subsequent discussions between the associate and evaluators clarify the observations and their actual or potential influence on student assessment. Once again, efforts should be made to avoid negative attacks and to focus on assisting the evaluator in positive ways to become aware of conscious and unconscious behaviors that affect evaluation.

While making rounds on the units during the performance examination, the associate is alert for verbal and nonverbal cues unintentionally given by the evaluators. For example, teachers often assist students with aspects of care when they are going about it awkwardly. They may also spontaneously interact with patients who direct questions to them, rather than waiting and allowing the student to assume responsibility for responding. Too, they may give clues in body language—standing position, facial expressions, hovering, silently offering physical assistance, directing questions to students or patients, and the like. These behaviors are so natural for many instructors that they creep in inadvertently. The fact that they actually occurred may escape awareness unless the teacher-turned-evaluator becomes sensitive to them. The associate can help in this regard, and thereby enhance the transition to more objectivity.

CRITERIA FOR EVALUATOR BEHAVIOR

Another strategy to assist instructors to learn and to implement desirable assessment behaviors is to establish a set of criteria for evaluating the behavior of evaluators. This strategy is most useful when the faculty participates in drafting the statements and when the focus is on the characteristics that facilitate the objective administration of the performance examination. These criteria then are used as a guide by evaluators and associates during and following the test to reorient their clinical assessment behaviors.

This strategy helps in at least two ways: (1) the faculty discussions required to formulate the criteria focus attention on desirable behaviors and on the need for all instructors to incorporate them during the test period and (2) the criteria provide an objective and generally acceptable standard for which evaluators will be held accountable. While the criteria relate to all aspects of the evaluator role, those specifically associated with the neutral observation of the students' competence to perform the critical elements are most important. Although the specific criteria may vary from one program to another, the most important point is that such a standard be developed and be used as one direct method of facilitating the positive transition to more objective evaluation.

In general the criteria involve the evaluator's behavior in relation to such concerns as the following.

- Direct and continuous observation of the student during the performance test.
- Use of critical elements and explicit examination protocol as the only grounds for judging the students' competence.
- Implementing all rules of the test consistently, as outlined in the examination study guide.
- Application of critical elements as written, without modification.
- Interactions with patients according to examination protocol.
- Interaction with staff to facilitate test procedures.
- Completion of all forms according to directions.
- Administration of the test in such a way as to minimize external stress on students.
- Protection of the patient/client at all times during the test.
- Maintaining an attitude of neutrality and detached involvement as prescribed by the role.

Such criteria potentially could serve more than one purpose, but in this context they are suggested as a way of helping in the reorientation and transition process. They crystalize the importance of the evaluators' behaviors and express the degree of control to be applied to these behaviors for all evaluators. Some evaluators may resent such controls or may interpret them as repressive; these faculty members also probably will have difficulty achieving the necessary level of objectivity and examination outcomes, unfortunately, will reflect the extent of their difficulty. Attaining a high-quality clinical performance examination is dependent upon an equally high degree of faculty cooperation in reorienting their assessment behaviors.

PSYCHOLOGICAL RESPONSES OF EVALUATORS

During the transition period, and even afterwards, faculty members experience a number of feelings that can have a direct effect on the examination process and outcome. Because of the potential power of these feelings they should be anticipated and dealt with when they arise. Some of the feelings are positive and tend to strengthen the test, others are negative and directly or indirectly undermine it. Some of the more frequently encountered faculty responses will be explored briefly to alert evaluators to the kinds of feelings they might experience.

ANXIETY

Almost every evaluator experiences some degree of tension and anxiety—before, during, and after a performance examination. This is natural, especially during the early transition period. Talking about it and openly sharing the feelings with other evaluators, the clinical associate, and other colleagues not directly involved will probably help the individual evaluator to understand the basis for the anxiety and to identify ways of coping with it. New evaluators wonder whether they are applying the test correctly, whether they are interpreting the critical elements appropriately, or whether they are being too lenient or too strict. They worry about their own potential for actual errors in judgment. Early in the process most evaluators also worry about the test's adequacy to measure the competence of students; hence they worry about the instrument itself as well as their ability to apply it properly. They question: Am I doing it right? Is the PCS sufficiently difficult? Does it test the right things? Are all the critical behaviors listed? Does it test enough really to document competence in nursing care? If the students pass on this occasion can I be sure they are good nurses?

Evaluators also feel the need for validation of their decisions, some more frequently than others. There is a constant internal struggle between the desire to use the instrument as designed and the need to incorporate personal judgments. The struggle is between the old familiar behavior pattern and the new one. Sharing specific experiences following the test episode helps evaluators to confirm or adjust their decisions and interpretations of the students' behavior. Experience with the test generally helps evaluators to gain more self-confidence.

Feelings of insecurity also emanate from the fear of being criticized by peers. Sometimes this relates to the incorrect application of critical elements or other aspects of the test, but most often the anxiety revolves around making pass/fail decisions about another teacher's students. Or, more particularly, the fear is that another evaluator will discover that "my students" are not passing the test, which somehow reflects on "me." This attitude is related to the belief that teachers are accountable for students' learning, and that positive or negative outcomes reflect on the teacher. To some extent this is true.

However, that point of view has been criticized in this text, as we have come to prefer that students be held responsible for their own growth and learning.

Teaching and Learning

There is, of course, some relationship between what the teacher teaches and what the student learns. Basically it is a matter of degrees of responsibility. For a criterion-referenced performance examination, however, the teacher makes known what shall be learned, assists students to use available resources, and provides objective methods for documenting achievement. The student is responsible for learning and for demonstrating competence against that predetermined standard. To the extent that this is accomplished, teachers (evaluators) can be free of the self-imposed anxiety about student behavior's reflecting on their own competence. This is a difficult goal to achieve but it is possible, and refreshing when experienced.

When other teachers objectively examine ''my'' students (hence, ''my'' teaching), it becomes a kind of peer review process. The natural resulting anxiety can become a stimulus to improve the quality of teaching. But, interestingly enough, it is not the teaching per se but rather the students' ability to demonstrate competence in testing situations that becomes the focus. As student ability is the preferred end-result of teaching, this kind of stimulus would seem to be quite desirable. This kind of anxiety, then, emanating from the performance examination can have—and should have—a beneficial effect on the teaching–learning process and on student outcomes. It initiates a different psychological investment in new kinds of teacher behaviors and learner outcomes.

Guilt Feelings

Most evaluators also experience guilt feelings because they do not engage in active teaching during the test period. This relates to another change in the frame of reference already discussed—namely, that this kind of evaluation (a performance examination) requires a separation between learning time and testing time, between teaching and evaluation, between clinical experience and documentation of competence. During the initial transition period, most evaluators continue to have the impulse to help, show, advise, correct, or otherwise engage in teaching behaviors. Experience in deliberately controlling these natural instincts along with assistance from other evaluators and associates help evaluators to exchange the guilt feelings for more appropriate feelings of satisfaction with being objectively neutral during the test.

Evaluators also experience another kind of anxiety. They wonder: What if the students fail? They could fail the test, fail the program, or, worse still, they might fail to perform as graduates. If final decisions rest on the outcome of a comprehensive performance examination, what happens when the students actually fail? If the student is a "good" student, has earned good grades, and otherwise "looks" satisfactory but fails the performance test, should the student pass anyway? be allowed to repeat the test? be given special dispensation? or just be failed, according to the examination protocol? Faculty frequently feel that they cannot allow students to fail on performance tests if they have been previously judged to be good students.

This kind of anxiety relates to a minor distrust of the examination and in its power to discriminate between competent and incompetent students. Obviously, the test must be developed and adequately pilot-tested to provide the basis for confidence. But once this is accomplished, faculty must use it as designed, even though some students might fail.

Initially, teachers may feel anxious about the use of such tests, but positive experiences are major incentives for change. It has repeatedly been shown that students who have an explicit standard to guide their learning and who know in advance that an objective performance examination is required rise to the occasion and learn. The standard outlines the expectations for their performance and they practice until they meet the standard—regardless of how long it takes or how many laboratory practice sessions are needed. They get help from peers or teachers or whomever. When they know that passing the performance test is just as essential as passing the written test and that they are held accountable for competence as defined in the examination study guide, the able and motivated students take the initiative and learn. Success is just as important to them as to their teacher—maybe more so. The transition is as difficult for teachers as it is for students, but with planning it can be accomplished with a minimum of anxiety.

Anxiety about the students, the success rate, and potentially negative reflections on the faculty and the program are ill-founded when the performance examination is incorporated as part of a total educational program. The instrument for judging competence in clinical performance is only one part—but a very important part—of teaching–learning approaches and responsibilities. In time, success experienced with performance testing will dispell most of the unfounded anxieties about it.

FATIGUE

The kind of tension described above usually results in varying degrees of physical and mental fatigue. The examination is an intense experience for both students and faculty, especially during the transition period. Each one is trying to achieve the designated expectations, fully aware of the consequences of failure. Under the stress of the testing situation students often make careless mistakes, or seem to be on the verge of making mistakes. This raises the stress level for both observer and student. Frequently, though, if they are allowed the opportunity students correct themselves before an error actually is committed.

However, observing students who are going through a high-tension examination is itself a stressful experience. The evaluator watches the student proceed cautiously and awkwardly, step by step, hesitating, thinking, trying. Things are not "quite right" but they are not wrong either. The evaluator thinks: No critical elements have been violated, but how much easier it would be if she would just . . . If only I could reach out and help her with just this part . . . Look out. She's going to contaminate the . . . no . . . she saved herself just in the nick of time. I thought for sure she would violate asepsis. I wonder if she realizes the problem . . . she's trembling so; the tension is interfering with her thinking. I know she can do it; I watched her two weeks ago. Be patient . . . watch . . . give her a chance."

This kind of mental struggle causes fatigue and exhaustion. The conflict between remaining neutral and wanting to help compels the muscles to tense in readiness. Every muscle strains forward to help, to show, to assist. Sometimes it is all the observer can do to hold back these natural teaching instincts. Not helping, when to do so would be customary, dramatically increases physical and mental fatigue because it requires deliberate and sustained effort.

After a day of such observations, evaluators have every reason to be tired. Experience, however, reduces some of the tension and the associated fatigue. But during the transition period these symptoms are ever-present reminders of the distinction between the role of the teacher and the role of the evaluator. They also force an awareness of new expectations and responsibilities during performance testing.

ANGER

Another feeling evaluators experience during performance testing is that of frustration and anger. Such feelings may be directed toward other instructors, the test itself, staff members, or the evaluator herself. Anticipating such feelings, accepting them as a part of the transition, and openly discussing them with colleagues can help to convert them from destructive impulses to growth-producing stimuli. A few examples will serve to illustrate the point.

Perhaps one of the common reasons for anger is that another instructor (evaluator) fails one of "my" students. Having someone else pass negative judgment on students can be interpreted as a negative reflection on the individual teacher who has been responsible for the student's learning. When one teacher previously has judged a student to be acceptable and that student later fails the performance test, the initial teacher may react with overt or covert resentment and anger.

Moreover, the experience of having the clinical associate reverse a pass/fail decision made by an evaluator may be even more distressing. This is done only on rare occasions but especially during the early period it can induce feelings of anger. Evaluators who tend to have a personal investment in their decisions feel threatened, undermined, and angry when they subsequently are reversed. The associate is usually the person who is most knowledgeable about the examination procedures, the one who oversees all of the individual tests and therefore is in a good position to exert more consistency on the entire assessment program. Part of her function is to interpret the test and its conduct according to the protocols established by the entire faculty; she is accountable to that body for her actions and to a certain extent for those of the evaluators as well. She has a sense of continuity and detachment that is not possible for individual evaluators because she is not directly involved in testing students. Because of the sensitive nature of the clinical associate's role, actions must be executed thoughtfully and objectively in order to minimize feelings of frustration and resentment that inevitably will occur.

The clinical associate also is the object of angry feelings when she calls the evaluators' attention to their ineffective behaviors during the test. Evaluators may or may not be aware that they have slipped back into the teaching role, and having the associate point out such behaviors for correction may not be appreciated at the moment. The manner in which such corrections are made is important, but so is the manner in which they are received by evaluators. The kind of anger that emerges from such interactions should be recognized as disruptive and should be discussed in a mature and candid way among those involved. The successful implementation of the test depends in large part on the willingness of all faculty members to accept new roles for themselves and others, some as evaluators and some as associates.

The Test and the Staff

Evaluators also may direct their anger toward the examination itself. A comprehensive clinical examination is not easy to implement, and evaluators may not personally agree with every prescribed critical element. Some situations may appear "special" and the evaluator will want to deviate from protocol. Or, when the test is administered exactly as required and a student unexpectedly fails, the teacher may react negatively to the test itself—as if it is responsible for the failure and for a decision that overrules her own. Sometimes when the test seems to be forcing a decision in a direction different from the prior opinion of the evaluator, she may be sufficiently distressed with the examination itself spontaneously to change the rules of conduct or the critical elements to suit the situation and the previous opinion. This can happen whether the decision is for a positive or negative outcome for the student involved. Evaluators who are angry with the test find ways to discredit it and to proceed by using their own opinions just as they have in the past. The consequences of such independent actions are clearly not in the best interest of the test, the students, the faculty, or the program. Teachers who maintain the attitude that their experience and subjective evaluation are more valuable than the structured testing procedures can destroy the effectiveness of objective examinations for an entire program. The transition is still in the early stages as long as some teachers chant: "I know a good student when I see one" or "My professional judgment is more valid that the test in this situation." Teachers who experience resentment when their prior assumptions about students are challenged by a properly administered objective performance examination still need assistance in adapting to the new frame of reference. Clearly, the process takes longer for some than for others, but the feelings require some kind of forward attention as long as they continue to occur.

Evaluators also may direct anger at the staff on the nursing-care units where the performance test is administered. This usually happens when someone, knowingly or unknowingly, interrupts or complicates the situation during the test. Problems result when staff members "help" by doing such things as implementing new orders that could have been delayed until later in the interest of the test without imposing any hardship on the patients. When staff members begin nursing care before students arrive, or forget to "hold" selected treatments, etc., evaluators feel justifiably frustrated. However, this kind of situation should be expected during the transition period and steps should be taken to minimize such episodes, Being angry at the staff only results in more difficult interpersonal relations and tends to reduce the spirit of cooperation that is essential for the success of the program. This problem emphasizes again the need for a long-term and comprehensive orientation for agency staff in order to minimize day-to-day and recurring problems.

Evaluators also may direct feelings of anger at themselves when feelings, old habits, or circumstances interfere with the proper administration of the performance test. Slipping back into teaching behaviors can be frustrating to the individual, especially if such actions result in an inadequate test of the students' competence that shows up later, or if the associate just happens to be making rounds at that time. Once again, practice and concerted efforts help to reduce these kinds of instances and the resulting frustrations. Replacing old habits and ways of thinking is a gradual process. Again, open discussions with colleagues in planned or spontaneous sessions often help to relieve the anger and to pave the way for a better approach the next time.

AN OPEN APPROACH

Dealing with anxiety or frustration is difficult, but concealing these feelings will not improve the situation. Faculty who feel guilty for experiencing anxiety or anger may not want to talk about it; on the other hand, they may talk a great deal about it but have no interest in changing their behavior or their outlook. This then becomes a group problem that needs attention in the best interest of the objective performance examination itself. How particular problems are handled will vary, depending on the faculty and the situations. However, the kind of problems listed here occur so frequently that they can be anticipated and a preliminary plan can be drafted in advance for dealing with them when they occur.

One other point: there is an interactive "mutual effect" of these behavioral responses for everyone involved. Sustained and unresolved feelings of tension, frustration, anxiety, or conflict in one person influence the other persons in that situation. Students who experience a high stress level convey that tension to the patient and to the evaluator. Anger or anxiety experienced by the evaluator is easily transmitted to students who already are experiencing their own version of resentment or anxiety. Therefore, it is especially crucial that evaluators neutralize their own feelings as quickly as possible to avoid negatively influencing students, patients, staff members, or others. The test is designed to document the students' ability to administer specific aspects of nursing care, not their ability to deal with unnecessary high levels of stress. Even though exploring feelings that emerge from and are directly related to the testing situation may be uncomfortable, it is more desirable than perpetuating behaviors that negatively influence students and their performance. The orientation plan for evaluators and students should include some proposed methods for minimizing these negative feelings and their potential negative effects on all of those involved.

POSITIVE FEELINGS

Not all of the feelings experienced by evaluators are negative. To illustrate this point, a group of RN students in a generic BSN program were required to learn certain assessment skills included in the earlier portion of the basic program. They had an outline of the essential behaviors for which they would be held accountable during the end-of-course health assessment performance test. In a matter of two to three weeks following a period of basic instruction, the students had practiced repeatedly until they felt confident in conducting a physical examination at the designated level. They assumed responsibility for their own learning—once they knew what the expected standard was and that they would be held accountable for demonstrating the level of competence outlined in the examination protocol. Even though the faculty initially were dubious, they were quite amazed when the students were able to "put it all together" in such a short period of time and to pass the rigid performance test. Even though they had learned differently, these RN students achieved skills comparable to those of the generic students. In this case, and in others, an explicit standard of expectation and the motivation to achieve usually form a winning combination.

Administering an objective test also results in feelings of certainty being assured of students' competence, and taking pleasure in actually seeing demonstrated accomplishment. After a period of arduous teaching and of investment in assisting students to learn, the experience of observing them meet an established standard of care without assistance is pleasant indeed. Success in these situations increases the teachers' confidence both in the teaching–learning process and in the students' ability to practice in the real world of work. It lays the groundwork for more realistic preparation for the next step—either as a more advanced student or as a graduate. The faculty also can use these experiences to reinforce positive teaching and testing behaviors for the benefit of future students. Exchanging feelings of confidence for those of insecurity has the potential of resulting in more objective teaching and testing in the clinical areas. Conducting the examination as prescribed and accepting the results also leads to less concern about potential legal problems, as decisions are based on established, objective procedures.

CONTROLLING EVALUATOR BIAS

The problem of evaluator bias keeps coming up because it impinges on almost every aspect of the performance examination. Unless it is brought under some system of control, subjectivity has the power to negate the expressed will of the faculty and to nullify the intent of objective examination. The test and the process are impotent unless they are applied by evaluators exactly as prescribed. The moment they are spontaneously altered to accommodate the wishes of an individual teacher, one or more of the fundamental concepts is violated and the process and outcome are weakened. For example, if in the opinion of one evaluator the testing time should be lengthened for a particular student because of her prior knowledge about that student, the concepts of objectivity, acceptability, comparability, and consistency have been compromised. If the evaluator selects a patient with more than the designated number of areas of care, or adds expectations not outlined in the critical elements, the conceptual foundation of the test is weakened.

Scores of independent actions by evaluators—too numerous to list—can occur. Basically, the problem of evaluator bias emanates from two sources: (1) incomplete knowledge of the specifics of the examination and its implementation or (2) deliberate violation of procedures. In spite of knowing all about the test, some faculty members may continue to look for ways to bypass established protocol and to modify various aspects of the situation. If evaluators look hard enough for loopholes or for excuses to modify the test, they probably will find them, much to their personal satisfaction but to the detriment of objective assessment. The strength of established traditions and habits should not be underestimated. A teacher still will "get a feeling in my mind" about the capability of students and act on those feelings. This occurs throughout the teaching phase—and it can be extremely useful in helping students to learn; but such feelings are not appropriate during the performance examination.

Evaluator bias also may be exhibited in the kinds of arrangements made before the test even begins. For example, even when the criteria for selecting patients are followed, the evaluator can influence student outcomes. The criteria are intended to facilitate comparability of testing episodes but of necessity they must be broad enough to accommodate the actual situation. The intent is that students should have patients who require the same level of care. However, it is quite possible for an evaluator to stay within the criteria but still choose patients whose care is more complex than intended for the test period. Some evaluators have "pet areas" they look for, or avoid, which tailors expectations to their own preference rather than to the intent of the examination. The teacher in them looks for the most complex situation and the opportunity to stretch requirements to the limits—or beyond.

Another way the evaluator can influence the examination is by knowingly or unknowingly communicating to the staff and/or patients before or during the test personal opinions that create certain impressions. These impressions then find their way into the interactions that occur during the test, with either positive or negative outcomes. Depending on the preexisting relationship between the staff and evaluator, these incidental cues may be ignored or unconsciously used while giving or receiving report or assisting students during the test. Although this is not the most common problem, it should be anticipated and avoided.

Interactive Factors

Controlling evaluator bias is dependent on at least five major factors, including: the examination philosophy, the clarity of the testing instrument itself, explicit procedures to control bias, reorientation and full cooperation by the faculty, and mutual sharing of the rules with students and faculty alike. These are complex interactive factors that have been mentioned earlier; each will be reviewed briefly, with the intent of focusing on the control of bias.

The initial factor that introduces more objectivity into performance evaluation is the separation of teaching–learning time and testing time. This automatically imposes two sets of conduct for faculty members, one focusing on teaching and associated "interventions" and the other focusing on neutral observations without intervention. When instructors accept this fundamental idea they can begin to exercise control on their conduct during the clinical test as they do during the administration of written tests. Also associated with this idea is the separation of theory from performance testing. Once this concept is accepted, teachers do not have to question students or verbally interact with them during the performance test. This encourages more detachment and more neutrality.

The clarity and objectivity of critical elements and procedural statements also are essential in controlling bias. In developing the test, value words—such as correct, appropriate, proper, good, or the like—are excluded, or at least kept to a minimum. Such words are ambiguous and subject to multiple interpretations, depending on the evaluator, the student, and other aspects of the situation. Consequently, they allow more subjectivity than can be tolerated. Critical elements also should be phrased in such a way that these value words are defined and thus have a common meaning. For example, instead of stating that the student should take the temperature correctly, the critical element defines correct by giving a range of acceptability: "obtains temperature within plus or minus 0.2 of a degree." Testing procedures also are expressed in unambiguous language to minimize the independent actions and personal preferences of evaluators. When every step of the examination process is outlined, evaluators are prohibited from exerting biased opinions, hence the test is more consistently and objectively administered. This means spelling out what evaluators should do for anticipated and unanticipated situations, even if the protocol is established only for who decides and under what conditions particular decisions are made.

Obviously, merely writing the statements will not control bias; faculty members must fully understand and use them. Involvement from the initial phase of deciding to use a performance examination to its full implementation requires a comprehensive plan to assist faculty members to understand and cooperate with objective performance testing procedures, including the deliberate and comprehensive control of bias.

One rather effective way to control evaluator bias is to make all aspects of the examination and rules of procedure fully known to students. When students and faculty both share the same examination guide, the tendency for evaluators to make spontaneous changes is greatly minimized. Students not only know what can be tested (the array of possibilities), they also know all of the conditions under which they will be tested. This includes how much time is allowed, the kinds of patients selected, the number of areas allowed, and what happens when unanticipated events occur. If an evaluator chooses patients who require too many areas of care or inappropriate areas, the student has the right to object, as these actions are clear violations of protocol. If the evaluator believes that a student should be failed because of a previously established opinion and prematurely interrupts or fails her or him for behaviors not listed in the critical elements, the student has the right to appeal. Therefore, the fact that students are informed of the potential content to be tested, the role and responsibilities of the evaluator, and of all other aspects of the examination accomplishes two purposes: it greatly minimizes the tendency to deviate from protocol because of personal opinion, while it also facilitates achievement of the established standard of practice. Although this open approach is quite different from the traditional faculty–student relationship, it is extremely useful in performance testing because it markedly enhances objectivity and consistency. It establishes a new kind of partnership in learning, in which demonstrated competence of a given standard of practice is the expected and desired outcome.

SPECIFIC PROCEDURES

In addition to the above-noted ways to minimize the diversity of personal preferences and opinions, certain other procedures should be implemented. Perhaps the most important of these is establishing a random basis for assigning students to evaluators, to patients, and to units.* Any number of ways could be used and the best preferred method will depend on factors associated with the test, such as its complexity, available resources, number of students, timing, etc. The main point is that objectivity is enhanced when students are paired with an evaluator at random rather than on some deliberate basis. For example, students could draw cards on which the evaluator and patient-

---

*See chapter 8 for details about scheduling arrangements.

assignment patterns are written, or sign up for a given time slot without knowing who their evaluators will be, or be assigned by random numbers to evaluators who are not their current teachers. The same objective could also be accomplished by other methods. If examinations are given at the conclusion of the first and the second year, faculty could "exchange students" during the testing periods. If a comprehensive end-of-program examination is used, teachers from the early semester could become the evaluators, or when economically possible part-time faculty could be employed as evaluators during the examination periods.

It also might be desirable for the faculties of two or more programs in a given geographic area to form a "testing consortium" in which they exchange faculty members to evaluate each others' students. They also could form an evaluator pool, with assignments made on a random basis. In fact, it would be quite possible to establish a regional testing center for performance evaluation in which all comparable candidates would be tested by prepared evaluators from different programs in the area.* Efforts could be made to assign faculty at times other than when their own students are being tested; however, this probably would become too complicated and is not necessary so long as random assignments are made.

SUMMARY

In summary, then, evaluator bias can be controlled fairly well if teachers are not permitted to choose the students they wish to evaluate; if students are not permitted to select their evaluators; if neither group knows in advance which patients will be assigned; and if neither group knows in advance which selected areas actually will be assigned. One more factor that helps to limit personal preferences and bias is knowing that a colleague is assigned the role of examination coordinator (clinical associate) and has the explicit responsibility of ensuring that evaluators conform to all aspects of the examination. By having faculty members rotate between these two positions, everyone can learn the dual expectations and perspectives, and probably will develop a more positive attitude toward both roles and the difficulties associated with each.

---

*Plans are underway to make the New York Regents External Degree performance examinations available at regional testing centers throughout the United States and ultimately to other nursing programs.

EVALUATOR RESPONSIBILITIES AT EXAMINATIONS

Evaluators have two basic roles during the administration of clinical performance examinations conducted in the real-life setting. First and foremost they function as observers, examiners, and reporters of the actions (and inactions) of students against a prescribed standard of expectations. They also simultaneously function as a patient advocate, protecting the patient from any harm or threat of harm during the testing episode. Each of these roles is essential and requires the evaluator's undivided attention. Neither one can be relinquished or jeopardized by carelessness; therefore, each role will be explored to highlight the evaluator's respective responsibilities. Becoming familiar with these roles is an important part of the comprehensive transition to performance examinations. While most of these considerations apply generally, some of the particulars may vary from one program or type of examination to another, and modifications should be made as necessary. Obviously, in simulated situations most of the points related to patient protection will not apply.

THE EVALUATOR

As previously indicated, the primary responsibility of the examiner is to function as an objective observer rather than as a teacher. This is true for the entire testing period, even though a "teaching-oriented" conference can be arranged afterwards if desirable to discuss either positive or negative results. The evaluator also is responsible for behaving toward students in a manner intended to neutralize the test-related anxiety and to foster the kind of relationship that promotes objective assessment. Students may attempt to set up more familiar kinds of interactions; however, the evaluator is obliged to maintain a "positive neutrality" to the extent possible, given particular situations.

The evaluator is responsible for selecting patients according to the predetermined criteria to ensure comparability of testing episodes. This means that each patient chosen needs the designated required areas of nursing care and the correct number of selected areas of care as specified in the examination guide. As most patients usually need the required areas, the evaluator can save time by scanning the kardex or charts and seeking assistance from staff to identify patients who need the selected areas of nursing care on the examination list.

Team leaders, charge nurses, or other designated staff nurses can be extremely helpful in expediting patient selection, once they are fully oriented to the test procedures. After patients are tentatively identified, a brief discussion with the staff helps to confirm the appropriateness of assigning them for testing purposes. The staff readily knows which patients require too much time, are too ill, are not as ill as they seem on paper, have complicating factors (such as a family or physician who would become upset with the testing situation), are expected to leave the unit for special therapy, etc. The evaluator is responsible for confirming that the patient actually needs the areas of care identified for the test, that the care usually can be accomplished in the designated time period, and that the patient's (and/or family's) cooperation can be expected. In time, evaluators become more experienced in identifying and confirming patients for clinical testing. The staff, other evaluators, and the clinical associate can be most helpful in efficiently making these assignments. The selection process is extremely important if the test is to be objective, comparable, and consistently administered.

Once patients are tentatively selected and approved by the staff, the evaluator visits them to obtain their cooperation; however, this must be accomplished in a manner that ensures as much neutrality as possible. The word "examination" is not used with patients—either by evaluators, by staff, or by students. The word "test" or "examination" influences the patient to behave in one of several ways, none of which is in the best interest of the examination. Some patients might take the word to mean that they are having some kind of test or examination (this actually has happened), which creates unnecessary anxiety and confusion and serves no good purpose. Some patients may feel very kindly toward the students and attempt to help them in various ways. Patients and students thus become allies in a conspiracy against the test and its consequences. Such behavior inadvertently reduces the objectivity of the situation and is very difficult to reverse once it has been set in motion. Other patients are too concerned about their own illness so that they react in a hostile manner and give the student trouble that otherwise would not have occurred. Sometimes the patient assumes an ally relationship with the evaluator, and together, they will "really" test the ability of the student. This reaction, whether overt or covert, also reduces the opportunity to conduct the examination objectively, and should be avoided. Therefore, the evaluator is responsible for seeking the tacit approval of the patient to allow the student "to administer nursing care" during the examination just as they would during the teaching–learning phase. The approach to the patient is the same, but the approach to the student is quite different.

Staying Uninvolved

But that is only step one. Step two requires the evaluator to remain as unobtrusive and uninvolved as possible while the student is giving care. This is extremely difficult and requires deliberate and concentrated attention throughout the test. One of the major difficulties is that faculty members rarely have had the experience of remaining in the patient's room while students are giving care without showing, telling, or coaching the student and engaging in professional–social conversation with the patient and/or student. However, during the test, the evaluator is responsible for remaining detached and uninvolved—professionally and socially—with both parties. To the extent possible, and depending on the need to move in for closer observation, the evaluator should try to remain out of the line of vision, especially the patient's vision. This can be done by sitting in a spot where the student's actions can be clearly visualized but where the patient is not constantly reminded of the evaluator's presence.

This kind of detached, neutral position also can be achieved by the evaluator's casually telling the patient in advance that she will remain in the room while the student gives care, but that the student will be responsible for total care. If a patient becomes too curious and a detailed explanation is required so that the neutrality of the situation is jeopardized, then the patient should not be selected for testing purposes unless absolutely necessary. In most care settings in which students also have their clinical learning experiences, patients willingly accept a casual explanation for the student assignment. Sometimes further explanation may be required but if possible it should be given after the test is finished. The primary point is that evaluators are responsible for establishing and maintaining an atmosphere conducive to the objective examination of the students' competence.

Other Factors

The evaluator also is responsible for expediting the administration of the examination by assuring that all essential supplies and equipment are available prior to beginning the test. In fact, routine items such as linen, equipment for taking vital signs, and the like can be collected by the evaluator and put in the patient's room while the student is writing the care plan. In tests in which it is appropriate, students probably will be held accountable for preparing medications, treatment trays, etc., but evaluators should be sure such equipment is on the unit to prevent unnecessary delays during the test. Unless it is critical that students secure the equipment and supplies, evaluators can do so in advance, thus allowing students to spend all available time in planning, implementing, and evaluating nursing care required by the test, thus making the test more efficient and keeping the time requirement to a minimum.

The prime responsibility of the evaluator is the meticulous and conscientious application of the critical elements and other designated examination guidelines as the only basis for passing or failing students. Evaluators are expected to have the list of critical elements actually in hand (on a clipboard or in a notebook) during all phases of the test. Student behaviors are not recalled after the test is finished; rather, each critical element is checked off as it is performed. On-the-spot documentation prevents problems' arising from errors in memory. In some instances critical elements may be evaluated at the conclusion of the test if that is the appropriate time for them to occur—e.g., recording the history and physical findings, recording intake and output, or finalizing other aspects of care. Evaluators are not permitted to change, to delete, to "stretch," or to intensify critical elements during the test because it suits their own preferences. They are obliged to observe and report the student's behavior in reference to the critical elements as written.

When students fail to meet a critical element, the test is interrupted and terminated—without jeopardizing the patient, of course. After the failure is declared (outside the hearing of the patient), the evaluator may assist the student or complete the particular aspect of care in progress, whichever seems most appropriate. This is in the patient's best interest and maintains positive relationships with the agency staff for future examinations. The critical element failed is identified and the details of the situation are objectively described in a space provided on the evaluator's copy of the test, which is the permanent record. Both student and evaluator must sign the description as it is a legal part of the test document and may be necessary in the future should the student appeal the decision. If the evaluator cannot specify the critical element (or guideline) and document the student's failure to perform it as written, grounds for failure are very questionable. In these cases, it is advisable to discuss the situation with the clinical associate (or another evaluator if the clinical associate position is not used) prior to making a final decision.

Some behaviors are less concrete than others, and because a minimum of three human beings (student, patient, and evaluator) are involved with every test, total objectivity is not possible in real patient situations. Some aspects of care fall into an ambiguous gray zone and need special consideration. Behaviors related to asepsis, physical jeopardy, emotional jeopardy, and interpersonal relations frequently fall into this gray area and require clarification before the pass/fail decision can be made. In fact, unless the evaluator is convinced that the patient actually is jeopardized, the student is allowed to continue with nursing care. If the student is incompetent, another more concrete error undoubtedly will occur to result in failure; if no specific critical element is violated before the completion of the test episode, the evaluator then must decide, in consultation with another uninvolved person, whether or not the specific behavior was indeed grounds for failure and can be defended legally if that becomes necessary.

Evaluators sometimes interrupt students too hastily when they think an error is about to be made; thus another responsibility of the evaluator is to allow students sufficient time to correct potential errors unless the patient is actually being jeopardized. Sometimes these situations are "cliff-hangers" and are very stressful. The evaluator must stand by, attentive to every movement, ready to step in at any second to protect the patient, yet also must allow the student the opportunity to recognize the potential error and to correct it independently. All of this should be accomplished, of course, without giving cues to the student that an error is about to be committed.

Fulfilling the role of evaluator also requires that the faculty member be fully responsible for completing all examination forms as specified. The primary document is the assessment record that lists all critical elements with a space for checking a pass/fail result for each one. It also includes such basic information as the patient's name, identification number, location and date of the test, as well as the student's name and identification number, and the evaluator's name. The nursing-care plan written by the student also is part of the permanent test record as it includes the areas of care tested, the student's outline of care, and the final analysis and evaluation of that care. For legal purposes, it also must be signed by the student and the evaluator at the conclusion of the test.

All of these forms (and others if necessary) must be carefully completed and filed. Ordinarily, they simply document the specific content and results of the test; however, they become extremely important if the student who fails appeals the evaluator's decision. In such cases, the evaluator's written description of the failure and all other aspects of the documents are reviewed by a committee of uninvolved faculty members along with the student's petition and description of what happened. Consequently, careful attention to all details on the forms is essential. The evaluator who observes the student during the test episode is responsible for completing each form for each student, as specified in the examination guide. The associate collects each record and reviews it for completeness before students and evaluators leave the testing site.

THE PATIENT ADVOCATE

In addition to being an objective observer, the evaluator also functions as the patient's advocate when the performance examination is conducted in an actual patient-care environment. The primary responsibility associated with this role is to protect the patient during the test period from any unnecessary discomfort, harm, or interruption of ongoing care. There are several nuances associated with this responsibility that deserve explanation in the interest of preparing evaluators for this aspect of their role.

The evaluator establishes an initial relationship with the patient (and sometimes with his family and/or physician), which is intended to protect his best interest (as previously described). Careful attention is paid to selecting patients and to informing them in general as to what to expect. Every effort is made to minimize potential anxiety or other forms of distress. In some instances the evaluator must decide in the interest of the patient's well-being to choose another patient, or even to terminate the particular test episode if it already is in progress. Obviously, such decisions should be made as soon as possible to protect the interests of both the patient and the student. The evaluator is responsible for assuring to the extent possible that the patient's condition or recovery is not jeopardized by the test itself.

Basically, the evaluator is responsible for becoming fully informed about the patient's illness, treatment, and nursing-care needs before the student begins the test episode. Only when the evaluator is knowledgeable about all aspects of the patient's care can she protect him from any actions or inactions by the student during the test. Evaluators who do not take the time to determine IV fluid requirements, for example, cannot know whether the student's care is accurate or not. Unless the evaluator understands the patient's symptoms, treatments, reactions and responses, or whether he should be in or out of bed, etc., she will have difficulty in objectively and accurately determining the student's competence. The ability to intervene to protect the patient will be acutely limited unless the evaluator is fully informed and attentive to the needs of the patient.

Evaluators are responsible for remaining with the student continuously during the implementation phase of the performance examination. All aspects of all assigned areas of care must be observed directly, otherwise decisions will be made based on assumptions, guesses, or intuition. Nor can the patient be protected from an incompetent student if the evaluator is absent for the moment—regardless of the reason. (The word "incompetent" is used here to describe the student who does not meet the critical elements that have been written to define the standard of performance expected of students at the particular level being tested). Students may ask evaluators to go get some needed supplies or equipment, someone may call the evaluator out of the room, the evaluator may be tired and need a break. Regardless of the reason, students cannot be allowed to continue with care while the evaluator is somewhere else. Such a rule is in the best interest of the patient and is mandatory for the conduct of an objective performance examination. The evaluator does not know what the student is doing unless she is there to observe. This is a fundamental point and must be observed. If the evaluator has to leave the room, the student should cease care and leave the room also—or at least not engage in any direct care until the evaluator returns. If the student leaves the patient to obtain drugs or equipment needed for care, the evaluator must accompany her. Thought and planning are required to fully implement this rule of conduct.

From the beginning to the end of the test episode the evaluator is responsible for being attentive to the patient's needs and any changes in physical or emotional status and safety. If, for example, the student leaves the patient's room without putting the siderails up and the evaluator follows without correcting the situation, the patient is in jeopardy and the evaluator is responsible. If the evaluator loses concentration and allows her thoughts to wander to personal matters or the pressures of the work ahead, she has become disengaged and is unable to fulfill the role of patient advocate, or of evaluator. One reason evaluators become so fatigued during clinical examinations is this demand for constant awareness on behalf of the student and the patient. Unless she is fully alert she will not be perceptive of the patient or of the student.

Finally, the evaluator also is responsible for ensuring that the patient is returned to the care of the staff at the end of the test in as safe and comfortable condition as possible. Evaluators may become so focused on the student and the test that they block out patient requirements. At the conclusion of the test episode, IV fluids must be regulated properly, siderails brought up and secured, intake and output charted, oxygen flowing as specified, traction functioning, etc. Before leaving the unit the evaluator must recheck the patient to be sure that all aspects of care have been completed and reported, and that he is safe. The evaluators also must listen to the student's report to the responsible staff member and read the recorded progress notes to ensure that continuity of care is maintained as well as to complete the assessment of the student for that situation.

CRITERIA FOR EVALUATING EVALUATORS

The responsibilities of the evaluator are comprehensive but the fulfillment of all of them is essential if the examination is to be administered as designed and the patients protected from unsafe or unpleasant experiences. Consequently, it is important that evaluators perform these two roles as specified. During the transition they may need particular assistance in doing this, but under most test circumstances they will continue to require some form of monitoring. The tendency to regress to teacher behaviors is too likely not to provide for some kind of periodic evaluation. The following criteria for evaluating evaluators is suggested both as a summary of these individuals' responsibilities and as a guide to help them adapt to the new aspects of their role. The clinical associate or some other designated person may use these criteria in observing the evaluators during the administration of the clinical tests, especially during the early transition period. Experience has clearly demonstrated, however, that continued monitoring helps to assure objectivity and consistency. As pointed out earlier, evaluators and clinical associates may have difficulty accepting each other's roles unless they are mutually engaged in the development and in the approval of whatever final test arrangements are made.

IN THE ROLE OF EXAMINER

1. Functions as objective observer rather than as teacher during the entire clinical examination.
2. Behaves toward students in a manner intended to neutralize their anxiety and to promote objective assessment of competence.
3. Selects patients according to predetermined guidelines.
4. Prepares patients for the situation in a positive but neutral manner.
5. Expedites the testing process by assuring that all necessary supplies and equipment are available prior to beginning the test.
6. Evaluates students during the test by using only the specified guidelines and critical elements.
7. Observes the student at all times during the entire testing episode.
8. Documents the completion, error, or omission of each critical element (or guideline) during the test, as each area is being performed.
9. Allows student to correct errors unless the patient is actually or on the verge of being jeopardized.
10. Terminates the testing episode when necessary at the time and in the manner specified by predetermined criteria.
11. Obtains clarification and corroboration from the clinical associate prior to failing a student when the situation is ambiguous or borderline (''gray areas'').
12. Completes all forms as specified as legal documentation of the test.

IN THE ROLE OF PATIENT ADVOCATE

1. Establishes relationships with patient, his family, and staff that promote the best interest of the patient.
2. Assumes full responsibility for knowing all essential aspects of the patient's nursing care prior to beginning the test.
3. Remains with the student continuously during all aspects of care to ensure the safety and well-being of the patient.
4. Intervenes to protect the patient from actual harm or immediate threat of harm during the test period.
5. Remains aware of and attentive to the patient's needs throughout the test episode, but interrupts the student only when absolutely necessary.

6. Assumes responsibility for assuring that the patient is left in as safe and comfortable a condition as possible, and that continuity of care is maintained through the customary oral and written reports at the conclusion of the test.

ONGOING PROBLEMS OF EVALUATORS

The kinds of problems evaluators experience, even after a sustained orientation, generally fall into three broad categories: regression to the teacher role, inconsistency in test administration, and premature interruption of test episodes. Because all of these problems have serious consequences for test outcomes, some examples will be described. As with other aspects of implementing performance examinations, when the faculty is informed in advance, they can prepare to deal with these problems as anticipated events. At least theoretically this should minimize their occurrence, and the disturbance they cause when they do happen. Because most of these problems have been mentioned earlier, this section serves as a review. Each of the faculty responses reflects difficulty with one or more of the basic concepts presented in chapter 3.

REGRESSION TO THE TEACHER ROLE

When teachers feel uncomfortable with the examiner role they can respond in one of several ways. In the beginning they may be very conscientious about being an evaluator but gradually slip back into more comfortable and familiar behaviors with students, even during the test episode itself. Some faculty members exhibit the must-teach complex. They simply "can't help it"; they have an overwhelming need to be sure the student really knows—knows the theory behind the action, knows the mistakes nearly made, knows what to do and in what sequence, etc. They regress to asking the student: "why?" Some evaluators are able to correct themselves, but others need external assistance. The problem emanates from a lack of acceptance of the fundamental distinction between teaching and testing and between theory testing and performance testing.

The come-to-the-rescue complex is similar but has the added nuance of wanting to assist the student. This typically happens when the student looks somewhat bewildered and is thinking through what should be done next. These feelings also come over the evaluator when the patient asks a question that is assumed to be difficult or embarrassing for the student. The teacher in the evaluator comes to the rescue, and assists the student by answering the question—sometimes even before the student has had time to utter a word in response. The teacher is indirectly saying to the student: "Just watch me and I'll show you how to deal with such touchy situations." The teacher also is saying: "You don't know how to answer the question; I'll do it for you." This kind of faculty response seriously compromises the objectivity and comparability of the examination. Either the faculty does not understand the distinction between the role of teacher and role of evaluator, or has not accepted and does not trust the performance examination as the sole means of documenting the clinical competence of students.

Teachers who have the mothering complex also respond similarly but usually become more emotionally involved. They feel strong impulses to help, to show, and tell as a way of saying: "I care about what you're going through. You're so nervous. I know you can do it (didn't I show you how myself?) I cannot watch without helping. Reducing the psychic trauma [the student's and the teacher's] can't interfere that much with the test." The teacher–evaluator who is overcome with the mothering complex becomes the socializer with the student and the patient in order to relieve the stress and to protect the student. However, this kind of behavior reduces the objectivity, consistency, comparability, and level of acceptability of the examination and thus must be dealt with openly if and when it occurs.

Discomfort with the role of objective evaluator also may result in the I-can't-decide complex. Teachers who are not used to making concrete decisions on the basis of observed behavior and in reference to a specific standard may have difficulty actually declaring that the student has passed or has failed. They may look for hidden nuances, interpret behavior out of context, or look for that which isn't there. They feel the intensity of the experience and its importance, especially when the total decision about clinical performance rests on this one test. Sometimes looking at every student action under a kind of microscope and/or taking it out of context can result in distorted observations and expectations. The evaluator becomes so burdened with the need to be perfect in the assessment that she cannot make the decisions with assurance. She becomes unnecessarily anxious about the consequences of passing or failing the student and is momentarily immobilized. She may lose sight of the essence of the role and feel uncertain about what to do when the student asks a question or when patient care is interrupted unexpectedly.

The insecurity of the I-can't-decide complex can be relieved by discussing the use of examination guidelines and critical elements, exactly as written, as the grounds for making pass/fail decisions. When gray areas arise, the evaluator is reminded to seek consultation with the clinical associate or other uninvolved person. The concepts of examination, objectivity, and consistency also need to be reviewed, to illustrate how they can help to minimize this kind of insecurity. Experience and external observations by the associate will also help.

At the opposite end of the spectrum from the mothering complex is the detached-authoritarian complex. When some teachers are uncomfortable or uncertain about the evaluator role they may respond by acting like policemen. Somehow they equate objectivity with an extreme degree of detachment that often is manifested as intimidation. Those who react this way also misunderstand the role of objective observer, because they assume that it precludes any feelings of human caring for the student and that cold detachment does not influence the student's performance. In reality, the students' level of anxiety is greatly intensified by an authoritarian evaluator whose actions and body language convey the expectation (and maybe the wish) of failure. The student may become totally unnerved by a stern-looking evaluator constantly peering over her shoulder, with arms crossed in front of her, clutching the clipboard as if in protection from letting her true feelings show. The student reads this evaluator's behavior as menacing, threatening, and uncaring, and may lose the concentration required for the examination. Many students cannot survive such intimidation and consequently fail, not necessarily because they are incompetent but because of the additional psychological stress imposed by the evaluator's behavior. It takes only a few moments to recognize an evaluator with the detached-authoritarian complex. If the examination is to achieve its purpose, these evaluators will have to be cautiously confronted and helped to move in the direction of observing with the perspective of positive neutrality: neither as a mother, nor as a policeman, but as a humane, caring, neutral, observer.

One other behavior response to the discomfort of the evaluator role can be described as the idealist complex. In this instance the evaluator shows regressing to the teacher role by requiring that the student perform everything perfectly during the examination. It is not enough that the student correctly completes all critical elements and guidelines as specified by the test; everything must be done with the quality consistent with the teacher's own personal performance and expectation. Evaluators with this complex have expectations that are excessively exacting and beyond the level of acceptability established by the examination. They impose their own standard over that required by the critical elements. Such evaluators often may comment: "Well, she did the critical elements but I didn't like the way she did it. She almost contaminated the field. She should have thought of it in advance so she wouldn't have to interrupt the procedure. She didn't rub hard enough. She used too many 4 × 4s. [etc., etc.]" Such comments reflect a lack of understanding of the demands of a comprehensive objective performance examination and a wish for ideal performance by students, regardless of the tolerance of deviation from that ideal allowed in the test itself.

These evaluators have not yet integrated the fact that a performance examination, like an objective written test, includes a reasonable sample of clinical abilities (not the totality) and establishes the level of acceptability of student performance as outlined in the critical elements. Regardless of the desires for perfection by the evaluator, the concepts of examination, consistency, comparability, sampling, objectivity, and acceptability will be seriously compromised unless this problem is confronted and resolved. It is a very difficult and emotionally laden issue, but to sidestep it would be to invite failure in the examination process.

INCONSISTENCY IN TEST ADMINISTRATION

The second category of ongoing problems experienced by evaluators involves difficulty administering the test according to the predetermined conditions, rules, and critical elements. Faculty members who are fully informed about the examination and their role as evaluator, yet who still persist in deviating from the established protocol probably are suffering from the I-know-best complex. Knowingly or unknowingly these evaluators may do such things as change the criteria for selecting patients, assign too many or too few areas of care, change the time allowed for the testing episode, begin too early or too late, or neglect to collect routine supplies or to assure the availability of equipment. They also are willing to change critical elements, to add or to delete them "depending on the situation."

The evaluator who "knows best" frustrates the possibility of conducting an objective, consistent, and comparable performance examination. When the rules are changed spontaneously by individuals, the test loses its credibility and usefulness. Therefore, like the evaluators with other problems, those with the I-know-best complex need special attention. The suggested label for the problem conveys the need for caution in attempting to help these teachers modify their behavior to become more consistent with expectations for the role.

PREMATURE INTERRUPTION OF TEST EPISODES

The third category of ongoing problems concerns evaluators who prematurely terminate the examination and fail students. These evaluators share the strong feelings of the idealist but are unable to wait to see what the student actually does. They are convinced early in the administration of the test that the student "has failed" and are impatient to declare it. Typically, they do not allow the student time to recognize and correct an error (before the patient is harmed); they assume that the student does not know, did not recognize, will not perform, etc. Their intuition, guess, hunch, or experienced insight take precedence over letting the critical elements and other aspects of the test itself determine the student's competence. They are experiencing the jumping-to-conclusions complex.

Some examples will illustrate the point. One student was completing comprehensive care of a patient who had a Foley catheter connected to a drainage bag. The student was quite successful in meeting all critical elements until near the end of the situation when she was making the bed. She completed one side, turned the patient, and moved to the opposite side. She was completing last touches on the bed and making sure the patient was comfortable when the evaluator told her to step outside, where she informed her she had failed. The student was shocked and asked why. The evaluator stated that she had failed to adjust the Foley tube, that it was draped too low to facilitate drainage. The student responded, quite legitimately, that she had not yet had time to do so; she had planned to fix the tube but the evaluator had interrupted her. The student subsequently appealed and the evaluator's decision was reversed.

Similar situations occur when evaluators assume that the student is going to contaminate the dressing or gloves, is going to forget to chart intake and output, or omit vital signs, etc., and interrupt before the student has the chance to correct the actual or potential problem. However, after such situations occur the teacher can never really be sure that the student would have corrected the problem, and that is just the point: unless the patient is actually being jeopardized or is in immediate danger of being harmed, the evaluator has an obligation to let the student continue. Obviously, the evaluator must be ready to prevent harm to the patient, but she also must allow the student every opportunity to demonstrate competence up to that point. This is a difficult lesson to learn; but over and over, evaluators are surprised that if they wait a few more moments, students often discover the potential error and correct it in time—on their own and benefiting from that learning.

SUMMARY

The conversion of teachers to objective evaluators is a long-term and difficult process. However, nothing else is more important—except the test itself—in accomplishing objective clinical assessment of the learner. Because of faculty's influence on the outcomes of the test, considerable attention has been focused on some strategies for conversion, the psychological responses that can be anticipated, the roles and responsibilities of the evaluator, and a review of ongoing problems that can be expected.

The preparation and use of a manual for evaluators probably will help during the initial and long-term transition. Such a manual, used in conjunction with the orientation discussion (interaction) sessions, could be useful in helping teachers to identify problems they are likely to encounter, and thus avoid some distress. The manual should include all requirements of the examination itself, rules of conduct and expectations for student and evaluators, conditions under which the test will be administered, responsibilities of evaluators and associates, the potential evaluator problems, criteria for evaluating evaluators, and any other information that will help the faculty move closer to objective clinical assessment of students. The manual as well as the testing process probably can be revised and improved with experience. However, anticipating the most likely problems will help in the transition and will minimize unnecessary anxiety and frustration.

CHAPTER 10

Multiple Uses of Performance Testing in Education and Service

The previous chapters were deliberately focused on the process of developing and implementing a comprehensive clinical performance examination. Suggestions have been made periodically about how such a test could be modified for a variety of uses at different levels in nursing education and in nursing service. This chapter describes these possibilities in sufficient detail to assist the reader to make necessary adaptations for a variety of particular purposes. The foregoing concepts, principles, criteria, problems, and other considerations are applicable in essentially all types of performance testing, regardless of the specific purposes. Therefore, the suggestions described below are made within the context of material in the previous chapters and are presented merely to illustrate the wide range of application of objective performance testing. This basic material should enable administrators, practitioners, and other leaders to create their own test versions if those already developed are inadequate for evaluating specific competencies essential in their own programs.

AVAILABILITY OF REGENTS EXAMINATIONS

Since 1976 the standardized written examinations in nursing (and other subjects) developed by the New York State Education Department have been available throughout the United States and many countries abroad by special arrangement with the American College Testing Program. These written tests are widely used for advanced placement and screening purposes by generic programs at the associate, baccalaureate, and master's levels and by career mobility programs. There has been a similar need for objective performance examinations; however, their complexity and the need for specially trained evaluators have limited their implementation outside the State of New York.

At the time of this writing plans are underway to establish regional (or statewide) testing centers for all three nursing performance examinations developed for the New York Regents External Degree Nursing Programs: The Clinical Performance in Nursing Examination (CPNE), the Health Assessment Performance Examination (HAPE), and the Professional Performance Examination (PPE). The Regents External Degree Nursing Program is interested in cooperating with other nursing programs to make one or more of these examinations available for a variety of appropriate purposes. As with centers for the administration of the written tests, the existence of performance testing centers in locations throughout the United States makes it possible for these tests to be used both by students in local on-campus generic or special-purpose programs or by those enrolled for one of the Regents External Degrees. It is conceivable that testing centers also could be used by those in nursing service or other nondegree programs in which the examination requirements are similar.

The possibility of using such testing centers opens up entirely new vistas for the uses of performance tests in education and in nursing service. It would be quite possible, for example, for two or more institutions and/or agencies cooperatively to develop a testing center for a particular geographic area. The combined resources of instructors and facilities would make it more economical and practical to use performance examinations. It is also conceivable that several institutions in densely populated areas could arrange for a testing center with a fulltime staff of trained evaluators. Individual fees with backup support from those who use the institution would finance its operation. Use of such centers by external-degree candidates also would help to generate revenue, so long as the tests required by the faculty were used as specified. It is even possible for such a full-time testing center to administer several versions of performance examinations to suit the specific needs of different programs if it has a well-trained staff of evaluators. A university nursing program or hospital center with a sufficient number of well-prepared in-service staff and facilities might be considered appropriate sites for area-wide testing centers.*

*For further information about the use of Regents External Degree Examinations write: Coordinator, Nursing Program, New York Regents External Degrees, Cultural Education Center, Albany, New York 12230.

SCHEDULING AND GRADING

CREATING A REALISTIC SCHEDULE

When performance examinations are used to determine ability at the end of a course or group of courses, they obviously must be scheduled and administered at that time. Basic considerations for scheduling this type of testing have already been discussed (see chapter 8). However, when performance examinations are used for screening, advanced placement, and admission or promotion purposes, different arrangements could be planned. For example, when a test of performance ability is required in addition to theory testing and/or other documentation, it can be considered like all other prerequisites to be satisfied prior to a designated date. This allows participants to make appointments over a period of several months, thus eliminating the stress of scheduling a large number of testees during a brief time period. If a comprehensive performance test is a prerequisite for admission to an upper-division BSN program or other nontraditional program, the availability of a testing center will enable students to make appointments throughout the year in order to meet that requirement. Or, if the center is only operational during the summer months or intersession periods, appointments could be scheduled then. The amount of scheduling time necessary depends on such factors as the length of the test, the number of students, and the number of trained evaluators available. Scheduling such examinations during certain months or throughout the year makes the process more realistic and serviceable to more individuals without necessarily interfering with other ongoing activities.

GRADES FOR PERFORMANCE EXAMINATIONS

Throughout this volume performance examinations have been described as criterion-referenced, competency-based tests that document mastery of certain designated abilities. As such, students are judged to be competent or not competent, as having met the standard (passed) or not having met it (failed). While this approach seems logical for this kind of performance test, in some situations a faculty may be required or may choose to assign grades or levels of achievement for clinical competence. This poses some difficulties, but one or more ways of assigning grades can be suggested.

For example, one approach might use a basic set of expectations as previously outlined, with areas of practice and critical elements that must be met with 100 percent accuracy. Students could contract in advance for a higher grade (A or B) based on predetermined regulations and requirements. Different criteria for patient selection could be used, with more complex patient situations required for those who want to document a higher level of accomplishment. In addition, those opting for higher grades could be tested on more selected areas and on critical elements that have a more limited range of acceptability (i.e., are more exacting). Gradations in clinical competence can be documented by increasing the complexity of the patient, the number of areas of care, and the stringency of critical elements. The number of patients to be cared for during the time period could be another variable for measuring higher levels of competence.

If grades of A, B, and C are used, predetermined criteria could be specified and students could be held accountable for their performance, either by contract or through some other arrangement. Regardless of the grading system, students need to know in advance (via the examination guide) the expectations held for them and the criteria for success. Then they are responsible for learning and for demonstrating competence according to that standard.

Students also could document a higher level of ability by combining actual performance with other measures, such as individual patient-oriented projects, case studies, interdisciplinary conference, patient teaching, or other clinical activities, depending on the competencies being tested. The content, level of student, etc., all influence the ways in which grades could be assigned to the student's performance. So long as the basic concepts and other principles are applied, letter or number grades could be attached to performance if this practice is deemed necessary. In one sense, grading of competence against a designated standard is a contradiction. Once the criteria have been identified, students either meet them or they don't. However, given the realities of some situations, gradations of competence above and beyond the basic standard may be required; if so, they can be defined and applied. Regardless of the requirements for specific grades, the key point is that in criterion-referenced testing, students are informed in advance and in detail of the standard of performance expected of them; thus they learn with that standard in mind, and must document competence through an objective performance examination.

GENERIC PROGRAMS

Many basic nursing programs are interested in using performance examinations as part of the assessment process for students throughout the program of learning. The need to objectively verify competence as well as knowledge exists for associate, baccalaureate, or other basic instructional programs, and emerges from the demands for increased accountability. The extent to which clinical testing is used depends on many variables; however, it is possible to combine some form of performance examination with theory tests at the conclusion of every course or term, if the faculty is willing to make that kind of investment. It also is possible to have one performance test at the conclusion of the program, or to have some combination between these two extremes. The tests could be actual, or simulated, or both. Some examples related to generic, nontraditional, and special-purpose programs may be useful.

ASSOCIATE DEGREE PROGRAMS

An associate degree program in New York and another in Florida have developed modifications of the comprehensive performance examination described earlier; they use it at the conclusion of the third semester. The traditional evaluation procedures are used for each course but students are expected to pass the performance examination as a prerequisite for entering the final semester of the program. They are aware of this from the beginning of the program and therefore prepare for it accordingly.

The faculty of the Florida program initially required the performance test at the end of the second semester but later decided that students would benefit from additional experience and that the test would be more valid (for its intended purpose) if it were given later. However, they were uncomfortable about waiting to give the test until the entire program was completed because the consequences of failure were too serious; therefore, the third semester was selected as the most appropriate time. By learning about objective performance testing for the comprehensive examinations, the faculty became more adept at improving the quality of clinical evaluation throughout the entire program. Simulated tests were also developed for use in the college lab during the first three semesters. Among other payoffs, these early experiences help the students to learn how to prepare for the comprehensive clinical examination.

Another associate degree program (located in New York) uses essentially the same approach. Simulated college laboratory performance tests are used throughout the program in conjunction with other assessment procedures; however, during the third semester students are required to pass a comprehensive clinical test. For several reasons the test is given in two parts: one patient-care situation (PCS) is required at the midpoint of the semester and a second PCS is given at the end of the term. If students fail the midterm PCS, they become more aware of their need for additional practice to meet the level of competence expected by the faculty. On the other hand, if they pass that PCS they tend to feel more confident and are likely to spend time concentrating on other clinical abilities. When students pass the second PCS (given at the end of the semester) they are judged successful; if they fail that PCS they are eligible for one repeat PCS arranged by appointment within the succeeding few days. Students must pass a total of two PCSs in order to pass the requirements for clinical competence; the PCSs are divided between the midterm and final periods of the semester to fit time constraints and the faculty's preference for this approach.

In both of these illustrations, clinical performance examinations are required for a student to remain in and complete the nursing program. Students frequently do not like such stressful experiences, but nonetheless they are required to pass. They are fully informed of all aspects of the test and of the expectations held for them. They are given every opportunity to learn, to practice, and to become accustomed to direct and continuous evaluator observation. They are held accountable for their competence in meeting the standard, regardless of their preference for more conventional and perhaps less stressful methods.

An "Ideal" Approach

Still another associate degree program (in the Midwest) prefers the use of some kind of performance testing at the conclusion of each semester. Originally, the faculty wanted to develop and to require a simulated performance test at the completion of each module within each course. Students would be expected to study the module, to practice in the college lab, and to pass a performance test of everything studied before being allowed to perform those areas in the actual patient setting. This arrangement might seem to be ideal; however, it has several disadvantages. Primarily, a large proportion of "learning time" would have to be converted to testing time, resulting in problems for both the faculty and the students. Students also would lose the benefits of cumulative learning, which was described earlier as being beneficial for some and essential for others. Moreover, they all would be expected to learn at the same rate and in the same manner, which may be unrealistic especially when the student body is quite heterogenous.

The faculty in that program later decided that a better approach might be to require simulated laboratory tests at the conclusion of each semester but to use a comprehensive clinical performance examination at or near the completion of the entire program. Ultimately they want to develop and use actual performance examinations at the end of each semester but they realize that this may be unrealistic or unnecessary, or that at best it may be a very long-range goal.

One suggestion to accomplish some aspects of this faculty's "ideal" plan might include a modification in use of the learning laboratory. For example, rather than being optional for students, the practice labs could be mandatory before clinical assignments are made. Furthermore, students could be paired (or clustered in "teams") for the practice sessions. In this arrangement one student would "perform" the area being learned while the other one (or more) observed with critical elements in hand, simulating the role of evaluator. Then they could switch roles, and learning would take place for both groups. Such learning experiences would also help prepare students for the actual examinations. General guidance and supervision by the faculty would have to be provided, of course, but students would be held accountable for passing the actual performance examination, and therefore would have to take these sessions seriously. The characteristics of the students, faculty, and available resources will determine the usefulness of such an approach.

Other Scheduling Procedures

It also is possible in generic associate degree programs to modify the performance test still differently. For instance, clinical skills could be tested at the end of each course, gradually adding more and more factors to be tested as the students progress. Two or three randomly selected procedures could be tested in the patient setting at the end of the first semester. This would require only a brief time per student—if the session were regarded as a test and not as just another learning experience in which "everything" (comprehensive nursing care) had to be done for the patient. At the end of the next semester, an expanded array of skills could be used as the basis for random selection. By the end of the third semester one or two PCSs could be required with an appropriate number of areas of care being assigned. In the beginning the objective is to test separate skills in the patient setting; subsequently the focus is on the integration of knowledge and skills in the comprehensive care of patients.

The advantage of this cumulative clinical testing approach is that students become accustomed to objective and consistent evaluation before they are tested more comprehensively; the disadvantages include time and cost requirements, potential jeopardy to patients, and potential legal problems. The cumulative clinical testing strategy is appealing but essentially the same advantages can be attained by using well-planned simulated laboratory tests followed by more comprehensive patient situations after the students are ready for such a challenge.

BACCALAUREATE DEGREE PROGRAMS

The same kind of clinical performance tests described in the previous section also could be used in generic baccalaureate nursing programs. The timing, the complexity, and number of such performance tests are obviously dependent on the same variables as previously discussed. A test with limited scope could be administered after initial clinical courses; or, a comprehensive performance examination with two or more PCSs could be administered at the conclusion of the program—along with other tests to document competencies expected of BSN graduates.

The kind of clinical performance examination described above involves the technical, hospital-oriented aspects of nursing care for adults and/or children. Other performance tests also may be desirable. For example, with use of the same concepts and criteria presented earlier, a test could be developed to document clinical competence in the area of community health nursing. Essential areas of care and critical elements could be specified along with the criteria for client selection and other precedural aspects. Actual situations could be used so long as sufficient control could be exercised to ensure that reasonably comparable testing episodes would be administered with consistency. A realistic sample of the kinds of competencies expected of a new BSN graduate could be randomly selected, according to predetermined protocol. Students might be tested on abilities such as assessing the health needs of the client, writing a plan, using community resources, collaborating with others on behalf of the client, and/or administering direct nursing care to the client in the home. It should be clear, however, that administering a performance test in the home or a community agency presents its own kind of complexities, all of which require attention. The same concepts previously described apply, and many competencies necessary in community health care could be tested by using simulation.

Specific Areas

Following the courses that focus on parent–child care, a performance examination could be given to test for the unique aspects of nursing care required in that area. Again, a sample of those special competencies essential in caring for mothers (parents) and infants in the prenatal and postpartum periods could be identified and defined for testing purposes. If theory is tested on appropriately designed written tests and general nursing care is tested on a performance test administered elsewhere in the program, then only the unique aspects of parent–child nursing care remain for this examination. It is quite possible that most of those special competencies could be tested by using a simulated examination. When the number of clients with essential characteristics is limited or sporadic, or when facilities are inadequate, or when the skills to be tested are highly complex, perhaps a simulated test of a random sample of those skills would be most desirable. As with other simulated tests, various anatomical models and mannequins could be used, or live subjects could be programmed to role play for testing purposes.

It would be quite possible to use a simulated test to determine the student's ability to do things such as hold, bathe, and bottle feed an infant; administer tube feeding and/or medication to an infant; teach one or both parents various aspects of prenatal care; teach a group of new mothers how to care for their babies; assist new parents to deal with the stress of their new role, and the like. When possible and desirable, well-child clinics, the nursery, and/or postpartum units could be used. The complexities, limitations, and potential problems must be seriously contemplated and resolved before the actual units are used. The number of available clients (parents and infants) is generally unpredictable, as are the needs they present. Therefore, except for large testing centers (medical centers or specialty hospitals) this may be a difficult area in which to require a comprehensive performance examination in the actual patient-care setting. Simulation may be more realistic.

Another example of a performance examination in a generic BSN program is at the conclusion of a course on health assessment. Whether this content is integrated throughout the curriculum or is presented in one or more separate courses, the beginning-level competencies required to take a health history, conduct a physical examination, and then analyze the findings can be tested without too much difficulty. If this content is presented in one or more assessment courses, the test could be given at that time (i.e., at the end of each course, along with other aspects of nursing care); if it is integrated throughout the curriculum, the test could be given at the conclusion of the entire program. The entire history and a random sample of areas in the physical examination could be tested with use of either programmed subjects (clients) or actual clients who meet certain predetermined criteria. Once again, all concepts and principles of objective performance testing must be assured.

Clients and Types of Tests

The kinds of problems presented by actual clients generally revolve around availability and comparability. The problems of using paid subjects as clients relate to their reliability in coming for the test and in their consistency in providing the desired history. Using simulated clients, however, allows maximum control over the nature of the health problems or complaints presented and the kinds of physical findings students are expected to detect. Basically healthy subjects can be selected and instructed (programmed) to relate a predetermined health-care need during the history phase. This restricts the vast array of potential complexities that could occur when actual clinic or hospitalized patients are used.

Faculties of generic BSN programs that want to institute a comprehensive program of objective clinical assessment of students probably will plan to develop and implement two or more performance examinations. It is important to realize that trying to integrate all aspects of professional nursing into one comprehensive clinical performance test may be impossible or even undesirable, for several reasons. Clustering competencies and testing them in separate examinations seems much more realistic, for both the development and the implementation phases. Faculty and students may be more successful with two (or more) rather than one culminating extensive performance test that is nearly impossible to administer and even more difficult to pass, given the level of stress that would be associated with it.

The New York Regents External (BSN) Degree Program provides an example of using multiple examinations. It objectively evaluates the students' competence in nursing by using three performance examinations in addition to the five nursing-theory examinations. The Clinical Performance in Nursing Examination (CPNE) tests the technical portion of nursing care and uses actual adult and child patients in a general hospital. It requires application of all phases of the nursing process. A second type, the Health Assessment Performance Examination (HAPE), tests the students' ability to conduct a comprehensive history and physical examination from a nursing perspective and to analyze the findings and make recommendations for health maintenance or care. Normal, healthy subjects are paid to play the role to allow for maximum control for comparability, availability, testing conditions, etc. This practice requires special training of clients but makes the test more realistic in the long run. Students also are tested on their ability to differentiate between normal and exaggerated abnormal heart and breath sounds by using an audio tape. While various aspects of assessment are included in other nursing tests, this examination is designed to document the students' competence by using a highly controlled set of circumstances.

The third performance examination used for the BSN External Degree Program is totally simulated and is based on video-recorded vignettes to test the students' competence in meeting the critical elements identified by the nursing faculty. The Professional Performance Examination (PPE) tests dimensions of practice such as leadership, collaboration, research process, clinical decision-making, management of client care, teaching, etc. The use of specially designed video tapes makes it possible to manipulate and to control variables related to the client's background, major health problems, nursing process, client spectrum, and practice setting, while ensuring adherence to objectivity, comparability, consistency, sampling, level of acceptability, and the other basic concepts.

Each of these three performance examinations tests different competencies and uses a different format. Together they represent major areas of beginning-level competencies expected of BSN graduates. Each one has its own special significance as well as its unique problems in development and implementation. Together they serve as examples of the different kinds of performance tests that can be used, singly or in combination. It is anticipated that ultimately all three performance tests will be available at regional testing centers for use in more conventional or nontraditional BSN programs throughout the country.

ADVANCED PLACEMENT INTO GENERIC PROGRAMS

The growing emphasis on moving all nursing programs into academic settings has markedly increased the need for valid ways to convert experiential learning of nondegree students into college credits. Written examinations, portfolio assessment, and references are useful, but evaluating clinical competence remains the most difficult problem in implementing a program of advanced placement. An objective performance examination, carefully developed and consistently implemented, permits the faculty of a generic program to assist many more students with previous experience in nursing. The combination of written tests and a performance examination will provide a more realistic and objective basis for accepting or rejecting nontraditional students. In addition to documenting abilities, academic and clinical limitations would be identified and could be used as the foundation for planning a program of learning consistent with the students' needs.

A clinical performance examination consistent with the level of entrance being sought by the student could be required along with all other prerequisites. Examination appointments could be arranged at the convenience of the faculty throughout the year or during designated periods, such as between semesters or during the summer months. This would give students ample time to plan for this requirement without unnecessarily overburdening the existing faculty. However, the existence of a performance testing center in the area (city, state, or region) would make it possible for students to take the examination at any time prior to the admission deadline. Such a testing program is appropriate for those seeking advanced placement in associate, baccalaureate, and even in master's degree programs. A few examples will illustrate the usefulness and variety of approaches that might be considered.

ASSOCIATE DEGREE PROGRAMS

In response to the increasing number of licensed practical nurses seeking admission, an associate degree program on Long Island established assessment procedures for advanced placement of LPNs. In addition to the customary general education prerequisites, these students are required to take four standardized proficiency examinations in nursing (from the Regents external associate degree battery) and a performance examination. The performance test is a modified shorter version of the Clinical Performance Nursing Examination (CPNE) developed by the Regents faculty. Based on successful completion of these prerequisites, which may be met throughout the year but must be met prior to a designated date, LPNs are admitted to the third semester of this generic associate degree nursing program. These written and performance tests document that the LPNs have academic and clinical competencies equivalent to other students entering the second year of the program.

A performance test designed for this level could either use a simulated or actual format, depending on the availability of faculty and other resources and the need for evaluation in the real-life setting. In geographic areas where LPNs tend to be clinically strong and generally have abilities comparable to beginning second-year associate students, use of a simulated performance test probably would be quite adequate. If the faculty prefers a performance examination in the actual patient-care setting but is unable to develop or implement one, a simulated test can be used with the stipulation that additional evaluation is necessary after enrollment. For example, these special students could be objectively observed in a quasi-performance test after admission, within a period of a few weeks. This kind of arrangement is problematic, especially for students who cannot confirm plans for remaining in the program until after this conditional period. However, it does allow the faculty objectively to evaluate basic skills by using an economical and realistic approach, and to convert prior learning to academic credit.

It would be possible to design a test version that uses an actual setting but is limited to one three-hour PCS. This would make the test reasonably economical in time and cost, and would provide the opportunity for real-life assessment. In order to provide an appropriate level of acceptability with use of only one PCS, *X* or *Y* areas of care could be required with 100 percent accuracy (instead of two or three entire PCSs that require 100 percent accuracy in all areas and critical elements). For example, the single PCS might specify that students pass two required areas of care (such as promoting personal hygiene or taking vital signs) and two of three selected areas of care (such as handling sterile dressings or irrigations). This would mean that the student must complete four of five areas of care with 100 percent accuracy, but sufficient flexibility is provided to allow for sampling and diversity.

Of course, it is quite possible to design such a test by using a whole array of combinations so that students are tested on a random sample of appropriate areas of care. It also is possible simply to require that students meet all designated areas in the PCS with 100 percent accuracy, but limit the areas to be tested—e.g., personal hygiene, vital signs, and medications; or hygiene, vital signs, and dressing; or vital signs, medications, and dressings. The particular areas to be included will vary, depending on such factors as faculty availability and resources; the permutations and combinations are almost limitless.

Tests such as those described above could be readily developed and implemented by using the simulated format. The array of potential areas to be tested, their critical elements, and all other aspects of the test would be made known to students, but the actual test would include only a sample from those possibilities. So long as the basic concepts, principles, and criteria are followed, a number of test versions could be used by associate degree programs interested in assisting LPNs, corpsmen, or other experienced individuals to obtain advanced placement in existing generic programs.

BACCALAUREATE PROGRAMS

Performance examination also serves a useful function for advanced placement for those seeking admission into baccalaureate nursing programs. These students usually are registered nurses from diploma or associate-degree programs, although corpsmen and those with other backgrounds in health care also may seek advanced placement. Use of a battery of standardized proficiency examinations in nursing* and a clinical performance examination increases the faculty's confidence in the students' abilities without placing restrictions on the merits of their past accomplishments. Objective testing documents and students' knowledge and competence regardless of how, where, and when they learned such skills.

As with the tests described for associate degree programs those for the BSN level could follow a simulated or actual format. A real-life situation is preferable, but circumstances may not permit it—in which case paid subjects could be used for a simulated version of the test. While students could be tested on one patient-care situation, two or three would provide a broader-based assessment approach. The ideal performance test at this level is a comprehensive examination

---

*Such as those developed by the New York State Education Department and made available through the American College Testing Program.

such as the Clinical Performance Nursing Examination. This requires that students pass a minimum of two adult and one child PCS with 100 percent accuracy with respect to the critical elements and in a real-life setting. This provides the degree of complexity, variation, and reality desirable to document clinical competencies at this level. However, it should be clear that when it is not possible to administer the full CPNE, modified versions (actual or simulated) can be developed and used to advantage. In some cases, a BSN program may begin with a limited modified version and over a period of two to three years make the transition to a more comprehensive version. Developing a performance testing center with well-qualified evaluators takes one to two years, but the process could be in progress during the same period of time.

For those BSN programs that allow nontraditional students to take challenge examinations for some or all courses, additional performance examinations may be necessary. For example, if skills in health assessment are required of the generic students, a performance test such as the Health Assessment Performance Examination could be used in addition to the Clinical Performance Examination. Similarly, performance tests could be used for other content areas. The problem of development, however, is a major one, and priorities must be established regarding which test to develop first. Given sufficient time, motivation, and economic resources, all clinical areas could be tested in this fashion. The CPNE, HAPE, and PPE developed by the New York Regents Program can serve as models for the development of other performance examinations.

MASTER'S DEGREE PROGRAMS

In time, faculties of master's degree programs in nursing will develop and implement performance examinations objectively to measure achievement at the graduate level. Such tests could focus on the clinical specialty areas as well as performance in functional areas such as teaching and administration. Some efforts already are underway in areas such as health assessment, midwifery, and pediatric practitioner programs. The same concepts and criteria are applicable; only the content and complexity change. Such examinations would improve the quality of learning and the level of competence of graduates of these programs, and would markedly increase the potential flexibility for teaching–learning strategies. Less emphasis would be necessary for structured learning patterns, enabling nontraditional students to have an equal chance to demonstrate abilities regardless of where the competencies were learned. However, because nursing education developed as it did, some residual problems experienced at the graduate level need special consideration. In time, entire master's degree programs will be developed using objective theory and performance examinations.

Nonnursing Baccalaureates

In the past, thousands of RNs obtained B.S. or B.A. degrees in disciplines other than in nursing—e.g., sociology, education, counseling, psychology, etc. In many cases, the local college did not offer a degree in nursing, or if it did spaces for RNs were limited or courses were offered at inconvenient times. Those nurses who desired a bachelor's degree but could not move to a different location or could not exchange the job for a classroom on a full-time basis nonetheless pursued their goal and obtained a bachelor's degree. Many of these nurses have made significant contributions to nursing and to their communities. Many also have been stimulated to continue their educational preparation at the graduate level. However, as requirements for admission into master's degree nursing programs have become more stringent, those RNs with nonnursing bachelor's degrees are meeting increased resistance when they seek admission.

The use of standardized written tests and objective performance examinations could resolve a substantial part of this problem. The graduate faculty could require that all entering students without a major in nursing at the baccalaureate level take a battery of written proficiency tests and performance examinations to document knowledge and skills comparable to those of the more conventional students being admitted. The particular background and ways of learning could be more flexible and therefore more students could be accommodated, which would meet their needs as well as those of the profession—i.e., more master-prepared nurses. Rather than basing judgments on assumptions about the students' preparation for graduate study, students could be given an objective chance to demonstrate their level of achievement and commitment to learning. The written and performance examinations already developed and previously described could be used for this purpose. Others could be developed as necessary to meet special needs of different graduate programs.

The objective of graduate education is to advance the knowledge and abilities of students and to prepare them for work in special categories of service to society. Certain prior learning and experience are essential for most students; however, the diversity of that learning and experience can be enriching—both to the individual and to the profession. Rather than deny additional education to capable individuals with nontraditional backgrounds, it is possible (and may even be preferable) to design objective and valid ways to assure that their competencies are equivalent to expectations for more conventional students. Appropriate examinations can document whether or not such applicants have a satisfactory undergraduate foundation to prepare them for graduate-level work. The attainment and demonstration of learning at the desired level is the responsibility of the student. The use of standardized theory and objective performance examinations would facilitate the advanced preparation of thousands of capable nurses with nonnursing bachelor's degrees. This is a service that nursing educators could provide at a time when the need for master-prepared nurses is becoming more imperative.

CAREER MOBILITY PROGRAMS

As more emphasis is placed on providing basic nursing education in academic institutions and on increasing the educational preparation for nursing practice, more experienced adult learners are seeking degrees in nursing. This movement affects associate, baccalaureate, and master's degree programs. Nontraditional, career mobility programs are being developed and expanded to accommodate the needs of such students as well as the needs of communities for further services. One of the problems almost universally encountered by these programs is converting the nonacademic learning of these students into valid college credits. As with other programs described above, standardized theory tests and objective performance examinations are extremely useful, both to the program and to the students.

For example, a one-year associate degree program in a southern state was developed for LPNs in an effort to increase the number of available RNs in the area. Among other entrance requirements the LPNs are required to take a comprehensive proficiency examination in fundamentals of nursing and a clinical performance examination. The performance examination is an adaptation from the CPNE and includes a sample of those skills essential for beginning the second year of an associate degree program. It is a simulated examination given in the college facilities. Even though a large number of students apply, it is designed to be administered by the limited number of available faculty. The faculty tried one version of the test but later revised it to include and to require more areas of care. With experience, the faculty members became more skillful as evaluators and more understanding of the process of objective assessment; these insights were useful in making the transition to a more valid examination to screen applicants for admission. This performance examination is an important determinant because the number of student spaces is restricted and the academic demands on students enrolled in this one-year nontraditional associate program are intense. The nursing faculty currently is redesigning the test so that each student must pass a total of three required areas of care and one of two selected areas of care, each with 100 percent accuracy of the stated critical elements. Appointments are arranged during specified periods throughout the year at the convenience of the existing faculty. Potential students are given the examination study guide, which includes all details about content and procedural expectations. They are held accountable for learning and achieving the standard; how they prepare and how long it takes is their responsibility. The faculty makes the standard known and objectively administers the examination as specified in order to screen candidates for the program.

On admission, therefore, students will have documented certain achievements in general education, in nursing theory, and in nursing performance. Based on this prior learning, students can move into content areas typically found in the second year of an associate nursing program. If students were admitted without a performance examination the faculty might find themselves having to backtrack and spend an excessive amount of time in assisting students with basic first-year skills. In a program that already is quite demanding, this kind of problem could cause serious hardships for both faculty and students. By requiring the demonstration of both knowledge and skills for admission, the students and faculty can proceed with the career mobility program as it is designed. The time required to administer the preadmission performance examination is well worth the payoffs, especially when the testing time can be spread over several months.

Clinical performance examinations also are valuable tools in other types of career mobility programs, such as the following: baccalaureate programs for RNs, two-plus-two programs, extended and external degree programs, etc. In each case, the diversity and flexibility of past learning requires an objective and valid assessment of performance as well as knowledge. Programs that are developed to build on previous experiences and learning usually find it more essential to document exit (and sometimes entrance) competencies than do conventional programs. The content of the particular performance test depends on the level of expectations and other factors; the process of administering it and the underlying criteria are the same as described earlier. The challenge for a given faculty is to adjust the standard, the level of acceptability, the sample of competencies, the location, and the type of situations to suit their type of program and students. Furthermore, they then can make the transition to objective clinical testing as smooth as possible for students, faculty, and others who are involved. Depending on the variables involved, the implementation of such testing could take from one to three years. Even those performance examinations already available require several months of transition, but their usefulness is unquestionable, especially in flexible, nontraditional, career mobility programs.

SPECIAL NONDEGREE PROGRAMS

Performance examinations also can be developed and used in many other programs, such as certificate programs in specialty areas, clinician and practitioner programs, continuing education programs, and extensive workshops. All of these types of programs have a common need to document that the learners have accomplished the designated level of expectation and that they indeed are competent to perform the skills essential for the new role. The use of a performance examination greatly enhances the possibility of using flexible learning strategies and experiences. Students in these kinds of programs come with markedly different backgrounds, yet they all are expected to exit with "the same abilities." The learning needs of one individual might vary considerably from those of another; the approaches to completing program objectives also might be radically different from one student to another. Consequently, flexibility is usually quite important.

A concluding performance examination, objectively administered, enhances the possibilities for successful learning in these types of special programs. Students know in advance what is expected and therefore can focus their learning time according to their particular strengths and weaknesses. They also know that learning and the objective demonstration of skills is mandatory, which is a potent simulus for achievement.

SPECIALTY CERTIFICATE PROGRAMS

The usefulness of performance testing in specialty programs is well illustrated by the following example. The director of a perinatal nurse clinician program in New York* decided that students would be better prepared for their new role if they were required to pass an objective performance examination at the conclusion of the four-month program. Therefore, she used the concepts and criteria associated with the CPNE and developed a simulated test covering a sample of skills essential in the program. Based on the first experience she modified the test for the next group of students, making it clearer and more objective. Yet again, she rewrote the critical elements and developed better testing models for the third group of students. Each time the test was administered she learned more about the content to include, how to adjust the level of expectation, and how to specify the critical elements without having them look like steps in a procedure manual.

The teaching strategies she used changed along with expectations for students' performance. From the beginning, students knew they would have to pass a performance test—exactly as specified in the study guide. Therefore, they learned and practiced accordingly until the standard of expectation was met. Some students had to practice much more than others; the more adept and able students coached and assisted the others, thus increasing the feeling of *esprit de corps* and mutual responsibility.

One of the areas included in the test is intubation of a premature infant in respiratory distress. As these nurses are responsible for lifesaving measures of premature infants (both in hospitals as well as in rural areas and in transit), they must be able to insert a tube into a trachea and administer oxygen in a matter of a few moments. During the program students learn how to do this and practice on models as well as on live infants when the occasion arises (under supervision, of course). However, at the conclusion of the program every student must intubate a premature model according to the critical elements established. One of the critical elements requires that the blade of the scope be properly inserted into the trachea in 15 seconds, thus allowing air to be exchanged.

On one occasion a student had learned the theory but was clumsy with the procedure, actually taking nearly 60 seconds to assemble the

*The author is indebted to Rita Kopf, Department of Nursing, Adelphi University, New York, for examples from her perinatal nurse clinician program and for other ideas about the application of performance examinations.

instrument and insert the blade. Her peers practiced with her as the examination day approached. They counted off the seconds with metronomic precision, coaching her all the while. Gradually she became more skillful and during the test she actually performed the critical element in 9 seconds instead of the 15 allowed. By practicing against a designated standard, knowing she must achieve it, she became competent. She even felt competent. Furthermore, she knew, and her teacher and her peers knew, that when an occasion arose that required her to respond immediately and with skill to restore respiration to a newborn in distress, she could do it. More importantly, she could perform the skill without clumsiness, while her mind was free to encompass and respond to other needs of the infant and/or mother.

Requiring the performance examination helped the students to learn according to the expectations of their role and the needs of clients. Passing such a test greatly increased the self-confidence and value as health professionals. It also helped the teacher sharply to focus the role of the clinician following graduation and to assure that students were adequately prepared for the actual work world. The use of the examination therefore enhances the possibilities that clients will be better served and that the nurses will be better able to meet the expectations inherent in the situation.

CONTINUING EDUCATION PROGRAMS

Performance examinations given at the conclusion of certain continuing education programs and workshops would more adequately document that learning has taken place. Mere attendance and the correct response to several true-false questions do not indicate that the person has learned or changed in ability to apply that which was presented at the meetings. When the continuing education program has a clinical or performance component, a limited but specific performance examination could be developed and used. The same principles would have to be incorporated to ensure that the test was at the appropriate level of expectation, etc. Obviously, only a small sample of the content could be tested and undoubtedly a simulated format would be adequate. However, a number of procedural problems would have to be resolved, especially when the group is large.

The suggestion of using performance examinations at the conclusion of clinically oriented workshops initially may overwhelm those planning such meetings, but the gradual application of the idea would, indeed, have an impact both on the expectations for the teaching and for the learning. Programs would be presented differently and participants would have an added incentive to learn. When a certain number of continuing education units (CEUs) becomes mandatory for renewal of the license or for employment, more individuals will attend such workshops. However, the basic question is: Will their attendance make any difference to their practice? Giving a performance examination (as well as a written test) at the conclusion of the program could make a significant difference. If improving the quality of nursing practice is the object of continuing education, then performance examinations could provide a potent stimulus for learning and for change. This practice could reduce the number of participants who sleep, knit, or gossip their way through the meeting yet still collect CEUs. Requiring successful completion of even a narrow-scope simulated performance examination based on a random selection of activities might help to shake up the workshop hideouts and to accomplish the intended objectives.

It should be clear, however, that not every meeting, workshop, or program is suitable for performance examinations. Tests are most appropriate for those programs that have a small attendance, those that have a practice component, and those that require two or more days for the same participant. Programs of a theoretical nature and those lasting several hours or even one day probably are less likely to need such an examination. Those most appropriate are workshops that are planned to involve a period of one, two, or three months for the same individuals and that focus on changing practice behaviors. Even meetings of two to three days' duration involving fewer than 100 individuals could use performance examinations if the focus is on some practice component and if enough evaluators are available. The practice component could relate to clinical care of patients but it also could relate to the practice of teaching or of administration. When the purpose of the program is changing performance behaviors and when there is sufficient time for learning and practice to take place, a performance examination may be a useful instrument.

The problems of development and implementation are similar to those already presented, but the ultimate outcomes make the efforts worthwhile. The important thing is to begin to use such tests by starting with a small sample of content, a small number of participants, and using the tests only for certain occasions. Those responsible for continuing education programs gradually will learn the basics of developing and implementing performance examinations for this special purpose. As with other educational programs, a period of transition is required; planning and careful implementation are essential to the success of such endeavors. The key points are to select certain areas of practice presented during the meetings, to define them, and to specify the critical elements for each area. Simple rules of conduct and preparation of evaluators to ensure consistency and objectivity are other essential points. Obviously, the scope, intensity, and impact of a performance examination are less exacting in continuing education than in basic programs preparing for entry into the profession. Resources, time, and purpose all have to be logically and systematically considered; the performance test must be developed and used within the context of the workshop and made known to participants in advance. If planners get carried away with enthusiasm, the idea could backfire and cause such hostility that learning and change will be blocked rather than facilitated. Common sense and sensitivity to realistic expectations are just as important for continuing education programs as for basic programs. The use of a performance examination under certain circumstances will facilitate the effectiveness of the program; however, it will not cure all the ills of practice or of continuing education.

CERTIFICATION

The certification program of the American Nurses Association (ANA) provides an opportunity for practitioners in special areas of practice to document their competence. Currently, that documentation generally is satisfied through references, a written examination, and certain other written projects. The addition of a performance examination would enhance the credibility of the practitioner who holds the certificate as well as ensure more consistency in the quality of practice among the entire certified group. As suggested in other programs, giving such an examination—appropriately developed and implemented—would have a significant impact on the quality of preparation for certification and (consequently) on practice thereafter. At first the scope and sophistication of the performance examinations probably would be limited; however, over a period of a few years both could be enlarged through a series of extensive revisions to measure the desired practice accurately and comprehensively.

LICENSURE

Another suggested application of performance examinations being discussed both in the United States and in Canada relates to licensure procedures. Currently, the initial license to practice nursing is dependent upon passing the written examinations and renewal of license merely requires paying a small fee and completing a form. With the increasing instances of incompetence among new as well as experienced graduates, several state boards of nursing are considering implementing some type of performance examination as a requirement for licensure. Years ago candidates for licensure were required to pass a practice test, such as setting up a procedure or simulating some technical aspect of nursing care. For several reasons that practice was dropped; however, there is a renewed interest in using a better version of performance testing to document ability to render care. Concerns about the competence of nurses—being voiced both by the public and by the profession—have stimulated a new inquiry into this use of performance testing. The need for increased accountability in practice is clear and demands a reassessment of licensure procedure. Passing a series of written examinations has not proved sufficient to guarantee safe and effective care to the public in nursing or in other disciplines.

Several approaches to this gigantic problem might be suggested. Because of the large number of individuals seeking initial licenses twice each year, a performance examination probably could not be administered by the state board at the time written tests are taken. (This problem was a key reason for deleting the practice component years ago.) However, basic nursing schools could be required to administer some version of performance testing, and students would be responsible for passing such a test to be eligible for initial licensure. In this case the performance examination would serve a dual purpose: completion of the program and eligibility for licensure.

The content of such examinations is another problem for discussion, especially if it is to serve two purposes. Perhaps some flexible guidelines could be established by the state board and the specific criteria could be worked out by each school. Or, one basic version of a comprehensive performance examination (such as the CPNE) could be adopted by the state board; other performance tests desired by the program could be used in addition to that one. This would assure a common denominator of practice expectations, and would assure at least that degree of competence for all graduates of a given type of program. Documentation of excellence or of more comprehensive scope of practice could be achieved through other means or additional performance examinations.

Another entirely different approach also could be implemented which relates to the idea of using regionwide performance testing centers. As described earlier, such centers could be established to serve many purposes, including testing needs of basic programs, career mobility programs, and in this case, requirements for licensure. If one or more centers were developed in each state, graduates preparing for licensure could be held accountable for making an appointment and passing the designated examination within a specified time period. More than likely, the performance test—or a portion of it—could be simulated, which would make it more economical and efficient to administer. Simulated tests can be developed to demand the degree of competence expected for a given purpose, and when administered by trained, objective evaluators they can provide assurance of practice abilities. Although actual performance settings would be ideal, more than likely the problems inherent in this kind of testing would militate against their use. In locales in which a performance testing center exists and is open all or most of the year, individuals could apply for simulated testing whenever they feel ready. This would be useful for initial licensure, but if some form of performance test is required for renewal of the license a full-time center would be mandatory.

The license to practice nursing could be likened to the license to drive a car. Initially the candidate must pass a theory test and a performance test. Thereafter, periodic tests are required. In some states, the theory and road tests must be retaken every few years to assure that drivers know the rules of driving and are safe on the road—at least during the test. Similarly, in nursing, theory and performance examinations could be required initially, with followup testing at given periods, say every four to six years. Continuing education programs would assist in the process but the basic responsibility would belong to the individual nurse, both to keep up with theory and to apply it in practice, at least at the designated level of competence.

A few state boards of nursing are contemplating the move to performance testing. Based on testing procedures the individual nurse could be issued an initial license and subsequently required to document continuing ability. Instead of a license renewal form, some state boards already are contemplating the concept of a certificate of competence, which would require the practicing nurse to document competence in practice. How this concept is implemented undoubtedly will vary, but the fact that such ideas are being seriously discussed suggests the need for more objective assessment of competence in nursing as a condition for practice. The development and implementation of performance examinations as a requirement for licensure is being envisioned by many leaders as one of the central means of improving the quality of care essential to the well-being of the public and of the profession.

NURSING SERVICE

As suggested throughout this volume, clinical performance examinations have applicability in both education and service settings. The purpose of such examinations is to provide an objective basis for declaring the competence of an individual; clearly, such procedures could be used to advantage in meeting a variety of needs in nursing service. Regardless of the specific content and application, the basic concepts and criteria related to development and implementation and all other considerations previously presented apply to uses in nursing service. Of course, certain modifications have to be made but these already should be evident to the service user. The specific purpose of the test, the number of participants, the number of evaluators, and similar factors will differ, but the need for objectivity, consistency, comparability, and other elements is exactly the same as in the educational setting.

Some uses for performance testing in service agencies include the following:

- screening for initial employment
- evaluation following orientation for new graduates
- evaluation following a refresher course for returning RNs
- evaluation following an intensive course for those on specialty units
- promotion to other positions in the same agency

In each case, those responsible for staff development or in-service education will go through the same process described earlier. The content for the test will be extracted from that which is essential to the particular course or program. A sample of areas of practice will be identified and defined for purposes of the test and critical elements will be specified according to the criteria. The rules of procedure will be specified along with the expectations for the behavior of those giving the test and for those taking the test. An examination guide will be prepared and given to each participant, allowing for sufficient time for its use in the learning process. A mechanism will be developed to inform participants in advance of the expectations and the consequence of failure. Those responsible for evaluating the performance of the participants will be held to the same rules of conduct as described for instructors in basic programs.

A planned period of reprogramming and transition is also just as essential in the service setting as in the educational setting; the anxiety level can be just as intense for nurses and in-service instructors as for students and teachers undergoing the same process. Plans for development and implementation need to be just as carefully pursued in the service setting in order to avoid major misunderstandings and problems.

Decisions about whether the test should be a simulated type or should take place in the actual patient-care settings depend upon most of the same variables discussed earlier. One major advantage, however, is that problems with the service agency staff probably will be minimized. However, potential problems in this category should not be underestimated or taken for granted. Including those staff members who are likely to be affected in all phases of planning is just as important in the transition in the service settings as it is in educational programs located on campus.

Basic aspects of the CPNE can be used for service purposes as well as for those situations already described. For example, following a three-month orientation program for new graduates these people could be given an examination focusing on a sample of the areas of care expected in their role. One approach might be to require, say, that one of two PCSs be completed with 100 percent accuracy. The PCSs might include for example, four required areas and two selected areas and be administered on two different units. The tests could be scheduled for the same day or spread over a period of a week or more, depending on circumstances. Diversity is possible so long as all of the basic concepts and criteria are integrated.

For specialty programs, such as a course for nurses in intensive- or coronary-care units, the test could be simulated and highly specific. Participants could be required to respond to a sample of certain emergency situations that could be simulated, to respond to data from an EKG reading and other physical findings, etc. The evaluation of competence, however, would be based on a set of predetermined critical elements. Regardless of the areas of practice to be included, participants would be required to perform the critical elements according to the conditions specified.

Similarly, clinical performance examination comparable to the CPNE could be administered to RNs following a refresher course to document their readiness to care for patients in the particular employment setting. Ideally, the test could be administered in the actual setting; however, it could be modified and given as a simulated test. Either way, the competence of the nurse to administer nursing care according to a preestablished standard would be evaluated consistently and objectively. Such an examination would provide a guide for the nurse to know the level of performance expected and would improve the quality of care.

Performance examinations to test for competence in areas related to management also could be developed and used before promoting individuals to such positions. Simulated tests could be developed related to making assignments, working out typical staff problems, assisting the staff to achieve their potential, and other functions.

Regardless of the particular content, the performance examination does not have to be lengthy, excessively complicated, or all inclusive. The concept of sampling is an important one, particularly when time and availability and staff are limited. When participants are given the array of possible areas to be included but actually are tested only on a random selection of those areas, the effect is similar. The learners must prepare for all areas because they have no way of knowing the particular ones that will be assigned. Consequently, it can be assumed that if they can perform the few randomly selected areas of care, more than likely they also can perform the others. However, this procedure reduces the need for testing time, which is an important consideration in any setting.

It is essential that a system of objective performance testing be implemented thoughtfully and gradually, especially in situations in which unions exist. Legal ramifications must be considered and advice may have to be obtained from the agency's legal consultant. In this regard, introducing performance testing in service settings may be quite different from the educational institution. At the outset, those involved in planning should consider legal consequences and anticipate how they will deal with such problems, before they actually occur.

SUMMARY

Different types of performance examinations can be developed and used in a variety of education and service settings. They have particular relevance for promotion within generic programs, for advanced placement in generic or career mobility programs, for specialty certificate program, for licensure, and for various uses in nursing service settings. The basic principles and problems involved in development and implementation are similar. The use of simulated or actual performance examinations tends to improve teaching and learning and to enhance the possibilities for more competent practice. When learners are held accountable for a specified level of practice and evaluators remain objective and consistent in administering the examination, quality of care can be expected to improve. In this case, the outcomes justify the time and effort spent to ensure appropriate development and implementation.

CHAPTER 11

The Final Phase: Pilot-Testing, Validity, and Reliability

The final phase of developing a performance examination involves comprehensive pilot-testing and the documentation of reliability and validity. Initial aspects of the evaluation of the test begin in the early phases of development and already have been discussed briefly. The groundwork for validity and reliability are initiated with the first draft of the test and to some extent are considered throughout the developmental process. This chapter, however, focuses on the problems and procedures associated with pilot-testing and take place after the examination is essentially developed. As with previous chapters, this one presents some practical approaches and suggestions related to different types of performance examinations. Consultation with testing experts is advised for this phase, as with earlier developments. The approach used is process oriented and the reader is referred to the extensive bibliography for background information and theory related to reliability and validity testing.*

Few objective performance examinations of the kind described in this volume have been developed; therefore, detailed information

---

*For theoretical and detailed discussion of reliability and validity, consult the bibliography; the following references are particularly useful:

(1) Millman, Jason. Criterion-references measurement. In *Evaluation in Education*. Popham, W. James, Ed. Berkeley: McCutchan Publishing Corp., 1974;

(2) Levine, Harold. Selecting evaluation instruments. In *Evaluating Clinical Competence in the Health Professions*. Morgan M., and Irby, D. Eds. St. Louis, C.V. Mosby Co., 1978;

(3) Ebel, R. L. *Essentials of Education Measurement*. Englewood Cliffs, N. J.: Prentice-Hall Inc., 1972;

(4) Shavelson, R. J., Block, J. R., and Ravitch, M. M. Criterion-referenced testing: Comments on reliability. Journal of Educational Measurement, 9:133–37; Summer, 1972;

(5) Popham, W. J., Ed. *Criterion-Referenced Measurement: An Introduction*. Englewood Cliffs, N. J.: Educational Technology Publications, 1971.

about such topics as their specific reliability and validity are difficult to find. Consequently, basic principles have to be adopted to achieve the primary purpose—namely, to provide reasonable assurance that the test accomplishes its objectives. The intent is to document objectively that students are capable of performing those competencies prescribed as relevant, appropriate, and essential for practice at a given level. Thus both content and procedures have to be evaluated before the examination actually is administered to students.

Basically two purposes are served by final pilot-testing procedures: (1) to make final adjustments in the testing process to assure that the examination can be administered smoothly and as designed and (2) to be sure that the test is a valid and reliable instrument by which accurate decisions can be made about the capabilities of the examinees. Some assistance can be gained from studying procedures used for norm-referenced tests; however, criterion-referenced and domain-referenced tests* or "mastery tests" present their own kinds of problems and must be evaluated differently. The classical approaches used for reliability and validity require a different interpretation, or even may have to be discarded with some criterion-referenced testing.

Most educational-measurement references focus exclusively on written examinations. Even those that discuss criterion-referenced tests emphasize the written format. Consequently, information about the development and evaluation of performance-type examinations is scarce. Therefore, procedures related to determining validity and reliability of performance-type, criterion-referenced tests are based on general principles that are adapted to this particular test format. The reader is cautioned to observe major distinctions between test evaluation procedures for norm-referenced and for criterion-referenced examinations, and to note differences in evaluating written and performance examinations. The purposes in determining test validity and reliability are the same, but procedures for test development and evaluation are significantly different.

VALIDITY

The function of a criterion-referenced test is to distinguish between those students who have and those who do not have certain prescribed capabilities. In this case, performance is not related to a normative or

---

*Some writers use the term "domain-referenced test" and others "criterion-referenced test."

external group, as is true for norm-referenced tests. Rather, students are judged on their ability to meet a prespecified standard, and are tested only on those "items" that are essential to a particular "domain" of practice (i.e., a well-defined set of tasks). This kind of test allows the evaluator to make a reasonably accurate estimate of the student's level of functioning and is not intended to discriminate variability among students. Students are not competing among themselves for gradations in achievement; rather, they are competing with themselves against a prescribed standard.

Validation procedures are intended to determine the correspondence between the predicted (desired) outcomes and the actual (empirical) outcomes. A test is valid if the sample of content faithfully represents the universe of behaviors about which decisions are being made. Validity addresses the accuracy of the inferences about the student's level of functioning that are made from the test results. The more valid the test the more accurate the inferences are regarding the student's status in terms of a previously defined "domain" or standard of performance. However, inferences about competence obviously depend upon the appropriateness of the test content, procedures, level of difficulty, and representativeness.

In the case of criterion-referenced tests, validity estimates are determined in relation to the purpose of the test; the process depends on the correspondence of test items with the objectives to which the test is referenced. Measurement of performance provides information relative to the predetermined criterion or standard. Test results are used as the basis for inferring the degree to which the individual possesses the characteristics (abilities) presumed to be reflected in the test. Both reliability and validity are improved by the specificity of the behaviors to be judged, by the clarity of the items (critical elements), and by the careful training of those who will make the judgments (evaluators).

Some authorities suggest that the most appropriate way to evaluate the validity of these kinds of tests is by a logical analysis of the domain definition, the item generation scheme, and the individual test items.* Translating this approach from a written-test format to a clinical performance examination requires the logical analysis of the specified areas of care, their definitions, and the critical elements specified. The definitions establish the scope of the competencies to be tested and the critical elements correspond to test items.

Basically, a panel of experts must determine that the areas

---

*See references by Millman (Bibliography) and by Levine (footnote, p. 304).

selected for inclusion and defined are a representative sample of the kinds of competencies expected for the given type and level of student being tested. This panel of experts probably should include the faculty committee developing the test as well as a number of other uninvolved experts on content. The objective of the expert review is to determine that those areas included are a valid or true reflection of appropriate and essential content. Such a determination can best be made if the panel of experts represents all of the clinical areas included in the test content. That is, the adequacy of the test content can be best evaluated if it is judged by those who are expert in those areas.

Furthermore, the method by which areas are selected and defined also requires analysis. As previously explained, clinical experts draft the test content and then subject it to the scrutiny of appropriate others. Based on feedback, succeeding drafts are prepared, each one more refined than the previous ones, and each one a more accurate reflection of the reality being represented. Clarification of words and intentions moves the test toward a more objective sample of practice to be documented.

Increasing refinement of the critical elements through a similar process finally results in the statement of precise behaviors (or "test items") that accurately represent the universe of expected competencies. The logical analysis of these individual items (critical elements) is a continuous process but also occurs at the time of final pilot-testing to assure validity, as will be illustrated shortly.

In addition to a logical analysis, validity also can be determined by experiment. Empirical validity is achieved by comparing the test results with other known factors that represent the same domain. For example, the validity of the test can be documented if students are judged successful on comparable content by using other methods or instruments. The test has concurrent validity if inferences about the students' competence can be documented through other means used at about the same period of time.

The test also may have predictive validity if other measures used subsequently corroborate the results of the performance test. For example, reevaluating the same individuals after completion of the program on a comparable domain of practice will determine the extent to which the test predicted success. Therefore, follow-up studies of students tested on performance examinations provide essential data about the test as well as the students.

In addition to the ongoing analysis of areas, definitions, and critical elements during the developmental process, some other procedures are suggested during the final pilot-testing period. For example, a number of individuals who are experts in the clinical content areas being tested could be asked to review and critique the test content. These individuals might be other faculty members (at one or more schools) or appropriate representatives from the service sector—including practitioners, qualified supervisors, or those in staff-development positions. Such individuals analyze the content for accuracy, for relevance, for objectivity, and for representativeness from a different perspective—one that is generally free of vested interests and hence more objective. The validity of the test is dependent on the degree of agreement among these experts.

A more critical evaluation of validity is provided by administering the test to two groups of subjects who have been carefully selected. One group is judged to be "qualified" by other means, and the second group is labeled "unqualified" by using the same criteria. For example, a comprehensive clinical performance test designed to be administered at the conclusion of a program could be administered to two groups of students. The first group, called qualified, already has successfully completed the program as judged by other acceptable means. The second group, called unqualified, has completed only a small portion of the program and, therefore, is not expected to pass the performance test. Neutral evaluators, who are not told which students belong to which group, give the test as faithfully as possible and compare the results. Those in the qualified group are predicted to pass the test because they already have been judged successful by other accepted methods. Those in the unqualified group are predicted to fail the test as they have not had the requisite study or experience. The test has construct validity if these predictions are substantiated by the test outcomes.

Problems and procedures related to such pilot-tests will be discussed later. The point here is that the validity of the performance examination must be evaluated and that one or more ways may be used. Confidence in the test is increased when two or more approaches are used and when the results have a high degree of correspondence.

RELIABILITY

Reliability refers to the consistency of test performance and thus to the consistency of the decisions that can be made based on test results. It refers to the extent to which the test is influenced by transitory factors rather than the true competence of the student. In developing and subsequently in final pilot-testing of the performance examination, consideration must be given to identifying and eliminating the errors inherent in the test and test procedures and thereby increasing reliability. As mentioned about validity, specificity of behaviors to be measured and the training of evaluators are essential. Reliability also is increased by increasing the number of individuals being tested (for the evaluation of the instrument), increasing the length of the test, increasing the number of observers (evaluators), and increasing the number of observations (i.e., patient-care situations and/or areas of care).

Repeated measures of the same individual on comparable items (test-retest) and multiple observations of the same individual at the same time also provide measures for estimating the reliability of the test. However, these approaches (typically used with written tests) present special difficulties when applied to performance examinations, which will become more evident later in this chapter. When two test versions can be given, reliability is determined by the percentage of agreement between the results, or by the proportion of examinees placed in the same decision categories by the tests (pass/fail). Agreement of decisions or consistency of decisions made by different evaluators (or made from different test versions) indicates test reliability.

All evaluation is subject to some degree of error. The objective of test construction is to produce a test that provides accurate and consistent information about those who take it. Repeated efforts must be made to eliminate aspects of testing that interfere with this objective. Stated another way, adequate test development and pilot-testing procedures are essential in order to assure a reasonable degree of test validity and reliability.

Levine* classifies test errors into five major categories, which deserve mention here:

1. Environmental errors, such as rushing the test or fatigue of examinees.
2. Processing errors, such as miskeyed responses or misinterpretation.
3. Classification errors, such as evaluators' disagreement about coding.

---

*Levine, Harold. Selecting evaluation instruments. In *Evaluating Competence in the Health Professions*. Morgan, M., and Irby, D., Eds. St. Louis: The C. V. Mosby Company, 1978, pp. 33–51.

4. Generalization errors, such as inadequate items or observations.
5. Bias errors, including rater prejudice, halo effect, or inconsistent application of expectations.

Each of these items is important especially as it relates to reliability of clinical evaluation. Most of them have been mentioned in previous sections but should be recalled for this discussion.

EXAMPLES OF PILOT-TESTING PROCEDURES

Throughout the test development period, various aspects of the performance test are subjected to tryouts or "minipilot tests" as a means of revising and refining the test. These trials provide essential data that cumulatively result in a more valid and more reliable test of the students' capabilities. Clarification of content categories, definitions, critical elements, and procedures is essential and requires repeated tryouts and revisions of the test form. As more of the test is completed more aspects can be tested out simultaneously to see how well the parts fit together. Ultimately, when all aspects of the test have been completed satisfactorily, it is ready for a series of final pilot-tests.

The nature and extent of the performance examination will dictate how the pilot-tests will be conducted. Some possible approaches are presented below, along with some of the problems that can be anticipated. The intent of this section is to suggest the kinds of methods that might be used rather than to explore the topic exhaustively. These methods probably will require modification, depending on the unique set of circumstances presented by the particular performance examination and the setting.

COMPREHENSIVE CLINICAL PERFORMANCE EXAMINATION

Throughout this text the development of a comprehensive performance examination has been explored. Less complex examinations can be extrapolated from this model. This same kind of test also will be used for purposes of examining pilot-testing; other examples will be suggested subsequently.

In addition to the procedures already mentioned, final pilot-testing requires the administration of the test in situations that resemble the reality of the actual test situation as closely as possible. This is comparable to a full dress rehearsal before the opening night of a play. Conditions, procedures, forms, content, and subjects should reflect the actual testing situation as much as possible—with one exception. A second group of subjects also takes the test as a control measure.

As indicated earlier, the two groups of test subjects should be as much alike as possible except for their predicted ability to pass the test. The qualified group consists of those who have learned the content being tested and already have been judged successful by other appropriate means. The unqualified group consists of those who have not learned the content and therefore are not expected to pass the test. However, subjects in both groups should be similar in other characteristics—such as age, previous experience, grade-point average, etc. To the extent possible, they should be selected on some random basis, although this can pose major problems. Both groups should have a specified amount of time to prepare for the test by using the same examination study guide and directions. Both groups are urged to participate in the pilot-test as seriously as possible.

The test results for the two groups reflect essential information about the test itself, including its validity, reliability, level of difficulty, appropriateness, representativeness, and readiness for actual use. Theoretically, the majority of the qualified subjects are expected to pass the test while the majority of unqualified subjects are expected to fail the test. Deviation from these predictions indicates the existence of serious problems in either content or process, or both. Such problems also may be associated with subject preparation, evaluator behavior, or inadequacy of the setting. Needless to say, subjects, evaluators, and agency staff must be adequately prepared and must comply with protocol for the pilot-testing in order to determine the reliability of the examination.

The process of administering the pilot-test should be essentially the same as for actual testing. For example, the time frame, selection of patients, critical elements, etc., should be as designed. However, by subjecting each group to the maximum number of test units (PCSs)—each one evaluated independently by a different observer—five sets of discrete observations can be obtained for each subject. (This is predicated on a test that requires three of five PCSs for passing.) This procedure is equivalent to giving each subject five parallel tests, each one observed by a different evaluator; it also allows comparisons for areas of care as well as for multiple critical elements. By retesting Required Areas in each PCS combined with different Selected Areas, commonalities as well as differences among subjects can be compared. Maximizing the number of PCSs per subject provides more data for judging both validity and reliability of the test. Obviously, more subjects in each group will provide more data for analysis, which increases the possibility for correctly evaluating the effectiveness of the test. However, several problems are associated with these points, and they will be explored later.

If the test results consistently allow decisions to be made according to predictions, the test is a valid and reliable indicator of the competence it represents. Accuracy of decisions and consistency of decisions are the desired objective. The pilot-tests, faithfully conducted, should provide the data base for determining the extent to which these objectives have been accomplished. The number of pilot-tests needed to confirm readiness for use depends on the test outcomes, the degree to which the test can be administered as designed, and the number of subjects to whom the test will be administered.

A HEALTH ASSESSMENT EXAMINATION

Some performance tests are limited to more circumscribed competencies; however, they also require evaluation to assure an acceptable degree of validity and reliability. The procedures already described are appropriate, even though some modifications probably will be made. For example, in a test designed to determine the student's competence in conducting a comprehensive health assessment of a client, the following procedures might be used.

After the test is declared to be essentially ready, it is subjected to a series of prepilot-tests to refine procedures, forms, and specificity of expectations. Analysis of these data is used to make final revisions preliminary to final pilot-testing. As described above, the test is given to a number of qualified and unqualified subjects, whose background and level of preparation are concealed from the evaluators. To the extent possible, the test is administered exactly as designed.

In the case of the Health Assessment Performance Examination (HAPE) of the Regents B.S.N. program, only one programmed client-subject (instead of five patients) is involved. Therefore, the subject is evaluated only once by one evaluator. While such observations yield helpful information, the reliability of the test can best be determined if the student-subject is tested at least twice or observed simultaneously by at least two evaluators. When two evaluators observe the same performance of critical elements and make equivalent decisions about outcome, the test provides a consistent and reliable index of competence. When the evaluators come to different conclusions about the same performance, errors still exist in content, procedures, student preparation, evaluator behavior, and/or test conditions. Such a finding clearly indicates the need for further analysis, test revisions, and subsequent pilot-testing.

Similarly, as illustrated below, the pass/fail results for the qualified and unqualified subjects indicate the validity of the test. Qualified subjects are predicted to pass if the test is an accurate reflection of the domain of practice it represents. Those who have neither studied nor had experience in comprehensive health-assessment procedures are not expected to pass a test of these competencies. The level of difficulty, representativeness of areas, appropriateness of critical elements, etc., are evaluated through such pilot testing for validity.

	Pass	Fail
Qualified subjects	Majority	Few
Unqualified subjects	Few	Majority

A SIMULATED EXAMINATION

Simulated tests also need to be subjected to pilot-testing similar to that already described. The same approach of using two groups of participants is applicable. Whether individuals are subjected to multiple parallel observations or to simultaneous observations depends in part on the nature of the test and the circumstances of pilot-testing. Performance tests of various nursing skills given in the nursing laboratory are usually brief and discrete. Both approaches probably could be used, which would improve both the reliability of the test and of the evaluators' judgments. Both aspects are important and should be included whenever possible, regardless of the type of examination.

Simulated video-taped examinations also allow more detailed pilot-testing because of the limited number of persons directly involved. For instance, only test participants and evaluators are present, in contrast to the complex clinical setting that simultaneously includes the patient, family, physician, and other health-care workers, in addition to the evaluator and student. The time required for simulated testing also makes it more amenable to a different kind of pilot-testing. The number of evaluators needed and cost factors also are quite different.

Pilot-testing of video-taped performance examinations is comparable to that of other tests, in that groups of appropriately qualified and unqualified student-subjects are randomly selected (to the extent possible), oriented, and given the test under conditions that closely resemble actual testing situations. Comparison of results for the two groups provides data about test validity and reliability, as well as other information about level of difficulty, time requirements, adequacy of directions, preparation of evaluators, etc.

All of these variables and similar ones must be considered when plans are being made for pilot-testing. The exact form of pilot-testing and the procedures used for determining validity and reliability will be based on these multiple factors, which indeed will vary from one situation to another. Every effort should be made to use the procedures that will provide the most information about the accuracy and consistency of the test. Whenever possible, test and measurement consultants should be used in planning for pilot-testing and documentation of the validity and reliability of the performance examination.

OPERATIONAL PROBLEMS IN PILOT-TESTING

Certain problems can be anticipated when one is pilot-testing either written or performance examinations; however, those associated with the latter are significantly more difficult and require considerable attention. Some of the problems associated with cost, time, sample size, compliance of subjects, support systems, and administrative procedures need to be discussed here. As in previous chapters, the problems presented are suggestive of those that should be anticipated; this discussion should not be regarded as being all-inclusive. Most of the difficulties described were experienced during the pilot-testing of the three Regents External Degree performance examinations. They may be less likely to occur in regular on-campus situations, or at least, not to the same extent. It should be recalled that in the Regents External Degree program there are no in-resident faculty or students. All committee members, evaluators, and student-subjects—as well as clients-patients are acquired elsewhere for any designated purpose or assignment. When faculty members are already employed and available and a student-subject pool already exists, the extent of the difficulties discussed below may be minimized.

TIME REQUIRED

One striking problem associated with comprehensive pilot testing is the amount of time required to complete the process. Even when some prepilot-testing is incorporated throughout the developmental phase, this final activity could take up to six or nine months. For example, after the faculty committee completed the Health Assessment Performance Examination, active and comprehensive pilot-testing began. Every subsection already had been prepilot-tested several times. The first evaluators were oriented, student-subjects were located and given materials; client-subjects were located and baseline history and physical examinations obtained; the test setting was identified and confirmed; and current drafts of the examination study guide and forms were prepared. The test was administered to the first eight subjects, and from that experience the faculty committee learned much regarding the test: the level of difficulty (it was assessed as being much too difficult, as none of the qualified subjects passed it), the time required, the need for clarification for clients and continued orientation for evaluators, revision of recording forms, etc. All of the test data and feedback from clients, students, and evaluators were used to revise and improve the test and testing procedures. Several weeks later the same procedure was repeated, with still more data obtained that led to more revisions. The process was repeated several more times before the data indicated that the test was valid and reliable.

A full eight months later the last of the final pilot-tests was administered. During these months, the test was repeatedly administered to both qualified and unqualified student-subjects. All the while evaluators and associates were becoming better prepared for their unique roles, the clients were becoming more accustomed to their role, the forms were being revised, the comprehensive study guide was completed, and the requirements for passing and applicable critical elements were modified to achieve the desired level of difficulty. All of these experiences provided essential information for the finalization of a performance examination that is a valid and reliable instrument for documenting the competence of students in the particular content area. However, nine months were required to accomplish just this last phase. (Development of the total examination took three years.) Time is necessary to secure appropriate examination subjects and clients, to revise materials, and to reorient all of those involved. The desire to speed the process along is understandable, but this must be balanced against the need for adequate documentation of the validity, reliability, and procedural functionability of all aspects of the examination. Haste and premature administration to actual students could result in serious problems. Anticipating from the outset that several months probably will be necessary for pilot-testing should help to reduce anxiety associated with the time requirements.

COST CONSTRAINTS

Another problem associated with pilot testing is the cost. Obviously cost is dependent on several factors, including the time required per test, additional payment for teachers to serve as evaluators, payment to students to take the test, payment to client-subjects, preparation of necessary test materials, the purchase of additional equipment (if necessary), and other incidental expenses. The pilot-testing of the HAPE described above costs approximately $30,000 (which is in addition to previous costs for development and prepilot-testing). These costs are significantly reduced if faculty members who serve as evaluators already are employed and the testing time is incorporated into their ongoing schedule. However, students tend to cooperate with more commitment when they receive payment. It may be possible to use clients without payment, but this introduces other problems also.

When actual clients are used for a health-assessment examination, very little control can be exercised over their presenting problems, the complexity of their background, and their willingness to comply with the test requirements. Comparability of testing episodes is threatened unless this entire set of problems is considered early in the test development. Finding subjects who are willing to play the client role for a small fee helps to ensure comparable test episodes, but it adds to cost and introduces other troublesome factors that will be discussed later. When actual hospital patients are used for the clinical performance test, payment usually is not required for pilot-testing or actual test administration. The CPNE as described throughout this volume uses such hospitalized adults and children and payments to them was not required. While this method reduced expenditures, the pilot-testing cost for the CPNE was still in excess of $30,000.

How much to pay students, client-subjects, and evaluators will depend on the setting, the time involved, and other local factors. The payment must be reasonably sufficient to assure compliance with test procedures. If too little money is offered the participants may feel no obligation to prepare or even to appear for the test, even though they previously agreed to do so. The total time involved, the incentive to participate, and the nature of the test all must be considered. For example, less money might be offered to a group of students to take a video-taped simulated examination (even though it requires three hours) than to a group of students who must commit an entire day (or weekend) to take a clinical performance in a hospital setting. The stress level as well as time and involvement are quite different for the two tests.

SAMPLE SIZE

Another problem in pilot-testing involves adequacy of the sample size. Hundreds of short paper-and-pencil tests can be given at a minimal cost and in a short period of time. However, because of the cost and time involved in administering performance examinations, the sample size usually is small. The reality of the situation must be considered when one is deciding how many pilot-tests should be given. There is no magic number that indicates how many subjects is enough. Obviously, a larger number is preferable to a smaller one. Primary consideration must be given to obtaining sufficient data to be sure that qualified students can pass, that unqualified students are screened out, that the instrument and procedures are reliable, and that decisions are consistently made.

To the extent possible examination subjects should be selected on a random basis. This is exceedingly difficult, especially when several hours are required and when stress and actual performance are involved. Even though every effort is made to secure a random sample for final pilot-testing, any number of factors might interfere with achieving this objective.

The experience of the final validation study for the CPNE illustrates several problems that can be anticipated in other performance examinations. Generally, the objective was to administer the CPNE to a group of 40 nurses who were newly graduated from NLN-accredited associate degree programs throughout the state of New York and to a comparable group of 40 first-year nursing students in the same programs. The test results for these two groups were compared to results for the external degree students. The schools were selected at random and their cooperation with the project was obtained. First-year students and those who were about to graduate were asked to participate and to provide information about their background and grade-point average. They were told they would receive payment plus expenses for preparing and taking the CPNE as prescribed. More than 200 individuals signed and returned cards, agreeing to participate. Appointments were made, evaluators assigned, etc. But repeatedly, test subjects did not appear, cancelled the day before the test, or started the test but left before completing it. Each of these situations cost time and money and frustrated the attempt to gain an adequate sample size. It seemed easy for both the students and the new graduates who agreed to participate to change commitments at the last minute. Some could not get time off from work, some had other personal preferences, some became too threatened, some were too tired, and some no longer felt a commitment.

Regardless of the reasons, repeated encouragement and follow-up, and the incentive of payment, pilot-test subjects cannot be forced to participate. When large numbers of test subjects are used (as with paper-and-pencil tests), some of these biases can be minimized; however, pilot-testing of lengthy performance examinations must allow for a higher tolerance. Naturally the best plans must be made and every effort exerted to secure an adequate sample, but in the long run reality will dictate the ultimate outcome.

The number of actual participants in the validity and reliability pilot-testing episodes, therefore, results from a balance between cost, time constraints, cooperation of test subjects, prior test results, and the purpose and nature of the test being evaluated. Rarely will it be possible to claim that enough students participated and that procedures moved along smoothly. Careful attention needs to be given to characteristics of those who participate and the potential influence of these factors on test results.

CLIENT BEHAVIOR

Some additional comments should be made about paid client-subjects who participate in pilot-testing and actual test administration. Considerable attention should be given to meticulous orientation for their part in the procedures. In our experience with the HAPE, those who agree to play the role of the client reported several kinds of problems. Most said they had never had such a lengthy history and physical examination; they were not prepared for this, or for the fatigue associated with providing such a comprehensive review. Many client-subjects found it difficult to "lie" by modifying their history to include only the programmed aspects essential to the test. Such programing is essential in order to control the potential array of variables the examinee must deal with and hence the control of comparability of the test episode. The client-subjects need help in realizing that the experience is a simulated health assessment that is designed as an examination. Without adequate orientation and subsequent discussion, they feel guilty and find it confusing to tell their history with prescribed modifications; sometimes they are "caught" in giving conflicting data, which compounds their guilt and discomfort. The better student is able to detect such inconsistencies when they occur. The objective, of course, is to prepare clients adequately so that such guilt and inconsistencies do not occur.

Client-subjects also need assistance during the orientation period to learn how much information to volunteer. Some individuals enjoy talking and do so readily. They want to help the student and thus "tell all." Others understand the purpose of the test and provide only the information required by the student's questions. Some tend to hold back and make the student probe for information. Over a period of time those who agree to serve as clients can be helped to provide essential and consistent information that requires comparable efforts from all of the students involved.

OTHER FACTORS

As illustrated in the above discussion, pilot-testing of examinations given in actual settings is different from that for simulated tests. Only two examples of simulated examinations have been used; however, as described elsewhere in this book, some simulated performance tests take place in the nursing laboratory and involve clinical nursing skills that may or may not require the participation of human subjects. In some situations, training models, mannequins, equipment or other students may be used. The reader is encouraged to adapt the previously described information to the particular kind of test being developed.

As stated, the period of pilot-testing can be used for the initial preparation of evaluators, clinical associate, and client-subjects (when they are necessary). Naturally, some orientation is given before the first trial (prepilot-test), but every pilot-test episode should be used to train evaluators, to refine procedures and materials, and to obtain data regarding the validity and reliability of the test. By the time of the final pilot-tests, everything and everybody involved should be ready for the administration of the test exactly as it will be given to students for its intended purpose.

If the data from the final trials are satisfactory, the test is ready for administration to actual students. There may be a tendency to keep refining and revising the test *ad infinitum*; however, once the test has been proved to be satisfactory is should be given and essential revisions made subsequently. As with all tests, a performance examination will need some modification after a period of use, depending on changes in the curriculum or in emphasis on content and practice components of the program.

Follow-up studies of those who have completed performance examinations help to determine further the degree to which the tests accurately and consistently reflect reality. Surveys, interviews, or observations can be used to collect data so that an analysis can be made comparing competencies included in the test and those essential in the practice setting. Graduates and their immediate supervisors both can be used to supply comparative data. Working with these findings, still other changes might be made in the performance examination, depending on its purpose and other characteristics. Thorough analysis of follow-up studies helps to increase confidence in the test's reliability and also to facilitate its use in predicting the subsequent success of those who pass it.

SUMMARY

The pilot-testing period is the final phase of developing a performance examination. It is critical and cannot be overlooked. Preliminary administrations of the test provide essential data about the test content and procedures, about the level of difficulty, and about the accuracy and consistency of the decisions made about students. A series of pilot-tests usually results in revisions and improvements in the test, various procedures, and use of related materials. During these early pilot-tests, evaluators, associates, and others are oriented and gain some experience in their new roles. Once the examination is "ready" it is administered to a controlled sample of subjects to obtain validity and reliability data. A series of test episodes is conducted until the findings indicate that the test consistently results in accurate decisions about those taking it.

Plans for pilot-testing should take into account the time and cost required as well as the problems that can be anticipated from student-subjects and client-subjects (when used). Pilot-testing is necessary regardless of whether the performance examination is a comprehensive clinical test involving actual patients, a quasisimulated test using paid subjects for clients, a video-taped simulated performance test, or a simulated skills performance examination given in the nursing laboratory. The exact procedures and extent of pilot-testing will vary accordingly; however, the central questions must be answered. Is the test a reasonable representation of the reality it samples? Is the level of difficulty appropriate for those expected to take it? Are the decisions made about students who take the test accurate? Can the results be consistently obtained by using different evaluators and subjects? Does the test function adequately in the setting? Are materials, forms, equipment, directions, and other procedural matters sufficiently refined for actual use? Are evaluators (and "clients") sufficiently prepared and reoriented into their expected roles? These and other such questions are answered by the pilot-testing episodes.

Follow-up studies on those who have completed the performance tests help further to establish reliability and validity. Revisions in the test usually are also made based on such studies after one or two groups have completed the program. This method facilitates improvements in the performance examinations, which include results of feedback from those in the practice setting—thus making the test an even better representation of reality.

Bibliography

Anderson, Diann H., and Saxon, Jean. Performance evaluation of nursing students. Nursing Outlook 16:56–58, May, 1968.

Anderson, Scarvia B., Ball, Samuel, Murphy, Richard T., and associates. *Encyclopedia of Educational Evaluation*. San Francisco: Jossey-Bass, 1975.

Aranata, N. C., and Miller, C. L. Philosophical systems of weighing clinical performance in nursing. International Journal of Nursing Studies 7:235–42, November, 1970.

Ashkenas, Thais L. *Aids and Deterrents to the Performance of Associate Degree Graduates in Nursing*. League Exchange, No. 99, New York: National League for Nursing, 1973.

Bailey, June T., McDonald, Frederick J., and Claus, Karen E. Evaluation of the development of creative behavior in an experimental nursing program. Nursing Research 19:100–8, March–April, 1970.

———. Learning for mastery. *Evaluation Comment I*. Los Angeles: Center for the Study of Evaluation of Instruction Program, May, 1968.

———. The critical incident technique in identifying behavioral criteria of professional nursing effectiveness. Nursing Research 5:52–64, October, 1956.

Bare, Carole E. Behavioral change through effective evaluation. Journal of Nursing Education 6:7–21, November, 1967.

Barro, A. R. Survey and evaluation of approaches to physician performance measurement. Journal of Medical Education 1051–93, November, 1973.

Barrows, H. S. *Simulated Patients (Programmed Patients)*. Springfield, Ill.: Charles C Thomas, 1971.

Special appreciation is given to Patricia Hyland for permission to use extensively the bibliography she developed for her dissertation: "Comparison of Achievement on the Clinical Performance Nursing Examination Between Conventional Associate Degree, Students and Candidates for the New York Regents External Degree Program," Teachers College, Columbia University, 1978.

Barrows, H. S., and Abrahamson, S. The programmed patient: A technique for appraising student performance in clinical neurology. Journal of Medical Education 39:802–5, August, 1964.

Blakeney, Hazle W. Evaluation of Student Achievement in Associate Degree Nursing Programs (unpublished Ph.D. dissertation). Teachers College, Columbia University, 1967.

Block, Doris. Evaluation of nursing in terms of process and outcome: Issues in research and quality assurance. Nursing Research 24:256–63, July–August, 1975.

Block, James H. *Mastery Learning: Theory and Practice*. New York: Holt, Rinehart and Winston, 1971.

Bloom, Benjamin S., Ed. *Taxonomy of Education Objectives: Handbook I, Cognitive Domain*. New York: David McKay, 1956.

———. Learning for Mastery. *Education Comment*. Los Angeles: Center for the Study of Evaluation, May, 1968.

———, Hastings, J. Thomas, and Madous, George F. *Handbook on Formative and Summative Evaluation of Student Learning*. New York: McGraw-Hill, 1971.

Bower, Fay L. Normative or criterion-referenced evaluation? Nursing Outlook 22:499–502, August, 1974.

Boyd, Joseph, and Shenberg, Benjamin. *Handbook of Performance Testing*. Princeton: Educational Testing Service, 1971.

Bradshaw, Carol E. Jack of all trades—master of none. Journal of Nursing Education 13:14–19, April, 1974.

Brady, Elizabeth H. To test or not to test. American Educator 1:10–14, 1977.

Brandt, Edna Mae, Hastie, Bettimae, and Schumann, Delores. Comparison of on-the-job performance of graduates with school of nursing objectives. Nursing Research 16:50–60, 1967.

———, and Metheney, Bettimae Hastie. Relationship between measures of student and graduate performance. Nursing Research 17:242–46, May–June, 1968.

Brodt, Dagmar E. A specialty for associate degree nursing program graduates: Increasing neophyte competency and confidence. Journal of Nursing Education 13:20–21, April, 1974.

Bruce, Matthew H. External accountability in education. *Instructor Accountability: Issues, Facts, Impact*. New York: National League for Nursing, 1976.

Campbell, John P., Dunnette, Marvin D., and others. The development and evaluation of behaviorally based rating scales. Journal of Applied Psychology 57:15–22, January, 1973.

Carrol, John B. Problems of measurement related to the concept of learning for mastery. Educational Horizons 71–80, Spring, 1973.

Carter, Joan H., and others. *Standards of Nursing Care: A Guide for Evaluation, 2nd ed.* New York: Springer, 1976.

Chuan, Helen. Evaluation by interview. Nursing Outlook, 20:726–27, November, 1972.

Combs, Arthur. *Educational Accountability: Beyond Behavioral Objectives*. Washington, D. C.: Association for Supervision and Curriculum Development, 1972.

Cox, Richard C. Evaluation aspects of criterion-referenced measures. In *Criterion-Referenced Measurement: An Introduction*. Popham, W. James, Ed. Englewood Cliffs, N. J.: Educational Technology Publications, 1971.

Crancer, Joann, Fournier, M., and Maury-Hess, S. Clinical practicum before graduation. Nursing Outlook 23:99–102, February, 1975.

Crocker, L. M. A performance rating scale for evaluating clinical competence of occupational therapy students. American Journal of Occupational Therapy 29:81–86, February, 1975.

———. Validity of certification measures for occupational therapists. American Journal of Occupational Therapy 30:229–33, April, 1976.

Cross, K. Patricia. The external degree: An introduction. Journal of Higher Education 415–25, June, 1973.

———, and Valley, John R. *Planning Non-Traditional Programs*. San Francisco: Jossey-Bass, 1974.

Curtis, Joy, and Rothert, Marilyn. Instruction simulation systems offering practice in assessment of patient needs. Journal of Nursing Education 11:23–28, January, 1972.

Davis, Betty G. Clinical expertise as a function of educational preparation. Nursing Research 21:530–34, November–December, 1972.

Davidson, Grace E., and Brock, Marie Anita. *The Associate Degree Practitioner and Nursing Service Needs*. New York: National League for Nursing, 1974.

DeChow, Georgeen H. Characteristics of associate degree education: Competencies of the graduate. *Preparing the Associate Degree Graduate*. New York: National League for Nursing, 1977.

DeTornyay, Rheba. Measuring problem-solving skills by means of the simulated clinical nursing problem test. Journal of Nursing Education 7:34–35, August, 1968.

Dressel, Paul L., and associates. *Evaluation in Higher Education*. Boston: Houghton Mifflin, 1961.

Dunn, Margaret A. Development of an instrument to measure nursing performance. Nursing Research 19:502–10, November–December, 1970.

Dwyer, Joyce M., and Schmitt, John A. Using the computer to evaluate clinical performance. Nursing Forum 8:266–75, March, 1969.

Dyer, Elaine D. *Nurses' Performance Descriptions: Criteria, Predictors and Correlates*. Salt Lake City: University of Utah Press, 1967.

Ebel, Robert L. *Essentials of Educational Measurement*. Englewood Cliffs, N. J.: Prentice-Hall, Inc. 1972.

Erickson, Richard C., and Wentling, Tim L. *Measuring Student Growth: Techniques and Procedures for Occupational Education*. Boston: Allyn and Bacon, 1976.

Fitzpatrick, Robert, and Morrison, E. J. Performance and product evaluation. In Thorndike, R. L., Ed. *Educational Measurement*. Washington, D. C.: American Council of Education, 1971, pp. 237–70.

Fivars, Grace, and Gosnell, Doris. *Nursing Evaluation: The Problem and the Process*. New York: Macmillan, 1966.

Flanagan, John C. The critical incident technique. Psychological Bulletin 51:327–58, 1954.

Flanagan, John C., and others. Evaluating student performance. American Journal of Nursing 63:96–99, November, 1963.

Forest, Betty L. *The Utilization of Associate Degree Nursing Graduates in General Hospitals.* League Exchange No. 82, New York: National League for Nursing, 1968.

Frejlack, Grace, and Corcoran, Sheila. Measuring clinical performance. Nursing Outlook 19:270–71, April, 1971.

Funkenstein, M. D., Daniel, H. The learning and personal development of medical students: Reconsidered. The New Physician 741–55, September, 1970.

Garvin, Alfred D. The applicability of criterion-referenced measurement by content area and level. In *Criterion-Referenced Measurement: An Introduction.* Popham, W. James, Ed. Englewood Cliffs, N. J.: Educational Technology Publications, 1971.

Geitgsy, Doris A. Behavioral competencies of the ADN graduate. In *Technical Nursing Dimensions and Dynamics.* Rasmussen, Sandra, Ed. Philadelphia: F. A. Davis, 1972.

Gerchberg, Louise R. *An Observational Method for Evaluating the Performance of Nursing Students in Clinical Situations.* League Exchange No. 60. New York: National League for Nursing, 1962.

Giardina, Richard C. The baccalaureate: Defining the undefinable. The Journal of Higher Education 45:112–22, February, 1974.

Gorham, William A. Methods for measuring staff nursing performance. Nursing Research 12:4–11, Winter, 1963.

Gould, Samuel B., and Cross, K. Patricia, Eds. *Explorations in Non-Traditional Study.* San Francisco: Jossey-Bass, 1972.

Gover, V. The NPSI: A nursing performance simulation instrument. Albuquerque, N. M.: American Nurses' Association Eighth Nursing Research Conference, March 15–17, 1972.

Griffin, Joann K. *Writing and Using Behavioral Objectives in Nursing Education.* New York: National League for Nursing, 1977.

Gronland, Norman E. *Measurement and Evaluation in Teaching, 2nd ed.* New York: Macmillan, 1971.

Hadley, Richard. New York Regents External Degree Program: A national examining university. American Nurse 9:8–10, November, 1977.

Hagen, Elizabeth. Appraising the quality of nursing care. Nursing Research Conference (ANA) 8:1–8, March, 1972.

Harris, Chester W., Alkin, Marvin, and Popham, W. James, Eds. *Problems in Criterion-Referenced Measurement.* Los Angeles: Center for the Study of Evaluation, 1976.

Hart, Wynelk Mims. The Evaluation of the Performance of Baccalaureate Students in Clinical Nursing (unpublished Ph.D. dissertation). Indiana University, 1974.

Hayter, Jean. An approach to laboratory evaluation. Journal of Nursing Education 12:17–22, November, 1973.

Hazeltine, Louise S., and Zeitz, Leonard. Evaluating clinical performance. Nursing Outlook 11:33–35, August, 1964.

Hertzberg, Hazel W. Competency-based teacher education: Does it have a past or future? Teachers College Record 78:1–21, September, 1976.

Heslin, Phyllis. Evaluating clinical performance. Nursing Outlook 11:344–45, May, 1963.

Heydinger, Richard B. The assessment of study performance: A model and the reforms. Mimeographed research report prepared for the 30th National Conference on Higher Education sponsored by the American Association for Higher Education (Chicago), March, 1975.

Hilliard, Mildred. *Orientation and Evaluation of the Professional Nurse*. St. Louis: C. V. Mosby, 1974.

Hinz, D. F. Direct observation as a method of evaluating clinical skills. Journal of Medical Education 41:150, 1966.

Hodgkinson, Harold L. Current factors affecting higher education. In *A CBC Primer: Report of a Conference: Competency Based Curricula in General Undergraduate Programs*. O'Connell, W. R. Jr., and Moomaw, W. Edmund, Eds. Atlanta: Southern Regional Education Board, 1975.

Hoffman, Richard. Introduction to Mars Hill. In *A CBC Primer: Report of a Conference: Competency-Based Curricula in General Undergraduate Programs*. O'Connell, W. R. Jr., and Moomaw, W. Edmund, Eds. Atlanta, Georgia: Southern Regional Education Board, 1975.

Holdman, H. *The Training of Simulated Patients*. East Lansing: Michigan State University (Office of Medical Education Research and Development; College of Osteopathic Medicine; College of Human Medicine), 1976.

Houle, Cyril O. *The External Degree*. San Francisco: Jossey-Bass, 1973.

Houston, W. Robert, and Howsam, Robert B., Eds. *Competency-Based Teacher Education: Progress, Problems and Prospects*. Chicago: Science Research Associates, 1972.

Hubbard, John P., and others. An objective evaluation of clinical competence—new techniques used by the National Board of Medical Examiners. New England Journal of Medicine 272:1321–28, June, 1965.

Hyland, Patricia. Comparison of Achievement on the Clinical Performance Nursing Examination Between Conventional Associate Degree Students and Candidates for the New York Regents External Degree Program (unpublished dissertation). Teachers College, Columbia University, 1978.

Irby, D. M., and Morgan, M. K., Eds. *Clinical Evaluation: Alternatives for Health Related Educators*. Gainesville: University of Florida, Center for Allied Health Instructional Personnel, 1974.

Johnson, Dale M., and Wilkite, Mary J. Reliability and validity of subjective evaluation of baccalaureate program nursing students. Nursing Research 22:257–62, May–June, 1973.

Johnson, Dorothy E. Competence in practice: Technical and professional. Nursing Outlook 14:30–33, October, 1966.

Katzell, Mildred E. Evaluation for educational mobility. Nursing Outlook 21:453–56, July, 1973.

Kelly, Ruth L. Evaluation is more than measurement. American Journal of Nursing 73:114–16, January, 1973.

Kerlinger, F. N. *Foundations of Behavioral Research*. New York: Holt, Rinehart and Winston, 1973.

Klein, Stephen P., and Kosecoff, Jacqueline J. *Issues and Procedures in the Development of Criterion Referenced Tests*. Princeton, New Jersey: Eric Clearinghouse on Tests, Measurement and Evaluation; Educational Testing Service, TM No. 26, 1973.

Knott, Bob. What is competence-based curriculum in the liberal arts? Journal of Higher Education 96:25–39, January–February, 1975.

Krumme, Ursel S. The case for criterion-referenced measurement. Nursing Outlook 23:764–69, December, 1975.

Kubo, Winifred, Chase, Lida, and Liton, Jane. A creative examination. Nursing Outlook 19:524–26, August, 1971.

Lamont, Campbell T., and Hennen, Brian K. The use of simulated patients in a certification examination in family medicine. Journal of Medical Education 47:789–95, October, 1972.

Law, Eva J. *The Associate Degree Practitioner and Nursing Service Needs*. New York: National League for Nursing, 1974.

Lenburg, Carrie B. *Criteria for Developing Clinical Performance Evaluation*. New York: National League for Nursing, 1976.

———. Emphasis on evaluating outcomes: The New York Regents External Degree program. Peabody Journal of Education. Nashville: George Peabody College for Teachers 56:212–221, 1979.

———. The external degree in nursing: The promise fulfilled. Nursing Outlook 24:422–29, July, 1976.

———. Nontraditional approaches to learning. AORN Journal, 26:48–53, July, 1977.

———. Nursing–the New York Regents External Degrees assessment model. In *Evaluating Clinical Competence in the Health Professions*. Morgan, M., and Irby, D., Eds. St. Louis: C. V. Mosby, 1978, pp. 259–70.

———. *Open Learning and Career Mobility in Nursing*. St. Louis: C. V. Mosby, 1975.

———. Shaping practice behaviors through performance examinations. Power, nursing's challenge for change. (Papers presented at the 51st Convention of the American Nurses' Association, Honolulu, Hawaii, June 9–14, 1978.) St. Louis, 1979.

———. Who shall be admitted to graduate study? Nursing Outlook 23:633–37, October, 1975.

Lessinger, Leon M., and Tyler, Ralph W., Eds. *Accountability in Education*. Worthington, Ohio: Charles A. Jones, 1971.

Levine, H. G., and McGuire, C. H. The use of role playing to evaluating affective skills in medicine. Journal of Medical Education 45:700–5, September, 1970.

———. Rating habitual performance in graduate medical education. Journal of Medical Education 46:306–11, April, 1971.

Lindsey, Margaret. Curricular developments. In *New Perspectives on Teacher Education*. McCarty, D. J., and others, Eds. San Francisco: Jossey-Bass, 1973, pp. 178–93.

———. Competency based teacher education: Historical, current and future perspectives. *Competency-Based Education: Theory-Practice-Evaluation*. Report of work conference sponsored by the Department of Curriculum and Supervision, College of Education, University of Georgia, May, 1975.

Litwach, Lawrence. A system for evaluation. Nursing Outlook 24:45–48, January, 1976.

Livingston, S. A. Reply to Shavelson, Block, and Ravitch: Criterion-referenced testing: Comments on reliability. Journal of Educational Measurement 9:139–40, Summer, 1972.

Lynch, B. L. Clinical evaluation: Rating scale development and use. Gainesville: University of Florida, Center for Allied Health Instructional Personnel, 1975.

Lysaught, Jerome P. *An Abstract for Action: National Commission for the Study of Nursing and Nursing Education.* New York: McGraw-Hill, 1970.

McClelland, David C. Testing for competence rather than for "Intelligence." American Psychologist 28:1–14, January, 1973.

McDonald, Frederick J. Evaluation of teaching behavior. In *Competency-Based Teacher Education: Progress, Problems, and Prospects.* Houston, W. Robert, and Howsam, Robert B., Eds. Chicago: Science Research Associates, 1972.

McGuire, C. Simulation technique in the teaching and testing of problem-solving skills. Journal of Research in Science Teaching 13:89–100, March, 1974.

McGrone, Helen F. Tape recorded evaluation: A method of teaching. Journal of Nursing Education 14:11–16, January, 1975.

McIntyre, Hattie M., and others. A simulated clinical nursing test. Nursing Research 21:429–35, September–October, 1972.

Mackenzie, R. S. Factors essential to evaluation of clinical performance. Journal of Dental Education 38:214–23, April, 1974.

Mager, Robert. *Preparing Instructional Objectives.* Belmont, California: Fearon, 1962.

Marriner, Ann. Student self evaluation and the contracted grade. Nursing Forum 13:130–35, February, 1974.

Mayhew, Lewis B., and Ford, Patrick J. *Reform in Graduate and Professional Education.* San Francisco: Jossey-Bass, 1974.

Mehrens, William A., and Lehmann, Irvin J., Eds. *Readings in Measurement and Evaluation in Education and Psychology.* New York: Holt, Rinehart and Winston, 1973.

Meskauskas, J. A. Evaluation models for criterion-referenced testing: Views regarding mastery and standard setting. Review of Educational Research 46:133–58, Winter, 1976.

Millman, Jason. Reporting student progress: A case for a Criterion-Referenced Marking System. Phi Delta Kappan, 52:226–30, December, 1970.

Millsap, Margaret. The development of mastery learning. *Coping with Change Through Assessment and Evaluation.* New York: National League for Nursing, 1976, pp. 13–26.

Montag, Mildred L. *The Education of Nursing Technicians.* New York: G. P. Putnam's Sons, 1951.

———. *Evaluation of Graduates of Associate Degree Nursing Programs.* New York: Teachers College Press, 1972.

Moritz, Derry Ann, and Sexton, Dorothy L. Evaluation: A suggested method for appraising quality. Journal of Nursing Education 9:15–34, January, 1970.

Muthard, J. E., Morris, J. D., Crocker, L. M., and Slaymaker, J. E. Field work experience ratings and certification examination scores as predictors of job performance and satisfaction in occupational therapy. American Journal of Occupational Therapy 30:151–56, March, 1976.

National League for Nursing. *Evaluation—An Objective Approach*. Report of the 1971 Workshops of the Council of Diploma Programs. New York: National League for Nursing, 1972.

———. *Coping With Change Through Assessment and Evaluation*. New York: National League for Nursing, 1976.

———. *Instructor Accountability: Issues, Facts, Impact*. New York: National League for Nursing, 1976.

———. *Accountability: Accepting the Challenge*. New York: National League for Nursing, 1976.

———. *Collaboration for Quality Health Care: Education of Beginning Practitioners of Nursing and Utilization of Graduates*. New York: National League for Nursing, 1976.

Nolan, Donald J. Open Assessment in Higher Education: The New York Regents External Degree. International Review of Education 23: 231–248, 1977.

———. Selection and certification: The New York Regents External Degree: An examining university in America. A paper prepared as a contribution to the Secretariat work on Selection and Certification under the Education Committee Programs, Organization for Economic Co-operation and Development, Paris, 1975.

Nyquist, Ewald B. The Regents external degree. *Associate Degree Education: Current Issues 1973*. Papers presented at the 6th Conference of the Council of Associate Degree Programs, Anaheim, California. New York: National League for Nursing, 1973.

———. The external degree program and nursing. Nursing Outlook 21:372–77, 1973.

O'Connell, William R., and Moosaw, W. Edmund, Eds. *A CBC Primer: Report of a Conference: Competency Based Curricula in General Undergraduate Programs*. Atlanta, Georgia: Southern Regional Education Board, 1975.

Ortelt, Judith A. The development of a scale for rating clinical performance. Journal of Nursing Education 5:15–28, January, 1966.

Pearson, Betty D. A model for clinical evaluation. Nursing Outlook, 23:232–35, April, 1975.

Phaneuf, Marie C. *The Nursing Audit: Profile for Excellence*. New York: Appleton-Century-Crofts, 1972.

Popham, W. James. The performance test—a new approach to the assessment of teaching proficiency. Journal of Teacher Education 19:216–22, Summer, 1968.

———, Ed. *Criterion-Referenced Measurement: An Introduction*. Englewood Cliffs, N. J.: Educational Technology Publications, 1971.

———. Minimal competencies for objectives—Oriented teacher education programs. Journal of Teacher Education 25:68–75, Spring, 1974.

———. Application of teaching performance tests in pre-service and in-service teacher education. Journal of Teacher Education 25:244–48, Fall, 1975.

———. *Educational Evaluation*. Englewood Cliffs, N. J.: Prentice-Hall, 1975.

Quirk, Thomas J. Performance tests for beginning teachers: Why all the fuss? Educational Technology 13:14–16, May, 1973.

Ramey, Irene G. Setting nursing standards and evaluating care. Journal for Nursing Administration 3:27–35, May–June, 1973.

Reisman, David. Instituting competency-based degree programs in a large public university. *Instituting Competency-Based Degree Programs in a Large Public University: Curriculum of Attainments*. Tallahassee: Florida State University, Center for Educational Design, 1975, pp. 18–24.

Rines, Alice R. *Evaluating Student Progress in Learning the Practice of Nursing*. New York: Teachers College Press, 1963.

Rogers, Suzanne. "Testing the R.N. student's skills. Nursing Outlook 24:446–49, July, 1976.

Rosen, Albert. Performance appraisal: Interviewing evaluated by proximal observers. Nursing Research 16:32–37, Winter, 1967.

———, and Abraham, Gertrude E. Evaluation of a procedure for assessing the performance of staff nurses. Nursing Research 12:78–82, Spring, 1963.

Ryan, Betty Jane. Nursing care plans: A systems approach to developing criteria for planning and evaluation. Journal of Nursing Administration 3:50–58, May–June, 1973.

Schmidt, Mildred, and Lyons, W. Credit for what you know. American Journal of Nursing, 69:101–4, January, 1969.

Schneider, Harriet L. Evaluation of the associate degree nursing student. Paper presented at a workshop for faculty in associate degree nursing and other health occupation programs. New York: National League for Nursing, December, 1973.

———. The development of a test based on a simulated clinical setting (unpublished Ph.D. dissertation). Teachers College, Columbia University, 1974.

Shavelson, R. J., Block, J. H., and Ravitch, M. M. Criterion-referenced testing: Comments on reliability. Journal of Educational Measurement 9:133–37, Summer, 1972.

Sherlock, Sarah L. Editorial: The missing definition of basic competencies. NLN News 25:2, February, 1977.

Simpson, M. June. The "walk-around" laboratory practical examination in evaluating clinical nursing skills. Journal of Nursing Education 6:23–26, November, 1967.

Slater, Dorothy. *The Slater Nursing Competencies Scale*. Detroit: College of Nursing, Wayne State University, 1967 (mimeographed).

Slaymaker, J. E., Crocker, L. M., and Muthard, J. E. *Field Work Performance Report Manual: Use, History, and Development*. Rockville, Md.: American Occupational Therapy Association, 1974.

State of Florida Department of Education: *Associate Degree Nursing Education: Assumptions and Competencies for Entry to Practice*. Talahassee, May, 1977.

Stevens, Delphie. A tool for evaluating clinical performance. American Journal of Nursing 70:1308–10, June, 1970.

Tate, Barbara L. Evaluation of clinical performance of the staff nurse. Nursing Research 11:7–9, Winter, 1962.

Tate, Barbara L. Evaluating the nurse's clinical performance. Nursing Outlook 10:35–37, January, 1962.

The Carnegie Commission on Higher Education. *Less Time, More Options: Education Beyond the High School.* New York: McGraw-Hill, 1971.

Thorndike, Robert L., Ed. *Educational Measurement.* Washington, D. C.: American Council of Education, 1971.

———, and Hagen, Elizabeth. *Measurement and Evaluation in Psychology and Education*, 4th ed. New York: Wiley, 1977.

Tinning, F. C. *Simulation in Medical Education.* East Lansing: Michigan State University (College of Osteopathic Medicine), 1975.

Tower, J. B. Development of a rating scale to measure learning in clinical performance. Journal of American Dietetics Association 60:440–45, May, 1976.

Trivett, David A. *Competency-Programs in Higher Education.* Washington, D. C.: Eric Clearing House on Higher Education, American Association for Higher Education, 1975.

Tschudin, Mary S. *Evaluation in Basic Nursing Education.* New York: G. P. Putnam's Sons, 1958.

Turner, Edward V., Helper, Malcolm M., and Krisha, David S. Predictors of clinical performance. Journal of Medical Education 49:4:338–42, April, 1974.

———. Testing for Accountability. In *Accountability for Educational Results.* Hastrap, R. W., and others, Eds. Hamdem, Conn.: Linet Book, 1973, pp. 159–162.

———. Historical efforts to develop learning on a competency base. In *A CBC Primer: Report of a Conference. Competency-Based Curriculum in General Undergraduate Programs.* O'Connell, W. R. Jr., and Moomaw, W. Edmund, Eds. Atlanta, Georgia: Southern Regional Education Board, 1975.

University of the State of New York. *The New York Regents External Degrees in Nursing: Monograph I.* Albany, N. Y.: University of the State of New York, 1976.

Vosburgh, P. M. Development of a rating scale to measure learning in clinical dietetics: II. Journal of the American Dietetics Association 60:446–49, May, 1976.

Wandelt, M. A., and Ager, J. *Quality Patient Care Scale.* Detroit: College of Nursing, Wayne State University, 1970.

Watkins, Carolyn. Student evaluation by computer. Nursing Outlook 23:449–52, July, 1975.

Wentling, Tim L. Measuring the achievement of competencies. Educational Technology 13:48–50, May, 1973.

Williamson, Janet A., Ed. *Current Perspectives in Nursing Education.* St. Louis: C. V. Mosby, 1976.

Wilson, Margaret A. Equivalency testing in development of health practitioners. Journal of Allied Health 3:103–9, Spring, 1974.

———. *Equivalency Evaluation in Development of Health Practitioners.* Thorofare, New Jersey: Charles B. Slack, 1976.

Wood, Lucilla, Ed. *Nursing Skills for Allied Health Services, vol. 3.* Philadelphia: W. B. Saunders, 1975.

———, and Freeland, Thomas. *The U.C.L.A. Allied Health Professions Projects: Nursing Occupations Progress Report.* Los Angeles: University of California, April, 1971.

Woodward, Elizabeth S. Reflections of an external degree graduate. Nursing Outlook 24:429–32, July, 1976.

Woolley, Alma S. The long and tortured history of clinical evaluation. Nursing Outlook 25:308–15, May, 1977.

Wozniak, Delores A. External degrees in nursing. American Journal of Nursing 73:1014–18, 1973.

INDEX